EVIL

MASTERS OF

HOUSE OF

Writer: CHRISTOS N. GAGE

Penciler: MANUEL GARCIA

Inkers: JESSE DELPERDANG, NELSON PEREIRA, JASON MARTIN, RICK KETCHAM & SCOTT HANNA

Colorists: NATHAIN FAIRBAIRN, BRUNO HUANG & CHRIS SOTOMAYOR

Letterer: DAVE SHARPE

Cover Artist: MIKE PERKINS WITH GURU eFX

Assistant Editors: MICHAEL HORWITZ & RACHEL PINNELAS

Editor: BILL ROSEMANN

Collection Editor: JENNIFER GRÜNWALD

Assistant Editors: ALEX STARBUCK & JOHN DENNING

Editor, Special Projects: MARK D. BEAZLEY

Senior Editor, Special Projects: JEFF YOUNGQUIST

Senior Vice President of Sales: DAVID GABRIEL

Editor in Chief: JOE QUESADA

Publisher: DAN BUCKLEY

Executive Producer: ALAN FINE

HOUSE OF M

MASTERS OF EVIL

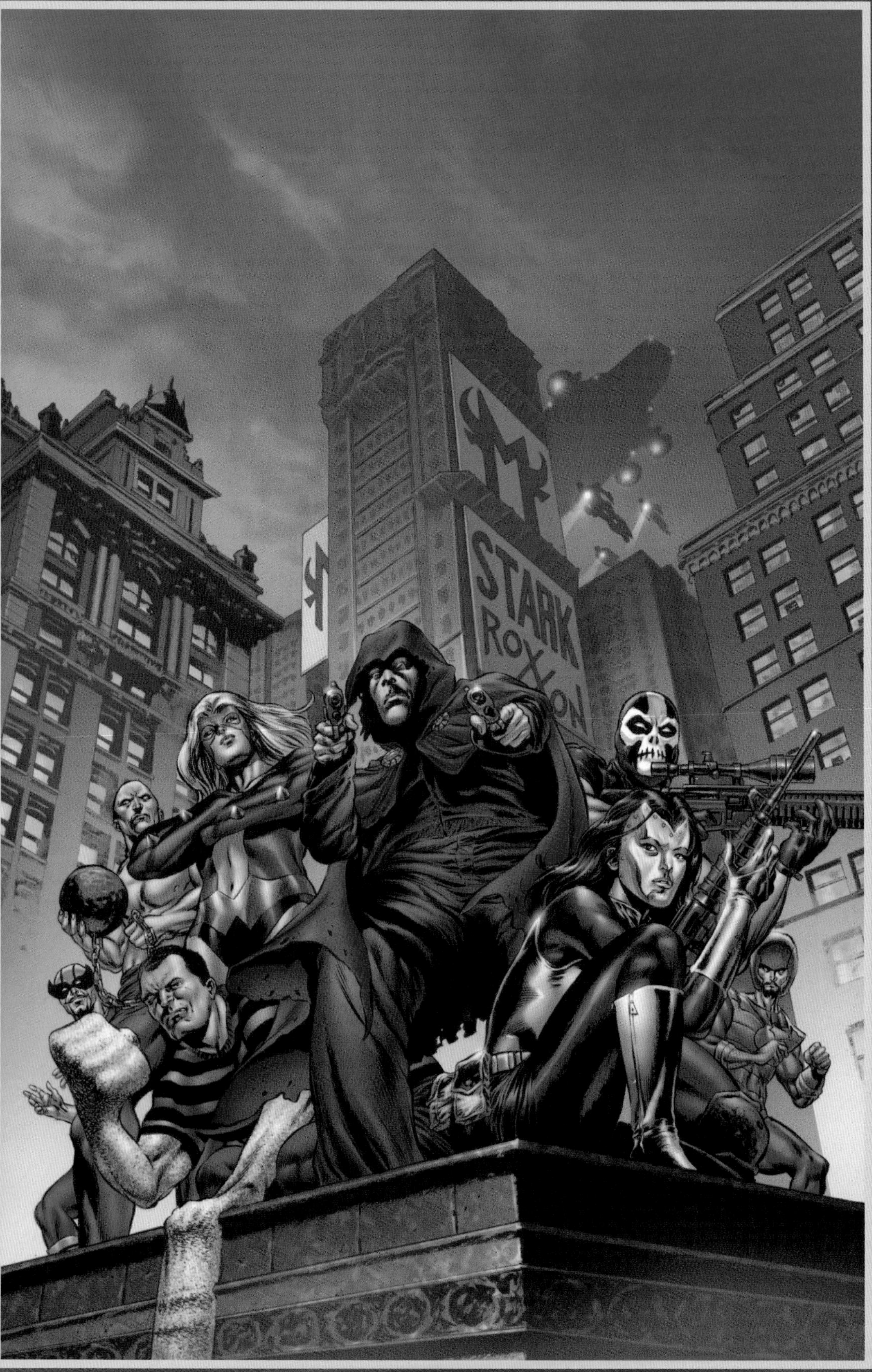
STARK
ROXXON

ISSUE #1: THIS THING OF OURS

The New Avengers and the Astonishing X-Men met to discuss the future of Wanda Maximoff, the Scarlet Witch – daughter of the powerful mutant terrorist Magneto. After losing control of her reality-altering powers and suffering a total nervous breakdown, Wanda had unleashed chaos upon her teammates, the Avengers, killing and injuring many of their number. Magneto intervened and took his daughter to the island nation of Genosha, where Charles Xavier – Professor X, founder of the X-Men – was to help her recover. But Xavier failed. So Wanda's friends and teammates gathered to decide whether such a powerful, unstable individual should live or die.

But Wanda's brother, Pietro – the former Avenger known as Quicksilver – refused to leave her fate in the hands of others. He urged Wanda to use her powers to remake the world into a place where their family's fondest wishes came true.

Everything burned to white. Reality as we know it vanished...

And was replaced by a society in which mutants ruled the culture, dominating most countries, religions and politics. A society in which normal humans – called "Sapiens" – are the oppressed minority, viewed as an evolutionary dead end, a species that will die out within two generations.

A kingdom united under Magneto's House of M.

In this world, the heroes we know live very different lives...and so do the villains.

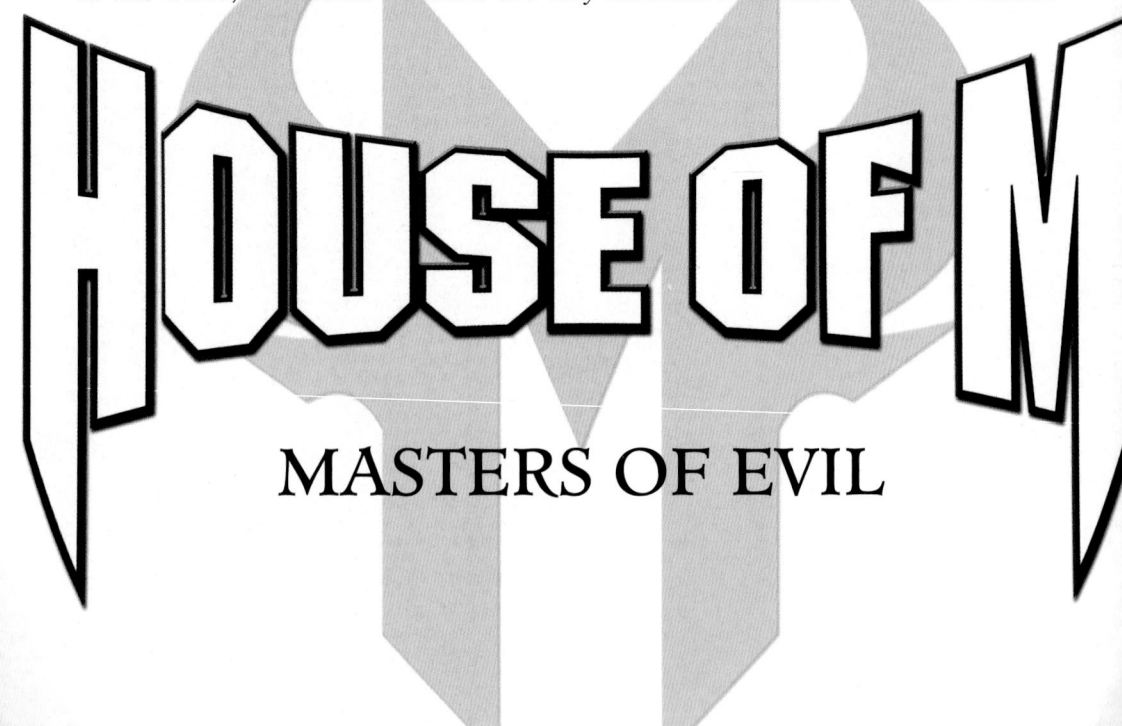

HOUSE OF M

MASTERS OF EVIL

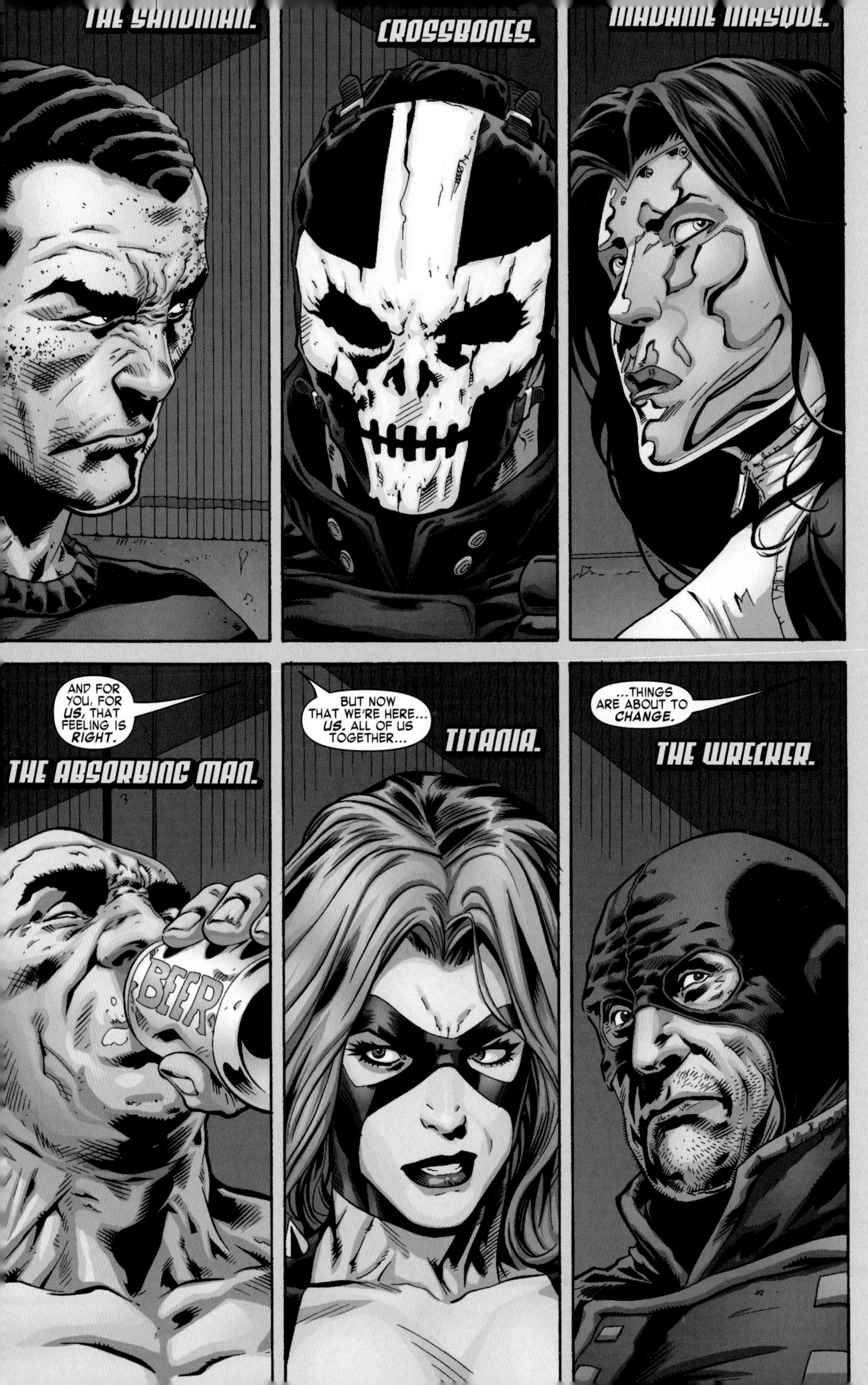
THE SANDMAN.
CROSSBONES.
MADAME MASQUE.
AND FOR YOU, FOR US, THAT FEELING IS RIGHT.
THE ABSORBING MAN.
BUT NOW THAT WE'RE HERE... US. ALL OF US TOGETHER...
TITANIA.
...THINGS ARE ABOUT TO CHANGE.
THE WRECKER.
BEER

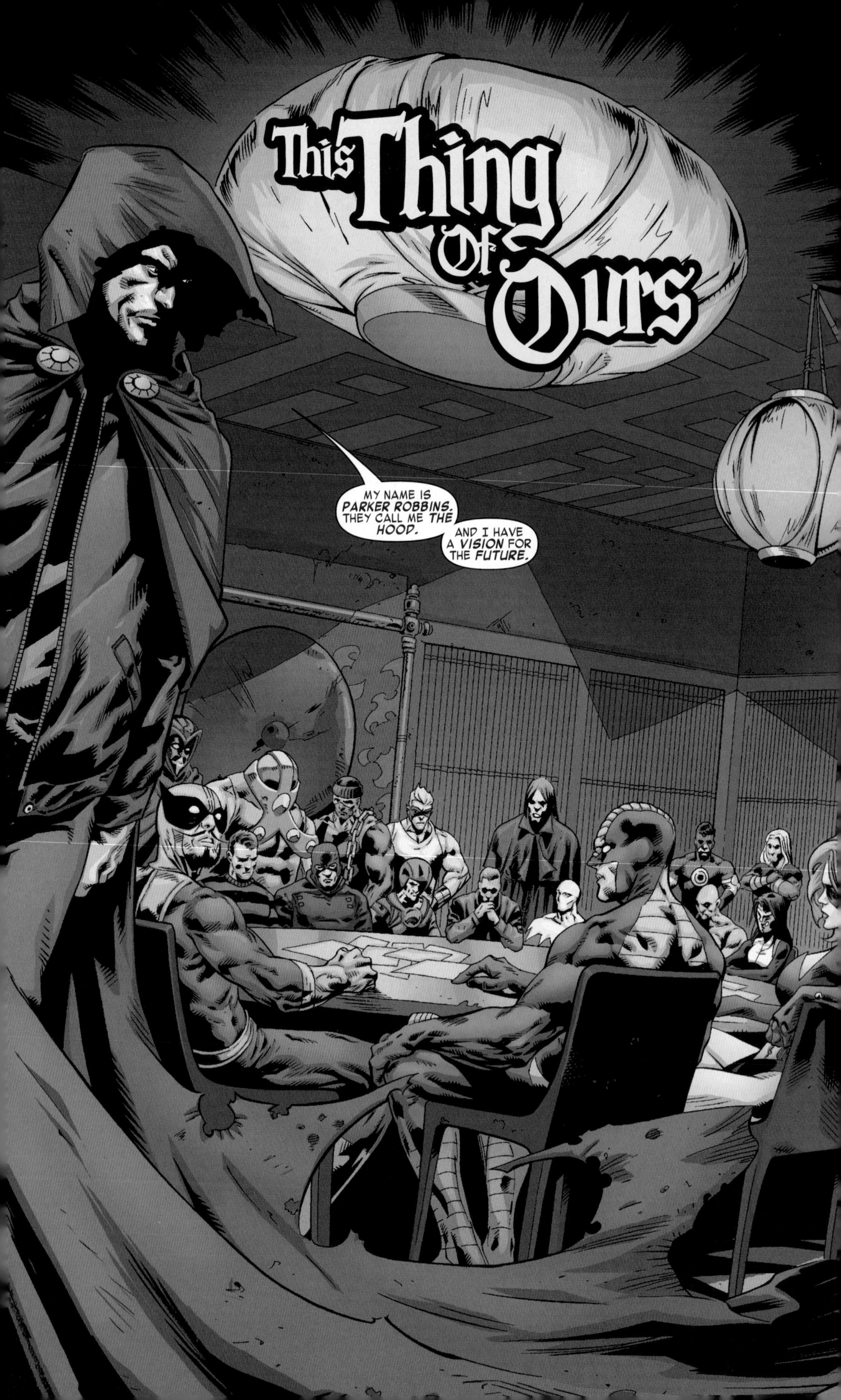
This Thing Of Ours
MY NAME IS PARKER ROBBINS. THEY CALL ME THE HOOD.
AND I HAVE A VISION FOR THE FUTURE.

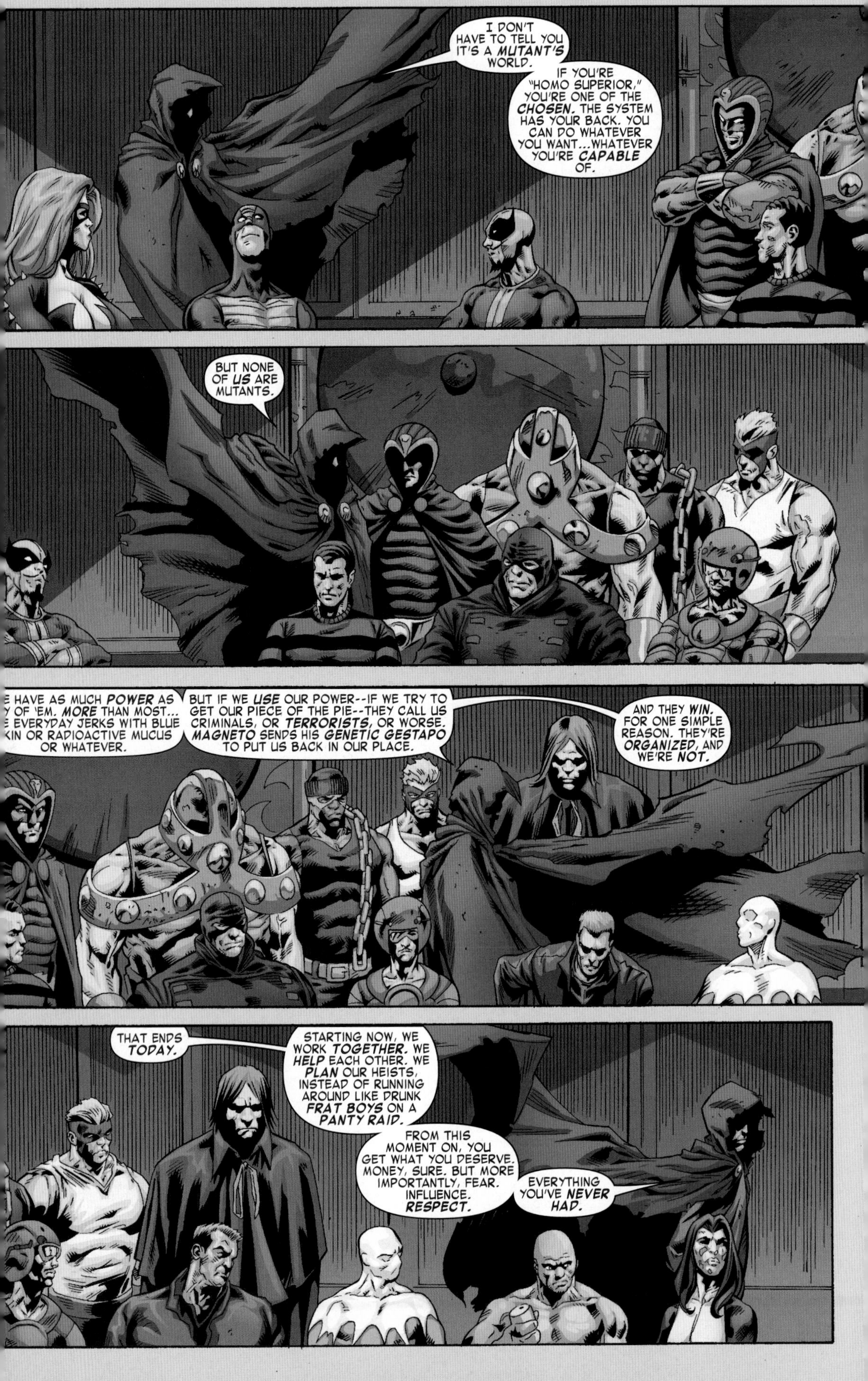
I DON'T HAVE TO TELL YOU IT'S A MUTANT'S WORLD.
IF YOU'RE "HOMO SUPERIOR," YOU'RE ONE OF THE CHOSEN. THE SYSTEM HAS YOUR BACK. YOU CAN DO WHATEVER YOU WANT...WHATEVER YOU'RE CAPABLE OF.
BUT NONE OF US ARE MUTANTS.
E HAVE AS MUCH POWER AS Y OF 'EM. MORE THAN MOST... E EVERYDAY JERKS WITH BLUE KIN OR RADIOACTIVE MUCUS OR WHATEVER.
BUT IF WE USE OUR POWER--IF WE TRY TO GET OUR PIECE OF THE PIE--THEY CALL US CRIMINALS, OR TERRORISTS, OR WORSE. MAGNETO SENDS HIS GENETIC GESTAPO TO PUT US BACK IN OUR PLACE.
AND THEY WIN. FOR ONE SIMPLE REASON. THEY'RE ORGANIZED, AND WE'RE NOT.
THAT ENDS TODAY.
STARTING NOW, WE WORK TOGETHER. WE HELP EACH OTHER. WE PLAN OUR HEISTS, INSTEAD OF RUNNING AROUND LIKE DRUNK FRAT BOYS ON A PANTY RAID.
FROM THIS MOMENT ON, YOU GET WHAT YOU DESERVE. MONEY, SURE. BUT MORE IMPORTANTLY, FEAR. INFLUENCE. RESPECT.
EVERYTHING YOU'VE NEVER HAD.

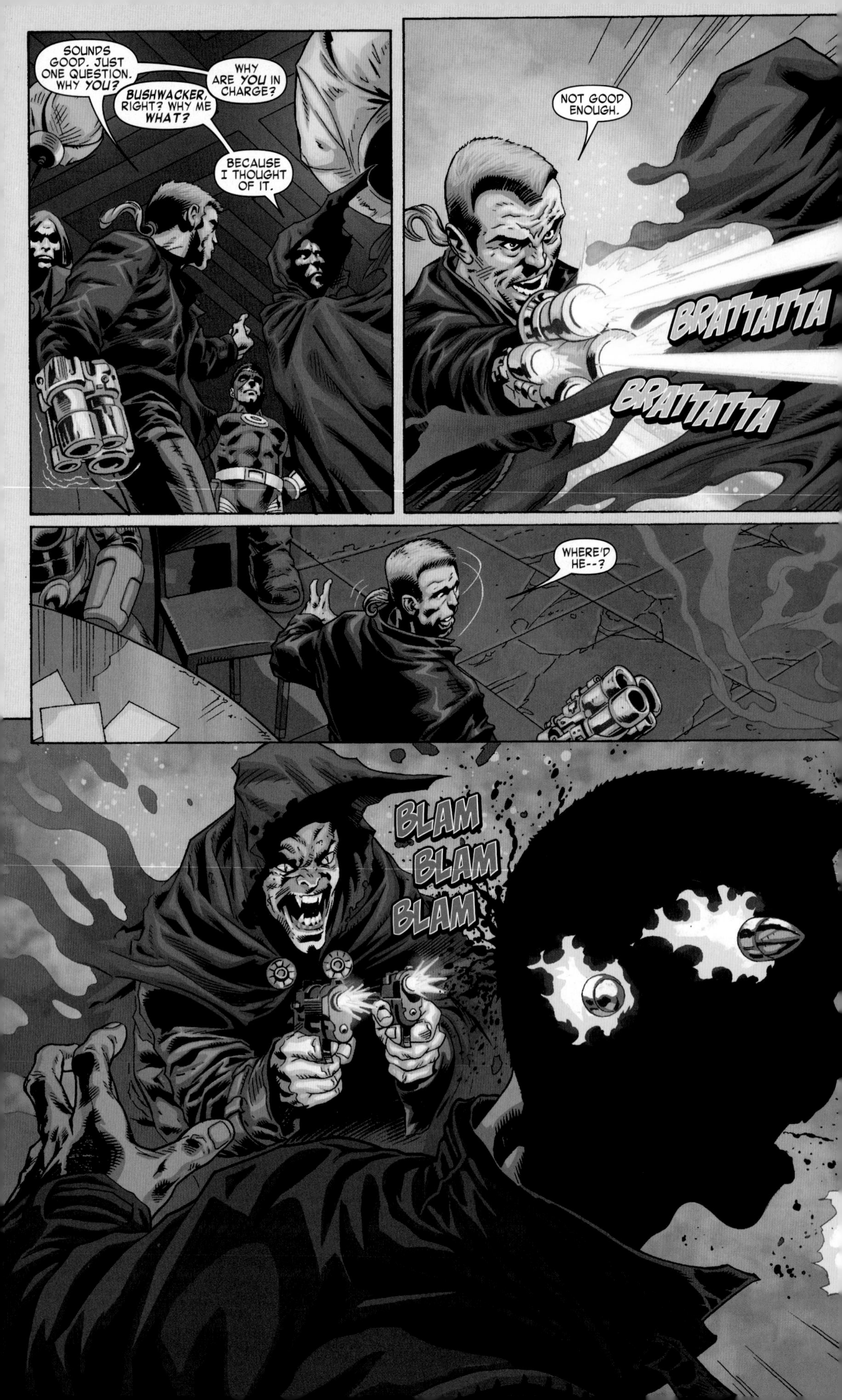
SOUNDS GOOD. JUST ONE QUESTION. WHY YOU?
BUSHWACKER, RIGHT? WHY ME WHAT?
WHY ARE YOU IN CHARGE?
BECAUSE I THOUGHT OF IT.
NOT GOOD ENOUGH.
BRATTATTA
BRATTATTA
WHERE'D HE--?
BLAM
BLAM
BLAM

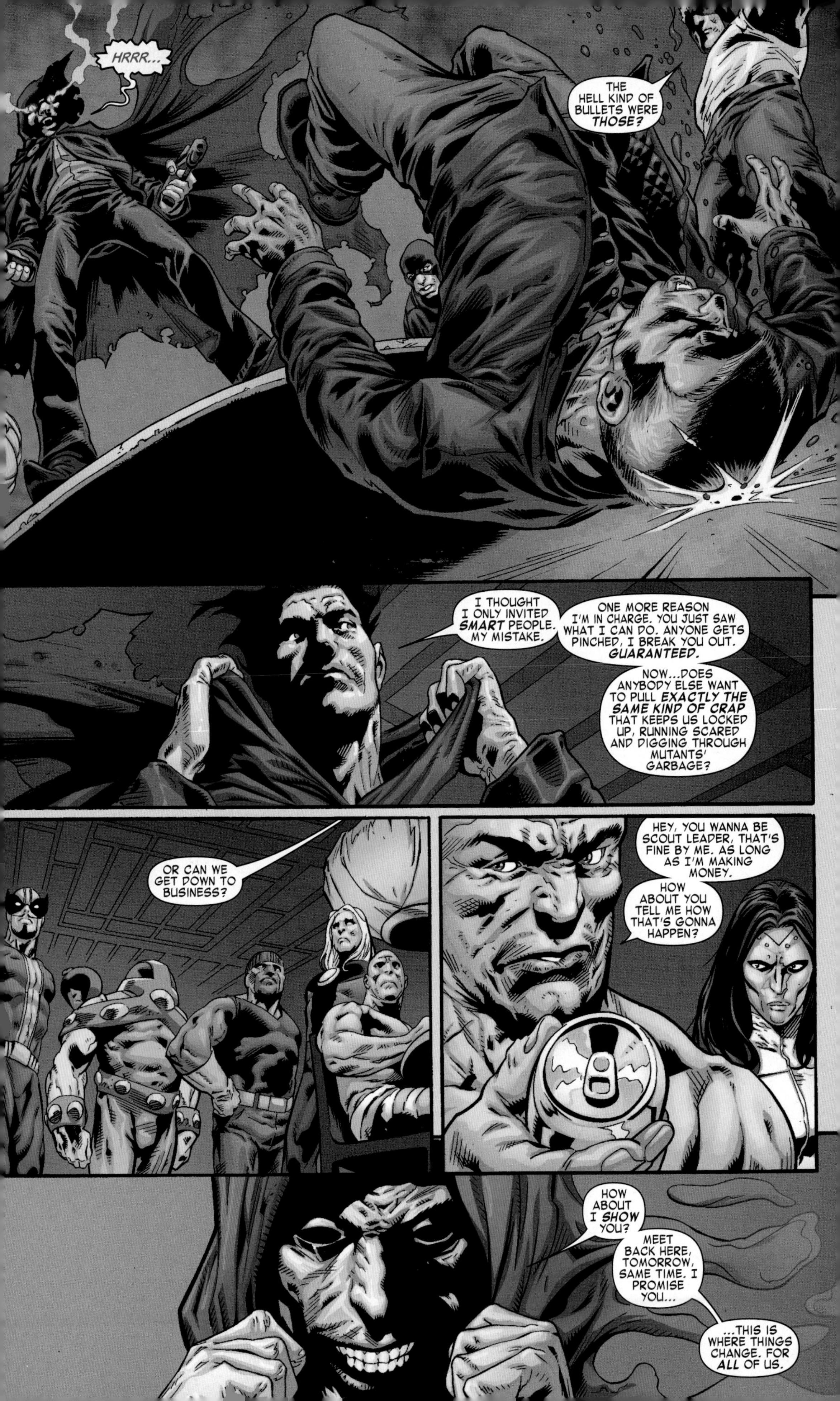
HRRR...
THE HELL KIND OF BULLETS WERE *THOSE?*
I THOUGHT I ONLY INVITED **SMART** PEOPLE. MY MISTAKE.
ONE MORE REASON I'M IN CHARGE. YOU JUST SAW WHAT I CAN DO. ANYONE GETS PINCHED, I BREAK YOU OUT. ***GUARANTEED.***
NOW...DOES ANYBODY ELSE WANT TO PULL ***EXACTLY THE SAME KIND OF CRAP*** THAT KEEPS US LOCKED UP, RUNNING SCARED AND DIGGING THROUGH MUTANTS' GARBAGE?
OR CAN WE GET DOWN TO BUSINESS?
HEY, YOU WANNA BE SCOUT LEADER, THAT'S FINE BY ME. AS LONG AS I'M MAKING MONEY.
HOW ABOUT YOU TELL ME HOW THAT'S GONNA HAPPEN?
HOW ABOUT I ***SHOW*** YOU?
MEET BACK HERE, TOMORROW, SAME TIME. I PROMISE YOU...
...THIS IS WHERE THINGS CHANGE. FOR ***ALL*** OF US.

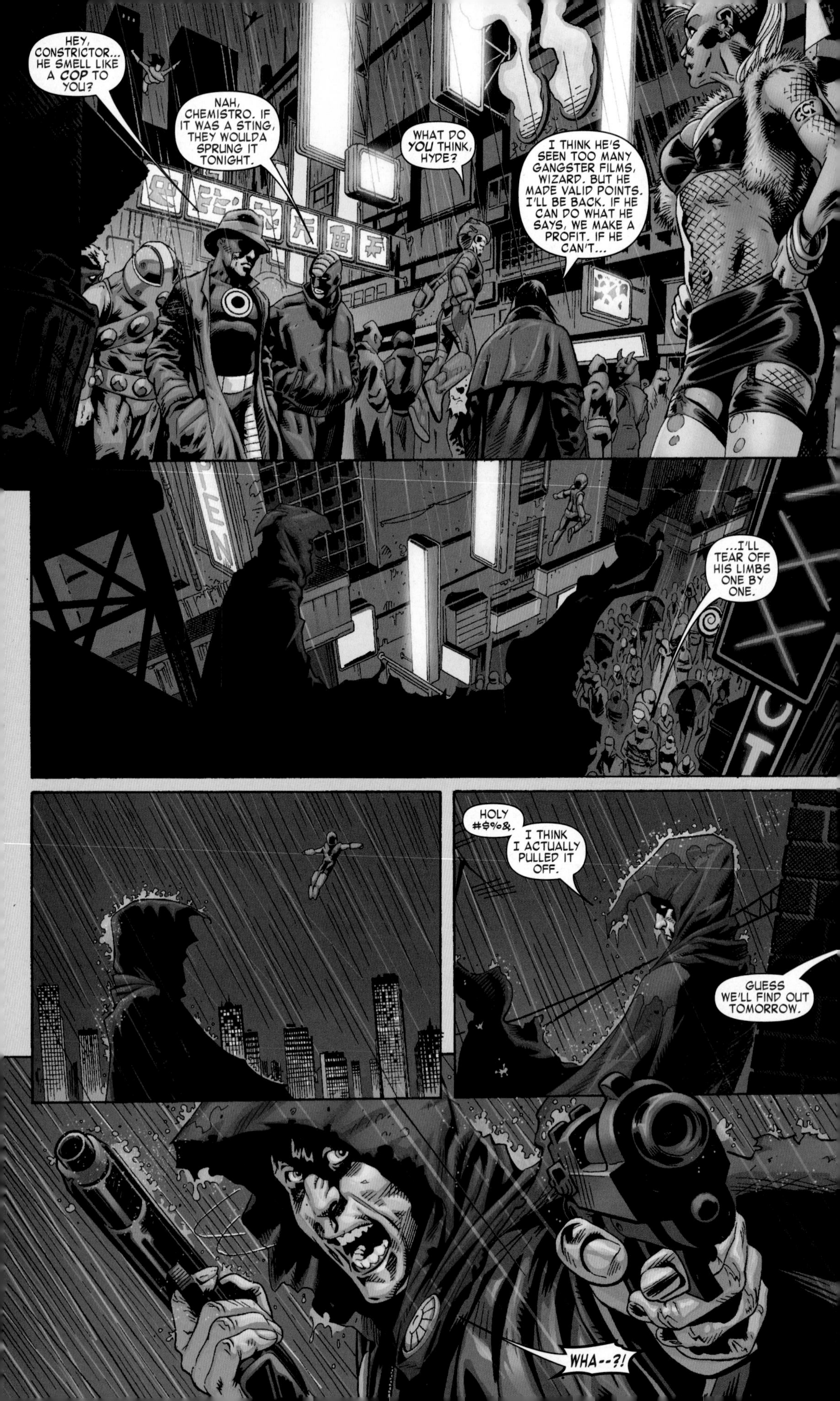
HEY, CONSTRICTOR... HE SMELL LIKE A *COP* TO YOU?
NAH, CHEMISTRO. IF IT WAS A STING, THEY WOULDA SPRUNG IT TONIGHT.
WHAT DO *YOU* THINK, HYDE?
I THINK HE'S SEEN TOO MANY GANGSTER FILMS, WIZARD. BUT HE MADE VALID POINTS. I'LL BE BACK. IF HE CAN DO WHAT HE SAYS, WE MAKE A PROFIT. IF HE CAN'T...
...I'LL TEAR OFF HIS LIMBS ONE BY ONE.
HOLY #$%&.
I THINK I ACTUALLY PULLED IT OFF.
GUESS WE'LL FIND OUT TOMORROW.
WHA--?!

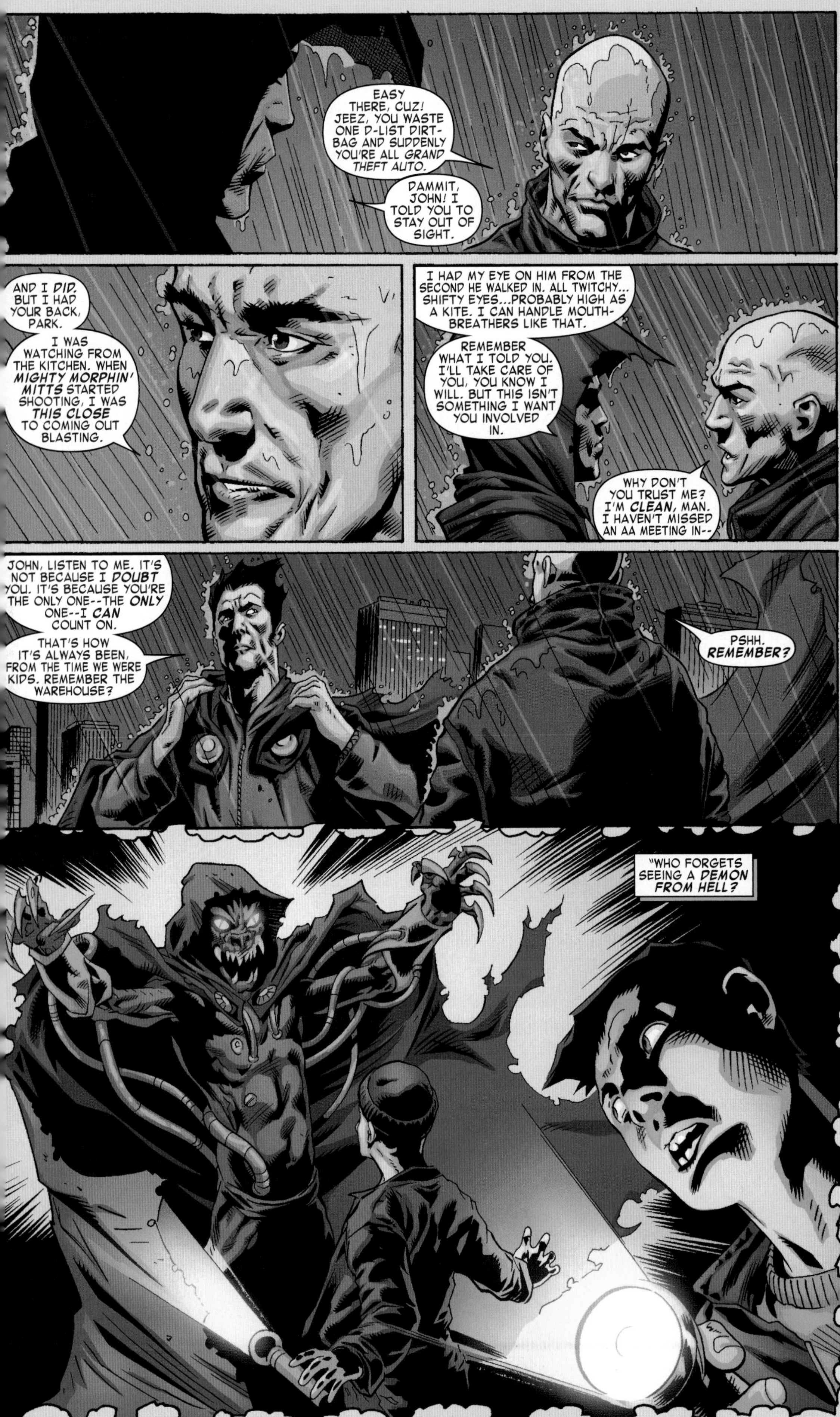
EASY THERE, CUZ! JEEZ, YOU WASTE ONE D-LIST DIRT-BAG AND SUDDENLY YOU'RE ALL *GRAND THEFT AUTO*.
DAMMIT, JOHN! I TOLD YOU TO STAY OUT OF SIGHT.
AND I *DID*. BUT I HAD YOUR BACK, PARK.
I WAS WATCHING FROM THE KITCHEN. WHEN *MIGHTY MORPHIN' MITTS* STARTED SHOOTING, I WAS *THIS CLOSE* TO COMING OUT BLASTING.
I HAD MY EYE ON HIM FROM THE SECOND HE WALKED IN. ALL TWITCHY... SHIFTY EYES...PROBABLY HIGH AS A KITE. I CAN HANDLE MOUTH-BREATHERS LIKE THAT.
REMEMBER WHAT I TOLD YOU. I'LL TAKE CARE OF YOU, YOU KNOW I WILL. BUT THIS ISN'T SOMETHING I WANT YOU INVOLVED IN.
WHY DON'T YOU TRUST ME? I'M *CLEAN*, MAN. I HAVEN'T MISSED AN AA MEETING IN--
JOHN, LISTEN TO ME. IT'S NOT BECAUSE I *DOUBT* YOU. IT'S BECAUSE YOU'RE THE ONLY ONE--THE *ONLY* ONE--I *CAN* COUNT ON.
THAT'S HOW IT'S ALWAYS BEEN, FROM THE TIME WE WERE KIDS. REMEMBER THE WAREHOUSE?
PSHH. *REMEMBER?*
"WHO FORGETS SEEING A *DEMON FROM HELL?*

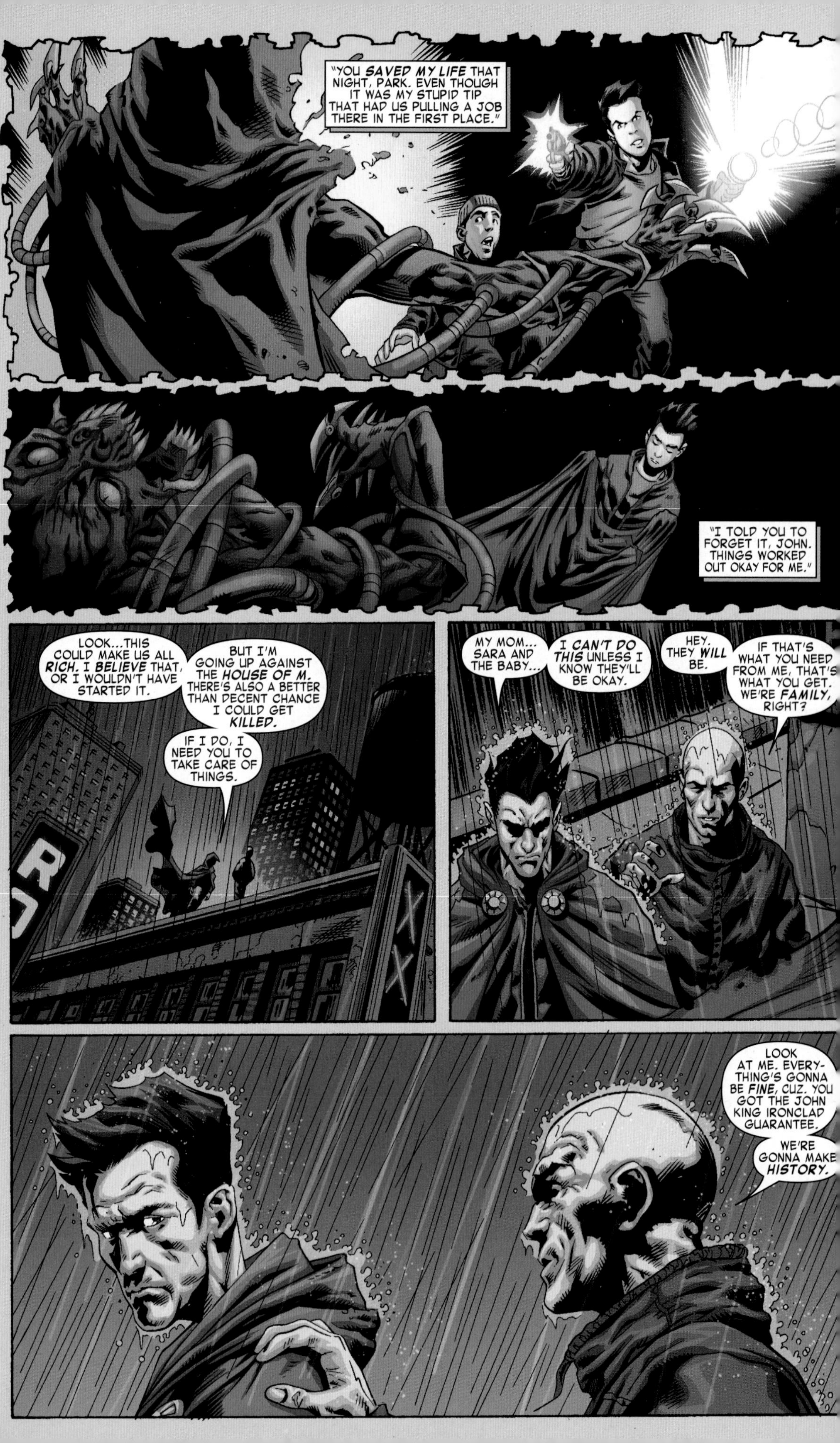
"YOU SAVED MY LIFE THAT NIGHT, PARK. EVEN THOUGH IT WAS MY STUPID TIP THAT HAD US PULLING A JOB THERE IN THE FIRST PLACE."
"I TOLD YOU TO FORGET IT, JOHN. THINGS WORKED OUT OKAY FOR ME."
LOOK...THIS COULD MAKE US ALL RICH. I BELIEVE THAT, OR I WOULDN'T HAVE STARTED IT.
BUT I'M GOING UP AGAINST THE HOUSE OF M. THERE'S ALSO A BETTER THAN DECENT CHANCE I COULD GET KILLED.
IF I DO, I NEED YOU TO TAKE CARE OF THINGS.
MY MOM... SARA AND THE BABY...
I CAN'T DO THIS UNLESS I KNOW THEY'LL BE OKAY.
HEY. THEY WILL BE.
IF THAT'S WHAT YOU NEED FROM ME, THAT'S WHAT YOU GET. WE'RE FAMILY, RIGHT?
LOOK AT ME. EVERYTHING'S GONNA BE FINE, CUZ. YOU GOT THE JOHN KING IRONCLAD GUARANTEE.
WE'RE GONNA MAKE HISTORY.

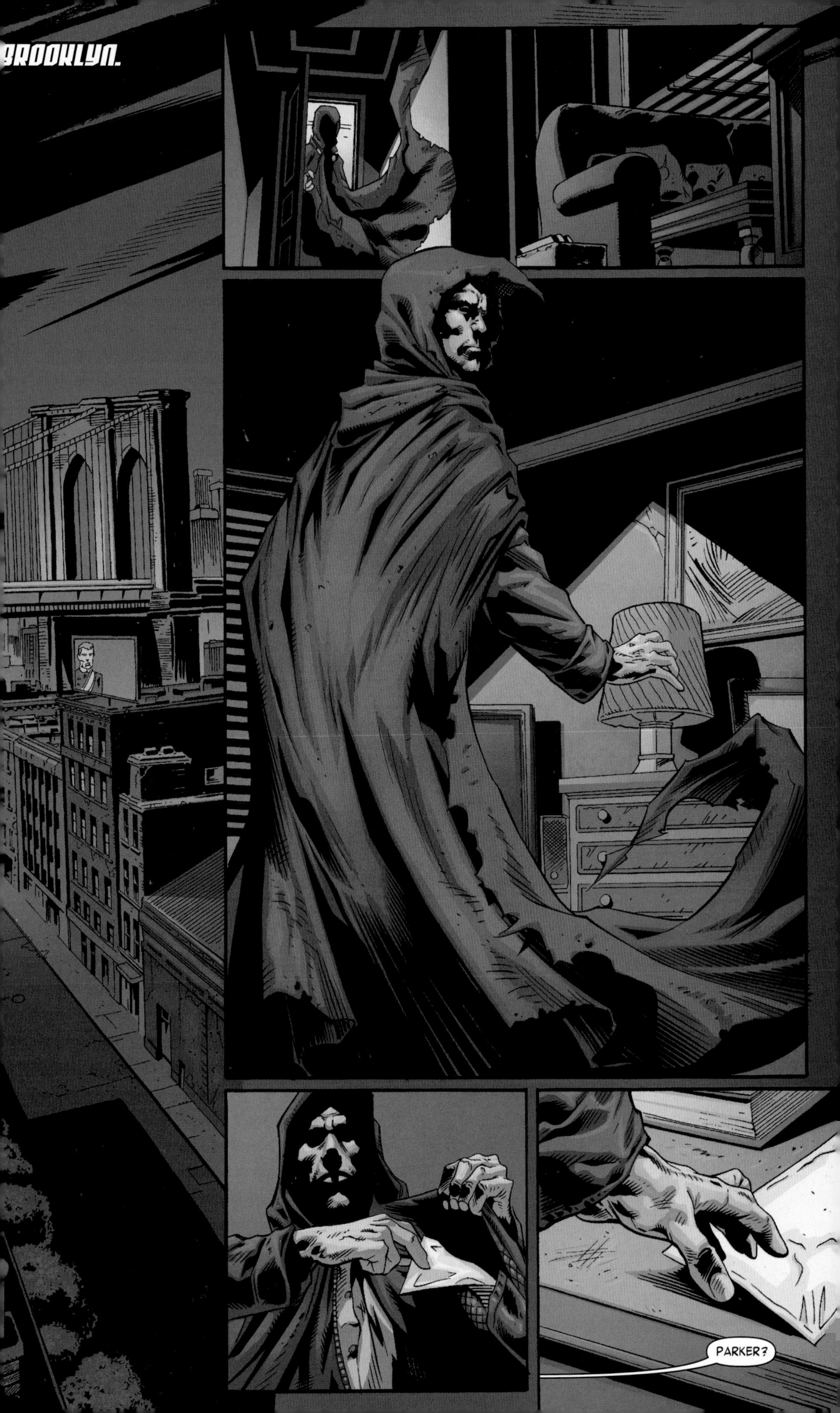
BROOKLYN.
PARKER?

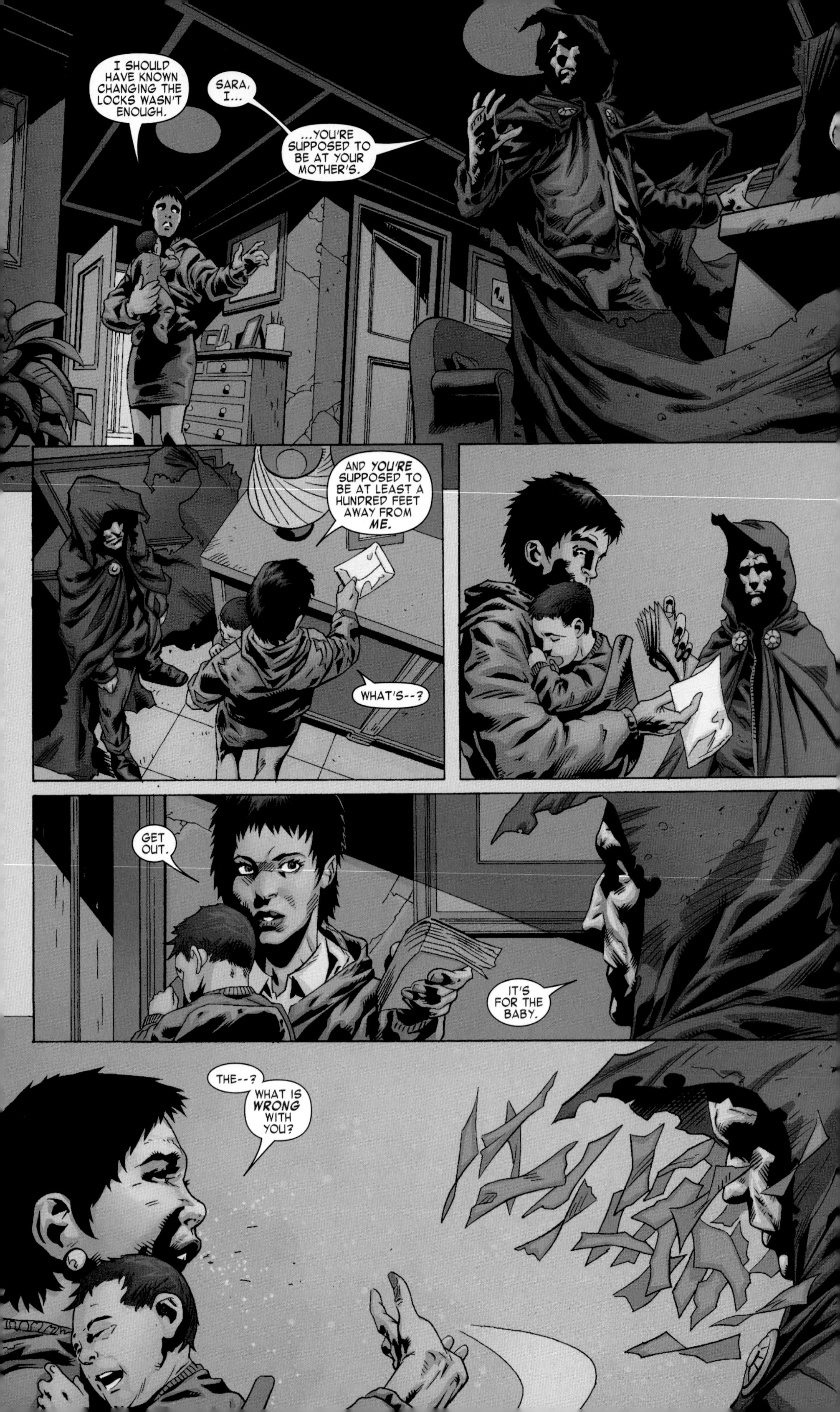
I SHOULD HAVE KNOWN CHANGING THE LOCKS WASN'T ENOUGH.
SARA, I...
...YOU'RE SUPPOSED TO BE AT YOUR MOTHER'S.
AND *YOU'RE* SUPPOSED TO BE AT LEAST A HUNDRED FEET AWAY FROM *ME.*
WHAT'S--?
GET OUT.
IT'S FOR THE BABY.
THE--? WHAT IS *WRONG* WITH YOU?

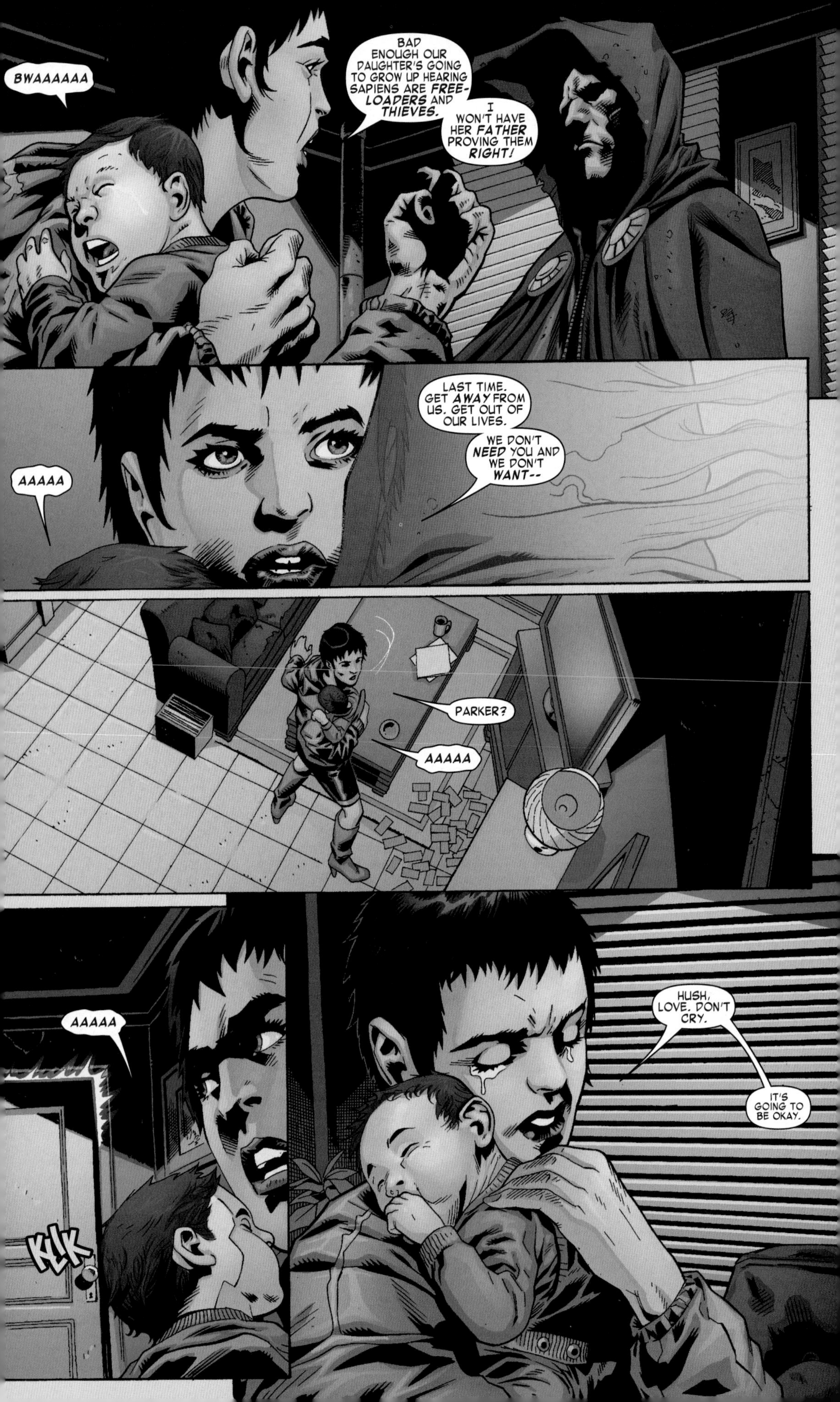
BWAAAAAA
BAD ENOUGH OUR DAUGHTER'S GOING TO GROW UP HEARING SAPIENS ARE FREE-LOADERS AND THIEVES.
I WON'T HAVE HER FATHER PROVING THEM RIGHT!
AAAAA
LAST TIME. GET AWAY FROM US. GET OUT OF OUR LIVES.
WE DON'T NEED YOU AND WE DON'T WANT--
PARKER?
AAAAA
AAAAA
KLIK
HUSH, LOVE. DON'T CRY.
IT'S GOING TO BE OKAY.

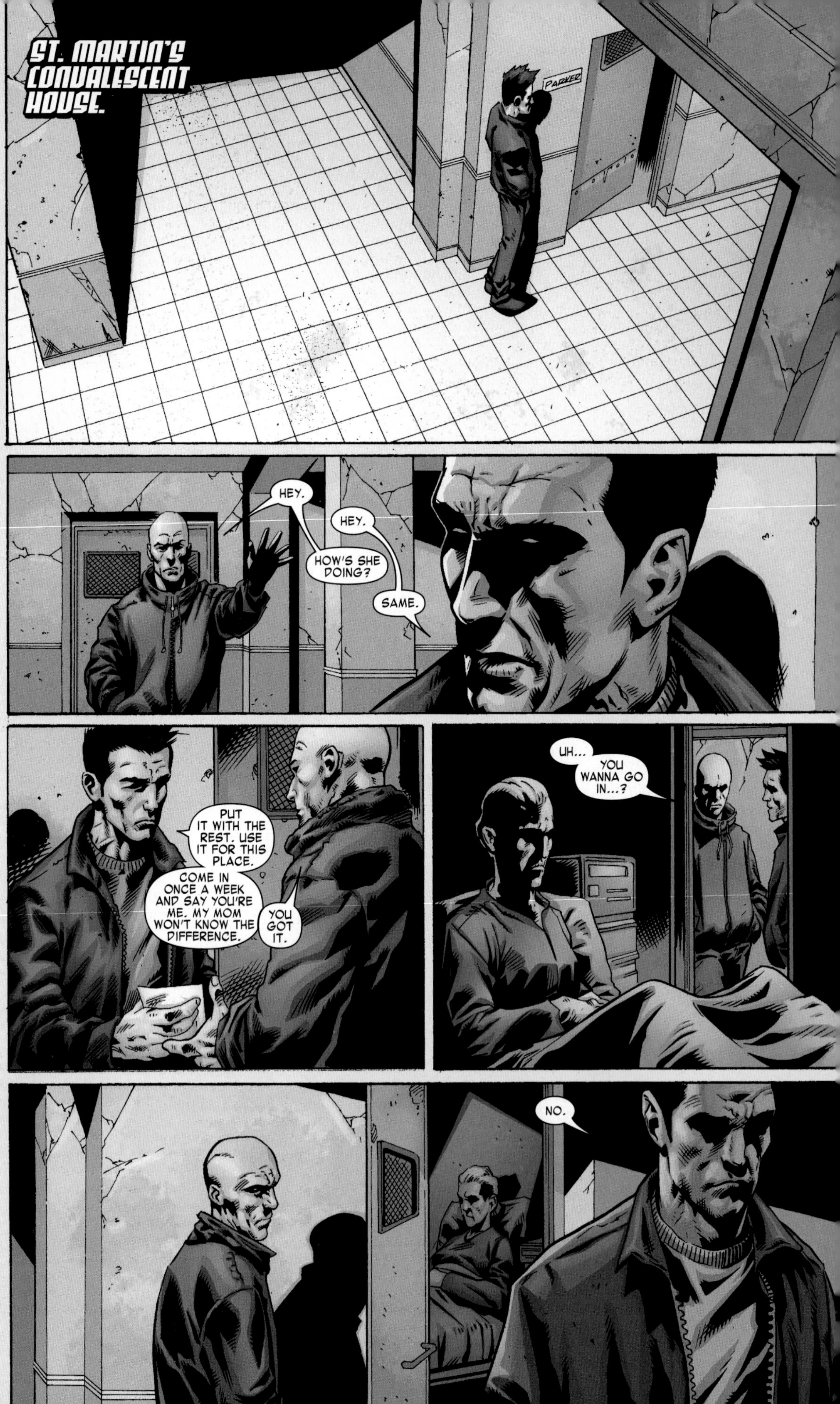
ST. MARTIN'S CONVALESCENT HOUSE.
PARKER
HEY.
HEY.
HOW'S SHE DOING?
SAME.
PUT IT WITH THE REST. USE IT FOR THIS PLACE.
COME IN ONCE A WEEK AND SAY YOU'RE ME. MY MOM WON'T KNOW THE DIFFERENCE.
YOU GOT IT.
UH...
YOU WANNA GO IN...?
NO.

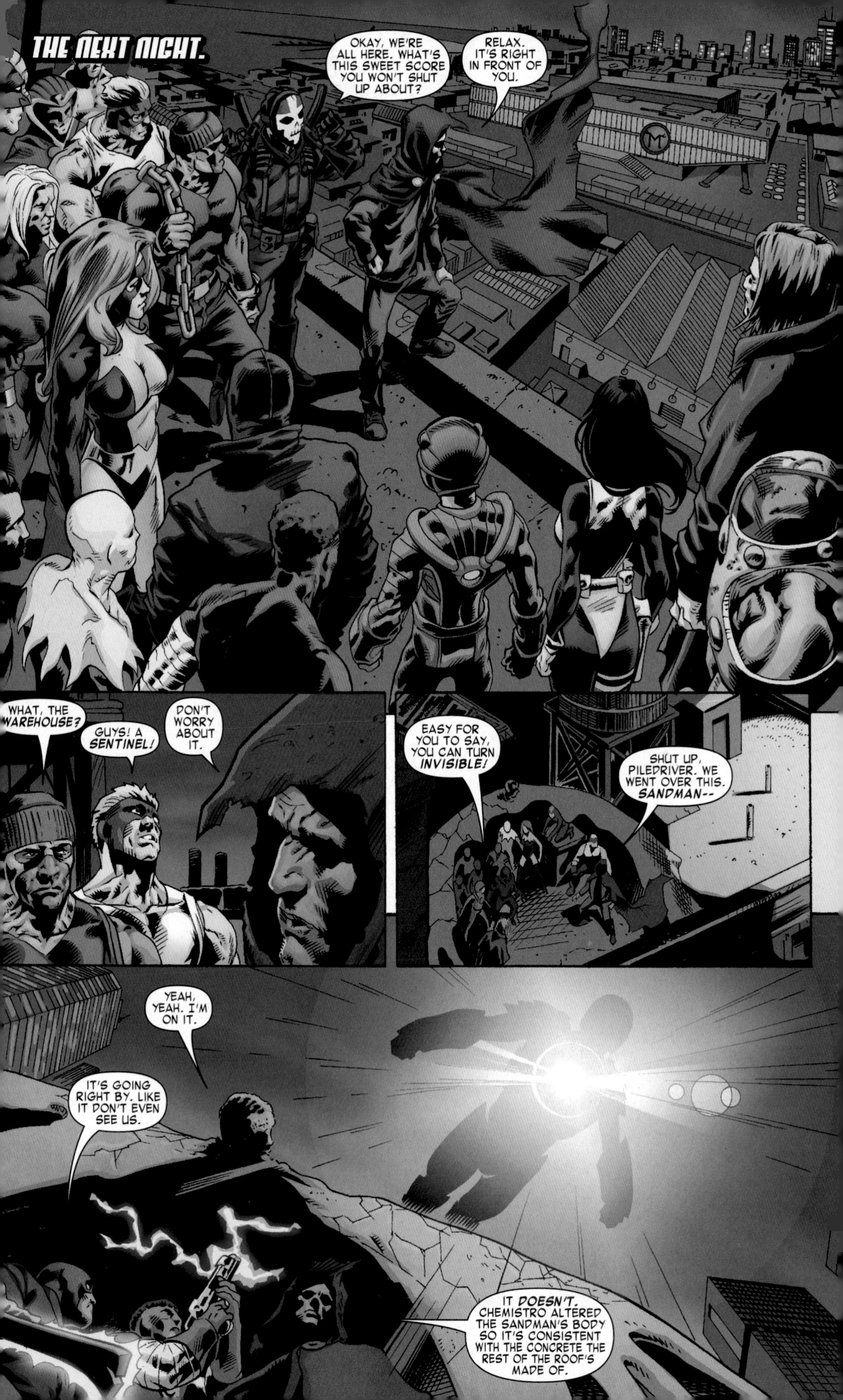
THE NEXT NIGHT.
OKAY, WE'RE ALL HERE. WHAT'S THIS SWEET SCORE YOU WON'T SHUT UP ABOUT?
RELAX. IT'S RIGHT IN FRONT OF YOU.
WHAT, THE WAREHOUSE?
GUYS! A SENTINEL!
DON'T WORRY ABOUT IT.
EASY FOR YOU TO SAY, YOU CAN TURN INVISIBLE!
SHUT UP, PILEDRIVER. WE WENT OVER THIS. SANDMAN--
YEAH, YEAH. I'M ON IT.
IT'S GOING RIGHT BY. LIKE IT DON'T EVEN SEE US.
IT DOESN'T. CHEMISTRO ALTERED THE SANDMAN'S BODY SO IT'S CONSISTENT WITH THE CONCRETE THE REST OF THE ROOF'S MADE OF.

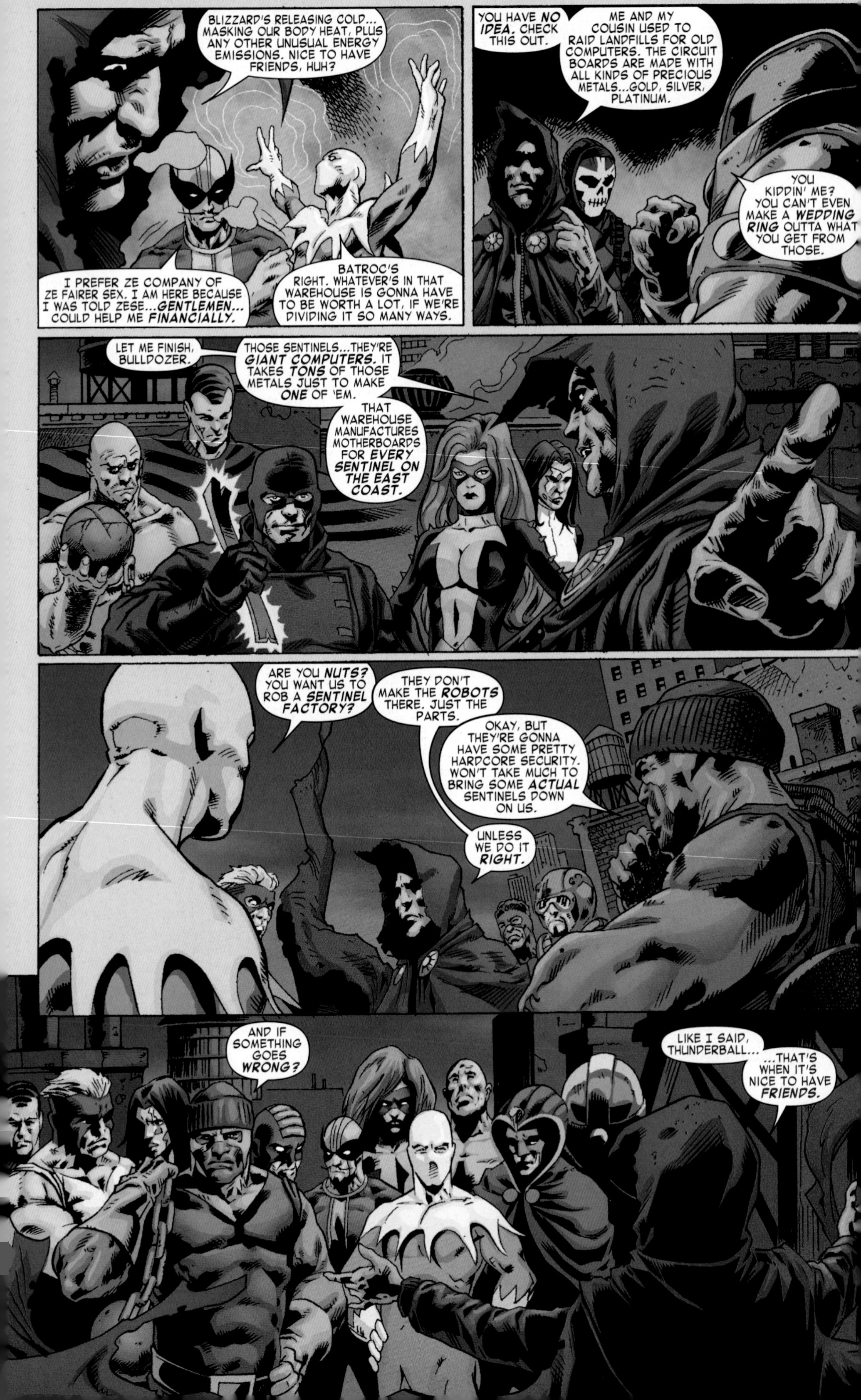
BLIZZARD'S RELEASING COLD... MASKING OUR BODY HEAT, PLUS ANY OTHER UNUSUAL ENERGY EMISSIONS. NICE TO HAVE FRIENDS, HUH?
I PREFER ZE COMPANY OF ZE FAIRER SEX. I AM HERE BECAUSE I WAS TOLD ZESE...GENTLEMEN... COULD HELP ME FINANCIALLY.
BATROC'S RIGHT. WHATEVER'S IN THAT WAREHOUSE IS GONNA HAVE TO BE WORTH A LOT, IF WE'RE DIVIDING IT SO MANY WAYS.
YOU HAVE NO IDEA. CHECK THIS OUT.
ME AND MY COUSIN USED TO RAID LANDFILLS FOR OLD COMPUTERS. THE CIRCUIT BOARDS ARE MADE WITH ALL KINDS OF PRECIOUS METALS...GOLD, SILVER, PLATINUM.
YOU KIDDIN' ME? YOU CAN'T EVEN MAKE A WEDDING RING OUTTA WHAT YOU GET FROM THOSE.
LET ME FINISH, BULLDOZER.
THOSE SENTINELS...THEY'RE GIANT COMPUTERS. IT TAKES TONS OF THOSE METALS JUST TO MAKE ONE OF 'EM.
THAT WAREHOUSE MANUFACTURES MOTHERBOARDS FOR EVERY SENTINEL ON THE EAST COAST.
ARE YOU NUTS? YOU WANT US TO ROB A SENTINEL FACTORY?
THEY DON'T MAKE THE ROBOTS THERE. JUST THE PARTS.
OKAY, BUT THEY'RE GONNA HAVE SOME PRETTY HARDCORE SECURITY. WON'T TAKE MUCH TO BRING SOME ACTUAL SENTINELS DOWN ON US.
UNLESS WE DO IT RIGHT.
AND IF SOMETHING GOES WRONG?
LIKE I SAID, THUNDERBALL...
...THAT'S WHEN IT'S NICE TO HAVE FRIENDS.

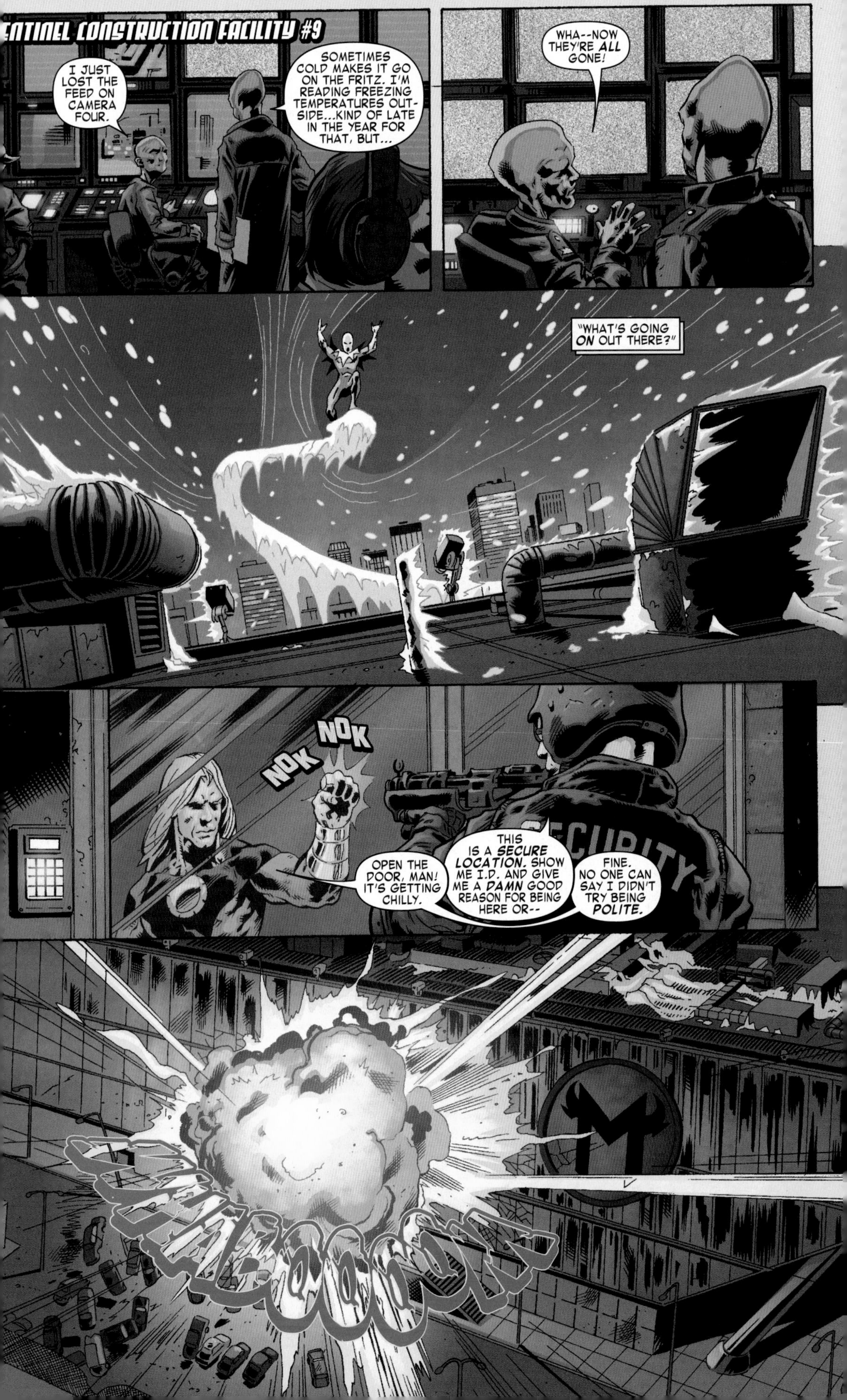
ENTINEL CONSTRUCTION FACILITY #9
I JUST LOST THE FEED ON CAMERA FOUR.
SOMETIMES COLD MAKES IT GO ON THE FRITZ. I'M READING FREEZING TEMPERATURES OUT-SIDE...KIND OF LATE IN THE YEAR FOR THAT, BUT...
WHA--NOW THEY'RE ALL GONE!
"WHAT'S GOING ON OUT THERE?"
NOK NOK
OPEN THE DOOR, MAN! IT'S GETTING CHILLY.
THIS IS A SECURE LOCATION. SHOW ME I.D. AND GIVE ME A DAMN GOOD REASON FOR BEING HERE OR--
FINE. NO ONE CAN SAY I DIDN'T TRY BEING POLITE.

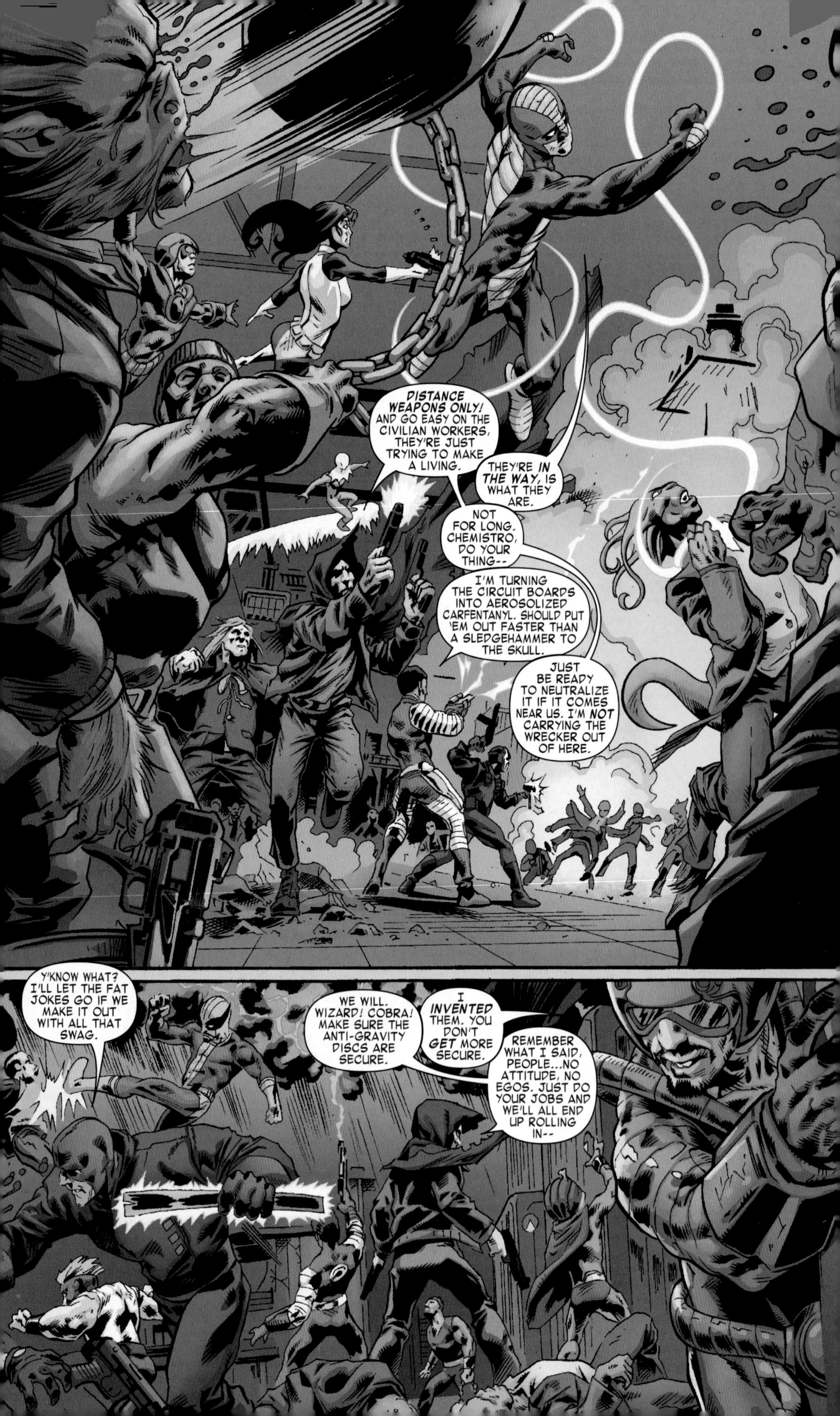
DISTANCE WEAPONS ONLY! AND GO EASY ON THE CIVILIAN WORKERS, THEY'RE JUST TRYING TO MAKE A LIVING.
THEY'RE IN THE WAY, IS WHAT THEY ARE.
NOT FOR LONG. CHEMISTRO, DO YOUR THING--
I'M TURNING THE CIRCUIT BOARDS INTO AEROSOLIZED CARFENTANYL. SHOULD PUT 'EM OUT FASTER THAN A SLEDGEHAMMER TO THE SKULL.
JUST BE READY TO NEUTRALIZE IT IF IT COMES NEAR US. I'M NOT CARRYING THE WRECKER OUT OF HERE.
Y'KNOW WHAT? I'LL LET THE FAT JOKES GO IF WE MAKE IT OUT WITH ALL THAT SWAG.
WE WILL. WIZARD! COBRA! MAKE SURE THE ANTI-GRAVITY DISCS ARE SECURE.
I INVENTED THEM. YOU DON'T GET MORE SECURE.
REMEMBER WHAT I SAID, PEOPLE...NO ATTITUDE, NO EGOS. JUST DO YOUR JOBS AND WE'LL ALL END UP ROLLING IN--

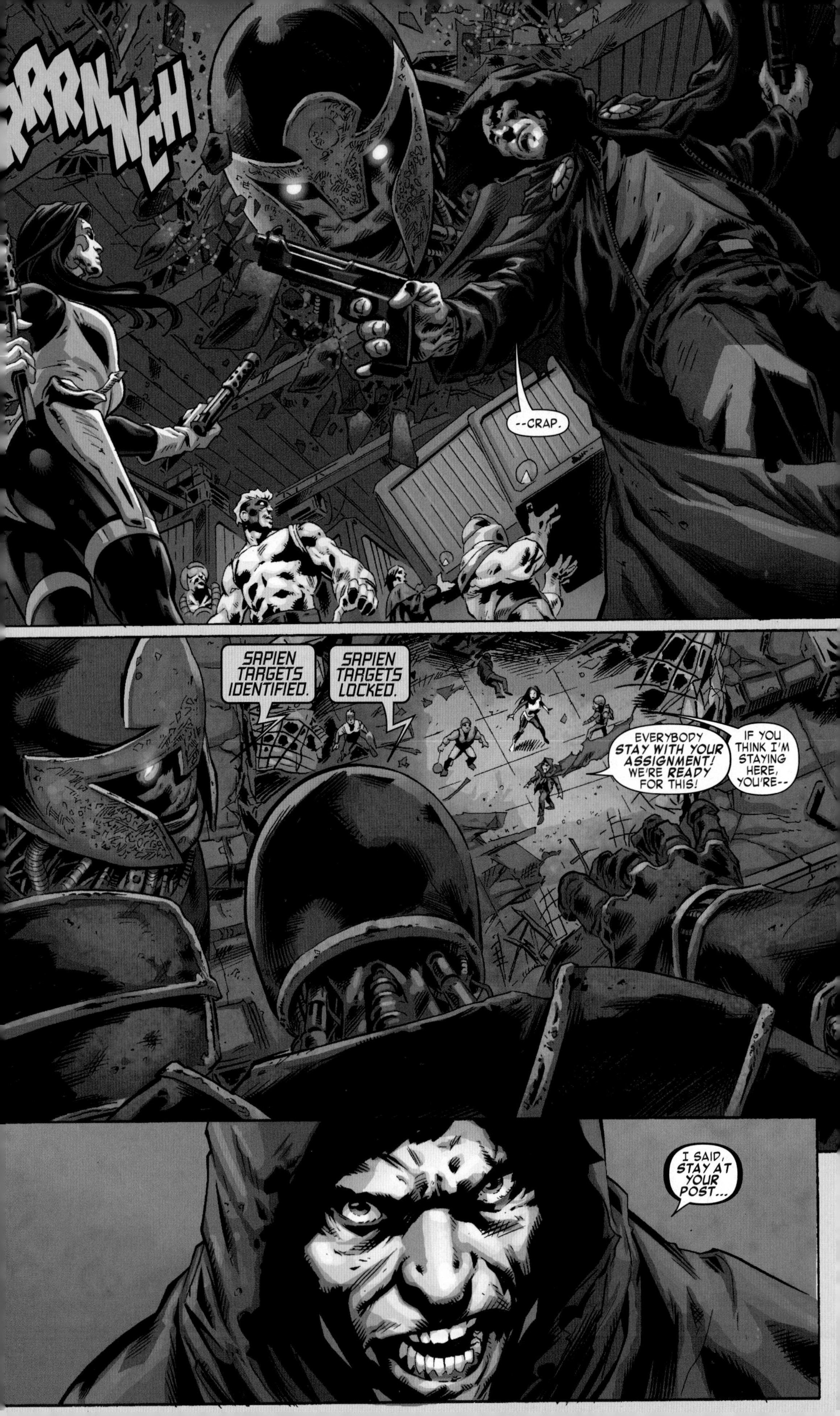
RRRNNNCH
--CRAP.
SAPIEN TARGETS IDENTIFIED.
SAPIEN TARGETS LOCKED.
EVERYBODY STAY WITH YOUR ASSIGNMENT! WE'RE READY FOR THIS!
IF YOU THINK I'M STAYING HERE, YOU'RE--
I SAID, STAY AT YOUR POST...

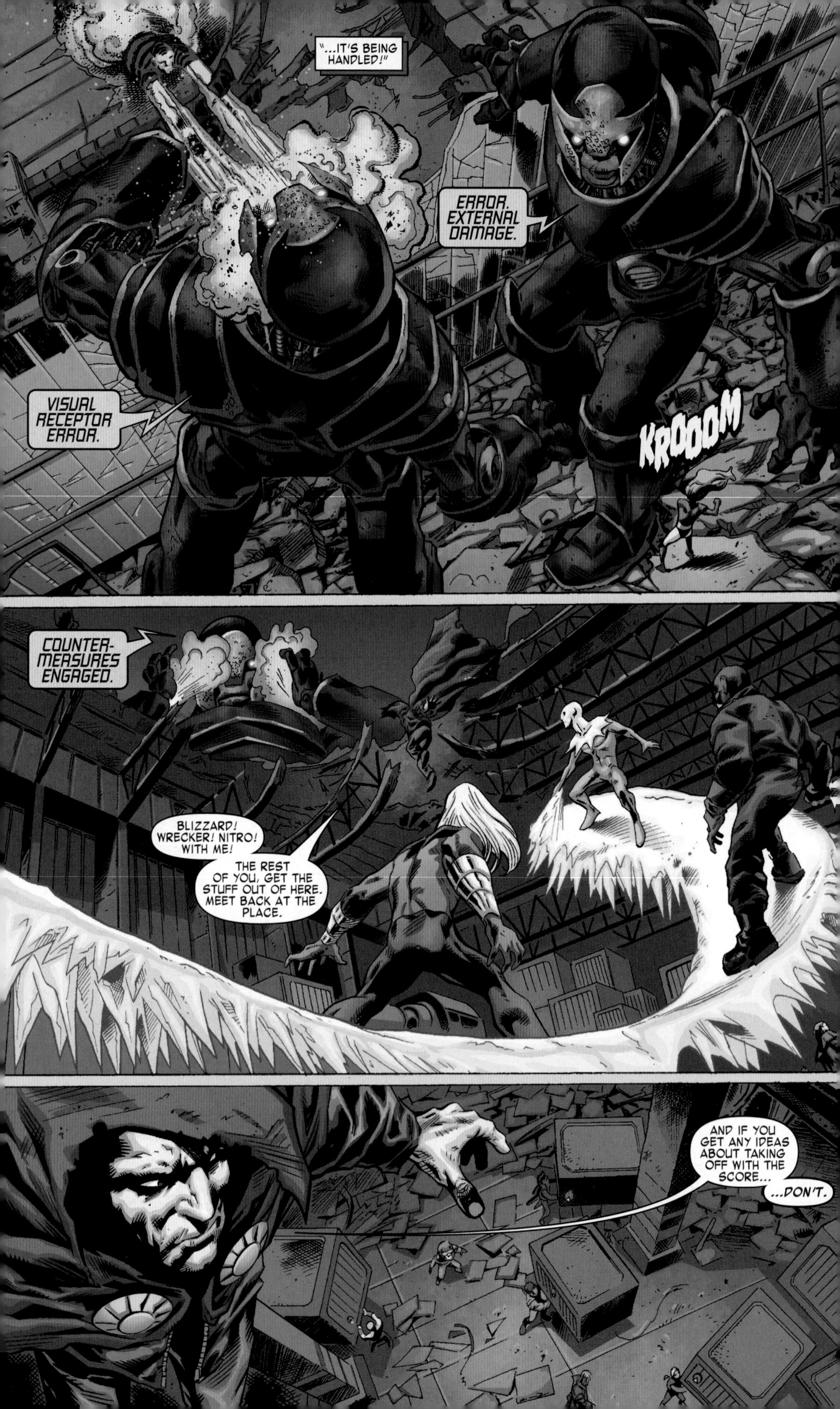
"...IT'S BEING HANDLED!"
ERROR. EXTERNAL DAMAGE.
VISUAL RECEPTOR ERROR.
KROOOM
COUNTER-MEASURES ENGAGED.
BLIZZARD! WRECKER! NITRO! WITH ME!
THE REST OF YOU, GET THE STUFF OUT OF HERE. MEET BACK AT THE PLACE.
AND IF YOU GET ANY IDEAS ABOUT TAKING OFF WITH THE SCORE...
...DON'T.

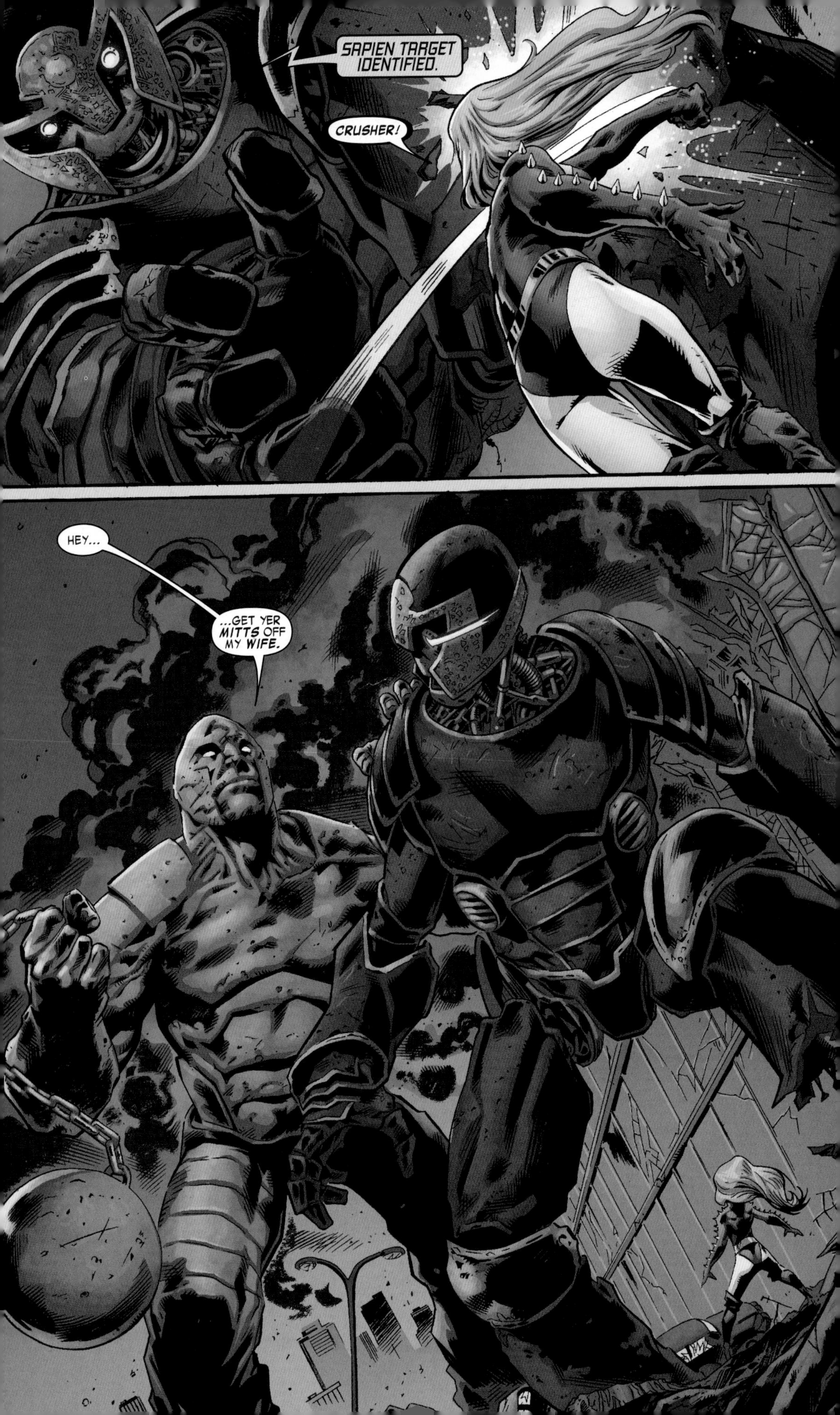
SAPIEN TARGET IDENTIFIED.
CRUSHER!
HEY...
...GET YER MITTS OFF MY WIFE.

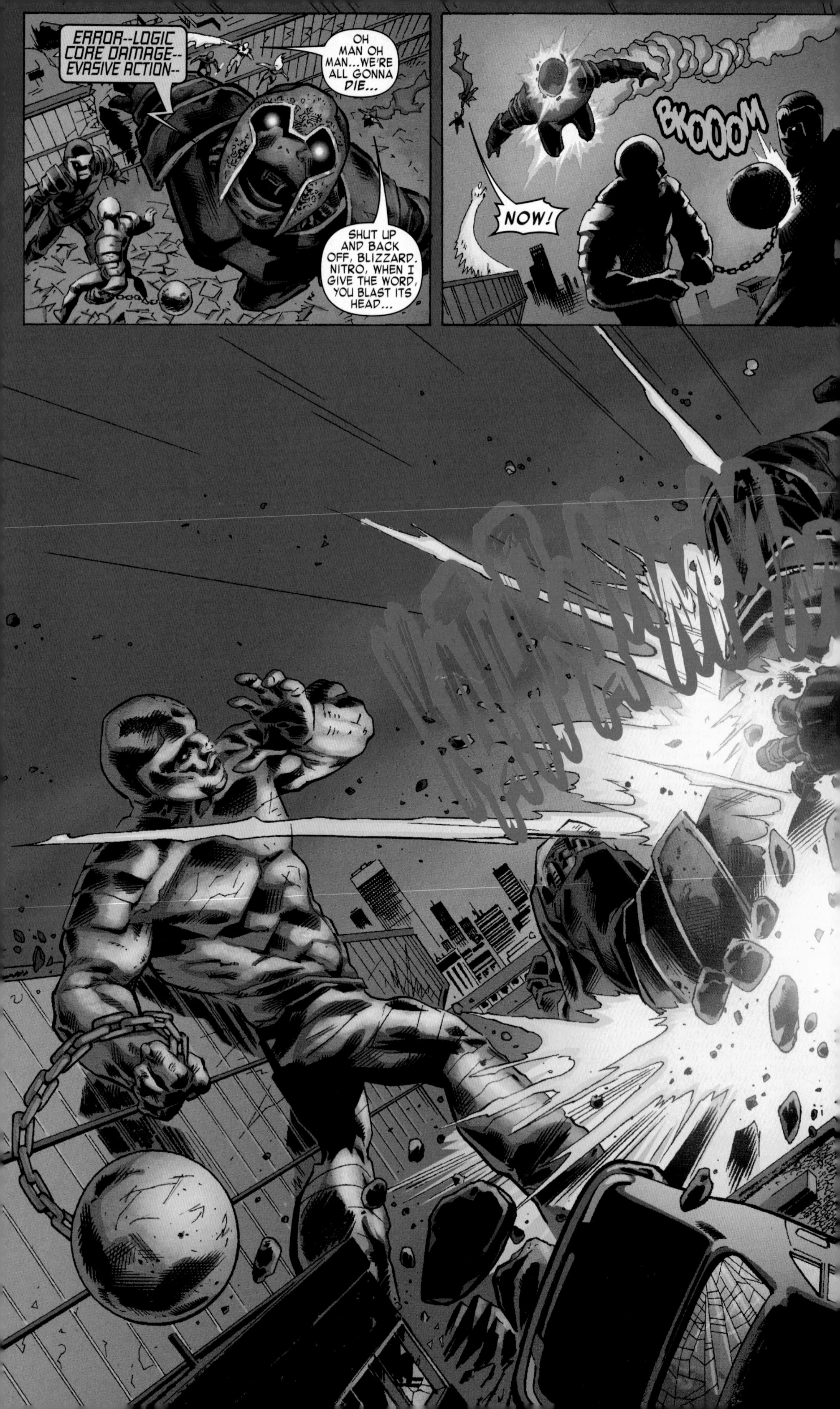
ERROR--LOGIC CORE DAMAGE-- EVASIVE ACTION--
OH MAN OH MAN...WE'RE ALL GONNA DIE...
SHUT UP AND BACK OFF, BLIZZARD. NITRO, WHEN I GIVE THE WORD, YOU BLAST ITS HEAD...
NOW!
BKOOOM

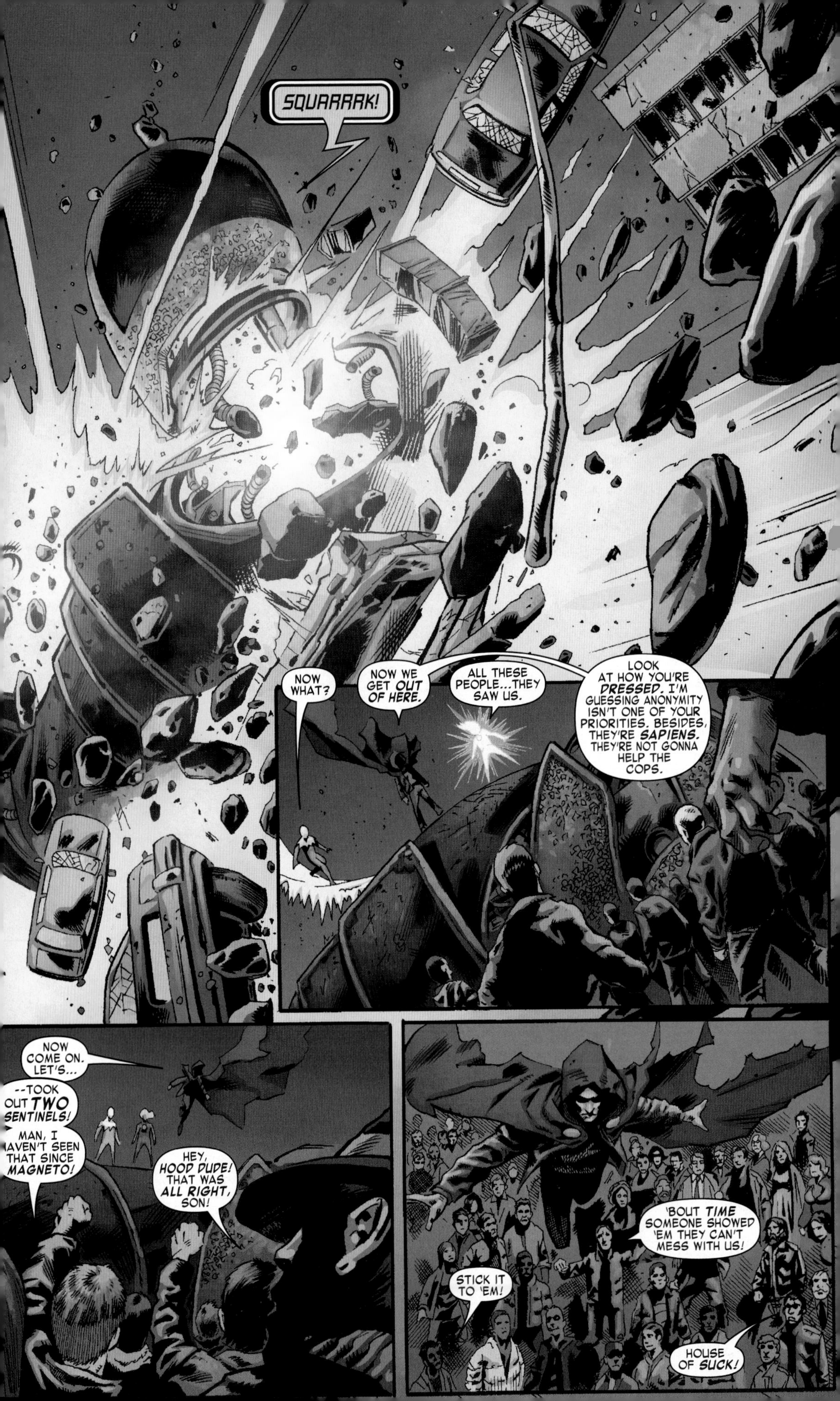
SQUARRRRK!
NOW WHAT?
NOW WE GET OUT OF HERE.
ALL THESE PEOPLE...THEY SAW US.
LOOK AT HOW YOU'RE DRESSED. I'M GUESSING ANONYMITY ISN'T ONE OF YOUR PRIORITIES. BESIDES, THEY'RE SAPIENS. THEY'RE NOT GONNA HELP THE COPS.
NOW COME ON. LET'S...
--TOOK OUT TWO SENTINELS!
MAN, I HAVEN'T SEEN THAT SINCE MAGNETO!
HEY, HOOD DUDE! THAT WAS ALL RIGHT, SON!
'BOUT TIME SOMEONE SHOWED 'EM THEY CAN'T MESS WITH US!
STICK IT TO 'EM!
HOUSE OF SUCK!

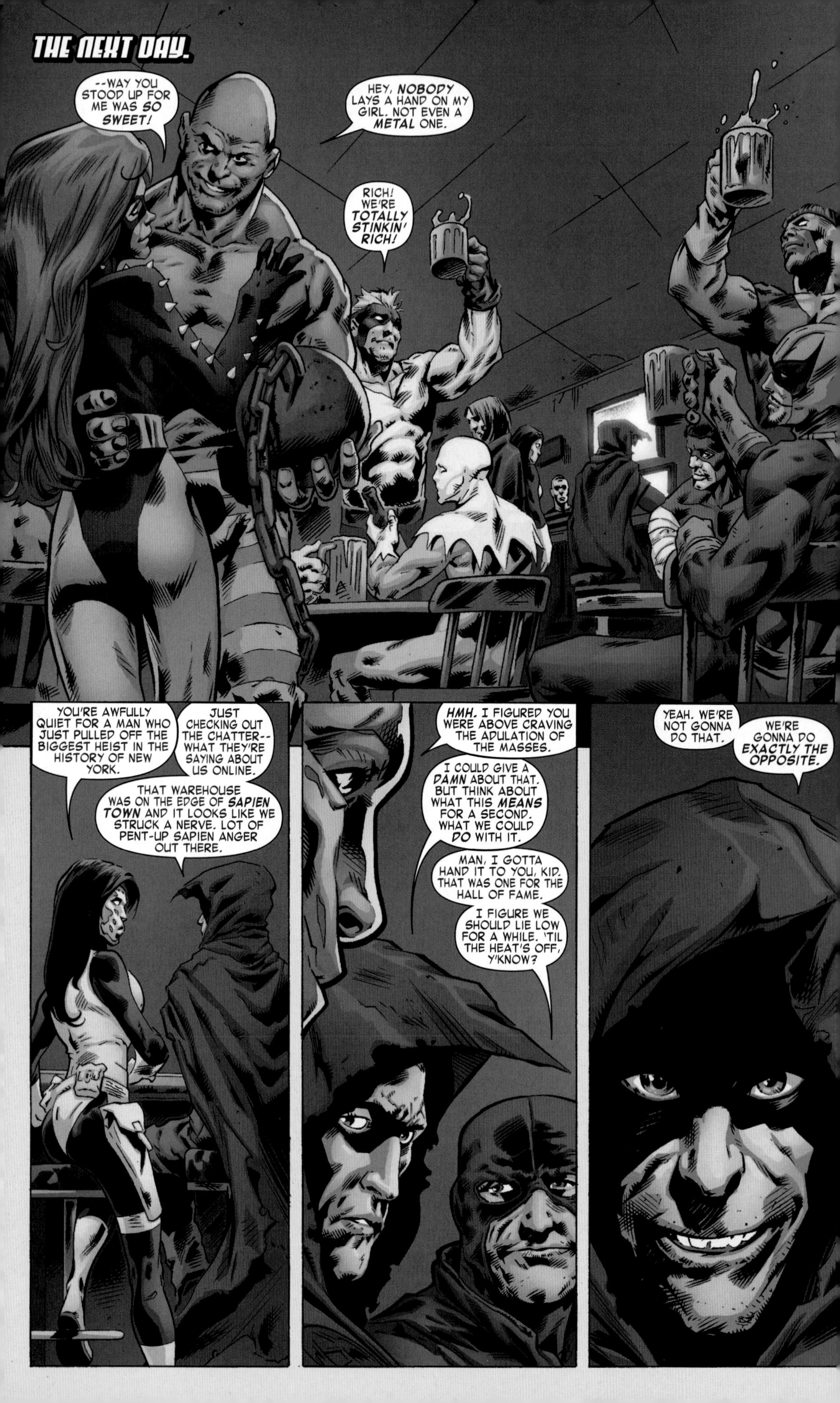
THE NEXT DAY.
--WAY YOU STOOD UP FOR ME WAS SO SWEET!
HEY, NOBODY LAYS A HAND ON MY GIRL. NOT EVEN A METAL ONE.
RICH! WE'RE TOTALLY STINKIN' RICH!
YOU'RE AWFULLY QUIET FOR A MAN WHO JUST PULLED OFF THE BIGGEST HEIST IN THE HISTORY OF NEW YORK.
JUST CHECKING OUT THE CHATTER-- WHAT THEY'RE SAYING ABOUT US ONLINE.
THAT WAREHOUSE WAS ON THE EDGE OF SAPIEN TOWN AND IT LOOKS LIKE WE STRUCK A NERVE. LOT OF PENT-UP SAPIEN ANGER OUT THERE.
HMH. I FIGURED YOU WERE ABOVE CRAVING THE ADULATION OF THE MASSES.
I COULD GIVE A DAMN ABOUT THAT. BUT THINK ABOUT WHAT THIS MEANS FOR A SECOND. WHAT WE COULD DO WITH IT.
MAN, I GOTTA HAND IT TO YOU, KID. THAT WAS ONE FOR THE HALL OF FAME.
I FIGURE WE SHOULD LIE LOW FOR A WHILE. 'TIL THE HEAT'S OFF, Y'KNOW?
YEAH. WE'RE NOT GONNA DO THAT.
WE'RE GONNA DO EXACTLY THE OPPOSITE.

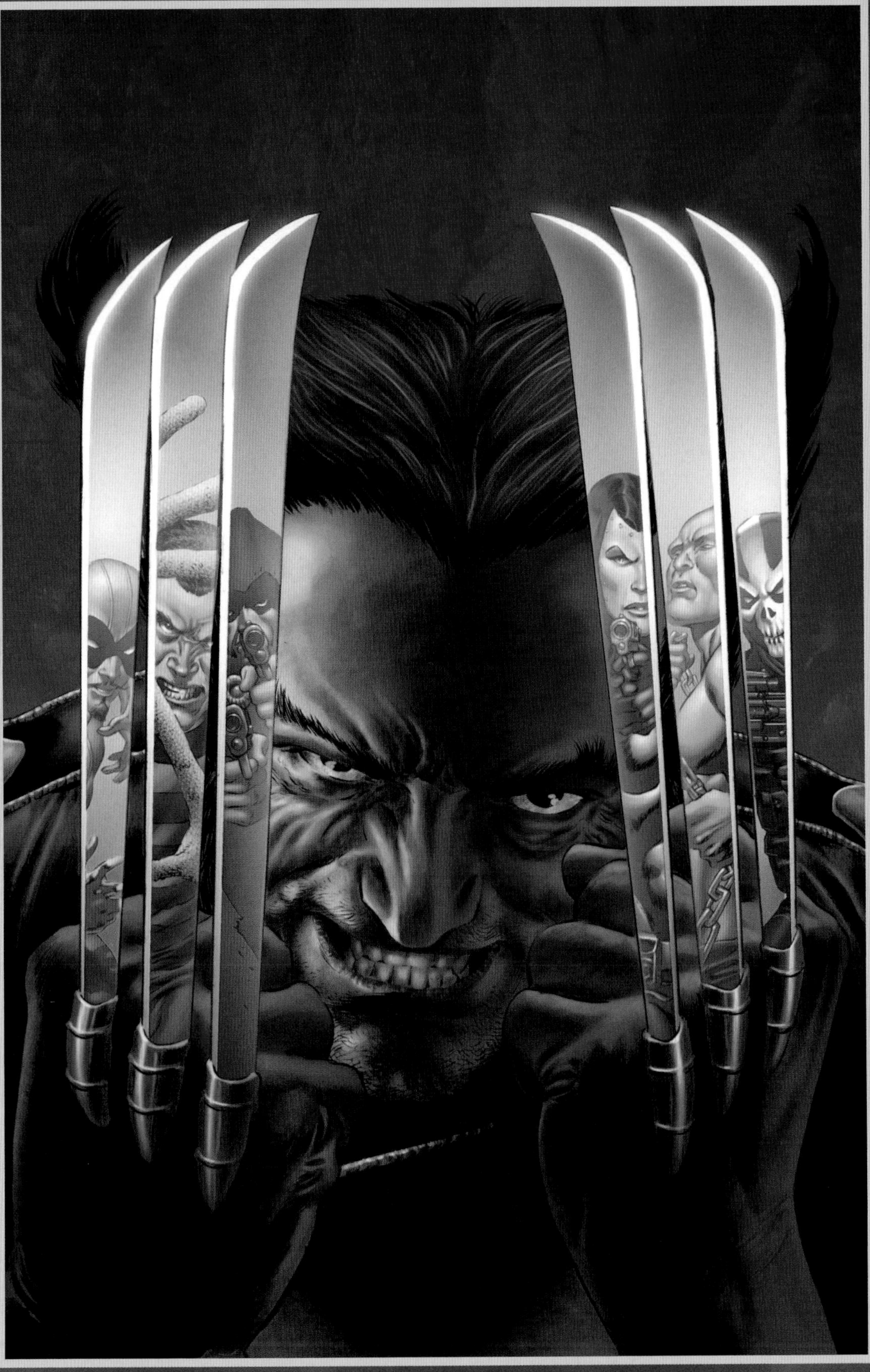

ISSUE #2: UNITY

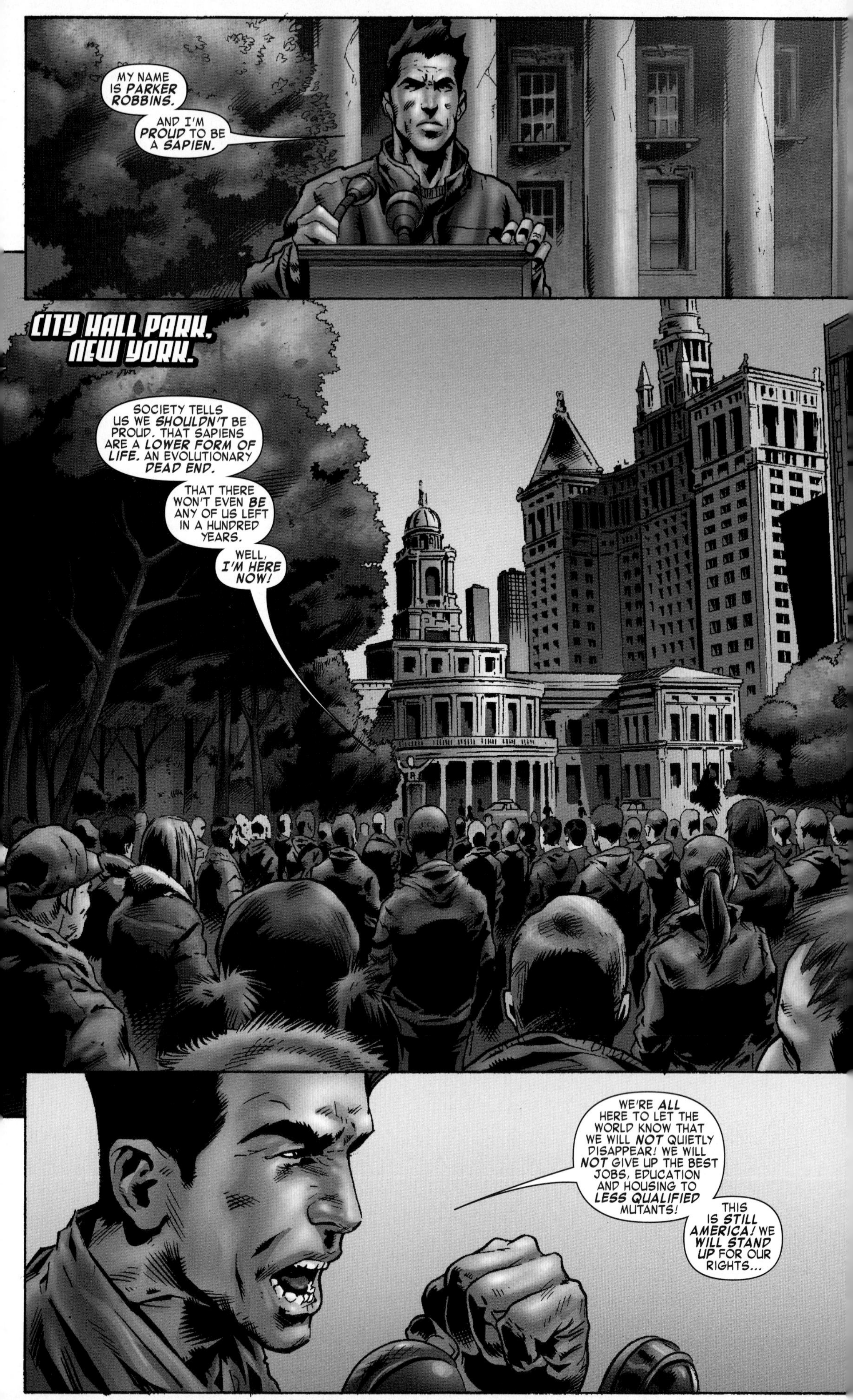
MY NAME IS PARKER ROBBINS.
AND I'M PROUD TO BE A SAPIEN.
CITY HALL PARK, NEW YORK.
SOCIETY TELLS US WE SHOULDN'T BE PROUD. THAT SAPIENS ARE A LOWER FORM OF LIFE. AN EVOLUTIONARY DEAD END.
THAT THERE WON'T EVEN BE ANY OF US LEFT IN A HUNDRED YEARS.
WELL, I'M HERE NOW!
WE'RE ALL HERE TO LET THE WORLD KNOW THAT WE WILL NOT QUIETLY DISAPPEAR! WE WILL NOT GIVE UP THE BEST JOBS, EDUCATION AND HOUSING TO LESS QUALIFIED MUTANTS!
THIS IS STILL AMERICA! WE WILL STAND UP FOR OUR RIGHTS...

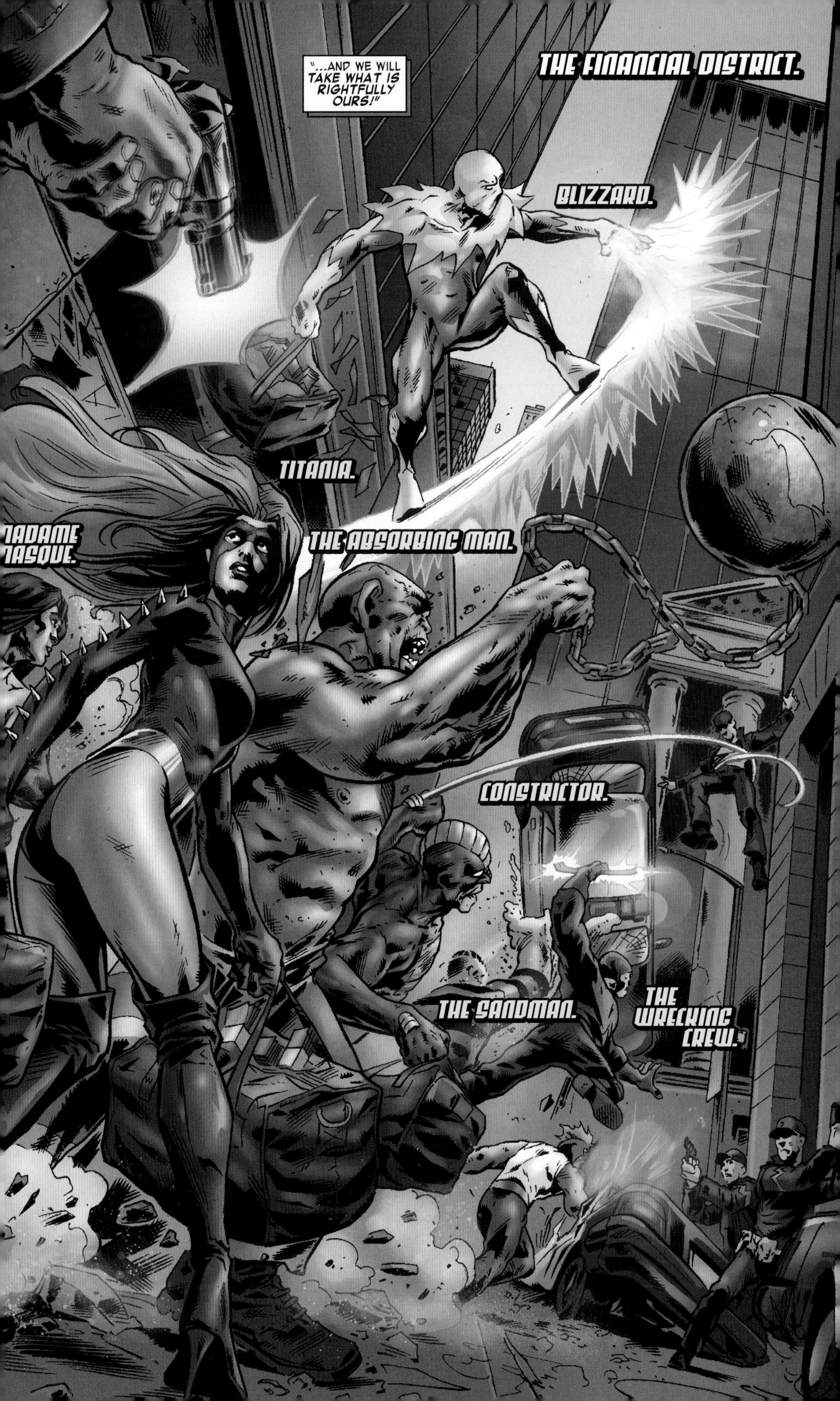

THE FINANCIAL DISTRICT.
"...AND WE WILL TAKE WHAT IS RIGHTFULLY OURS!"
BLIZZARD.
TITANIA.
THE ABSORBING MAN.
CONSTRICTOR.
THE SANDMAN.
THE WRECKING CREW.

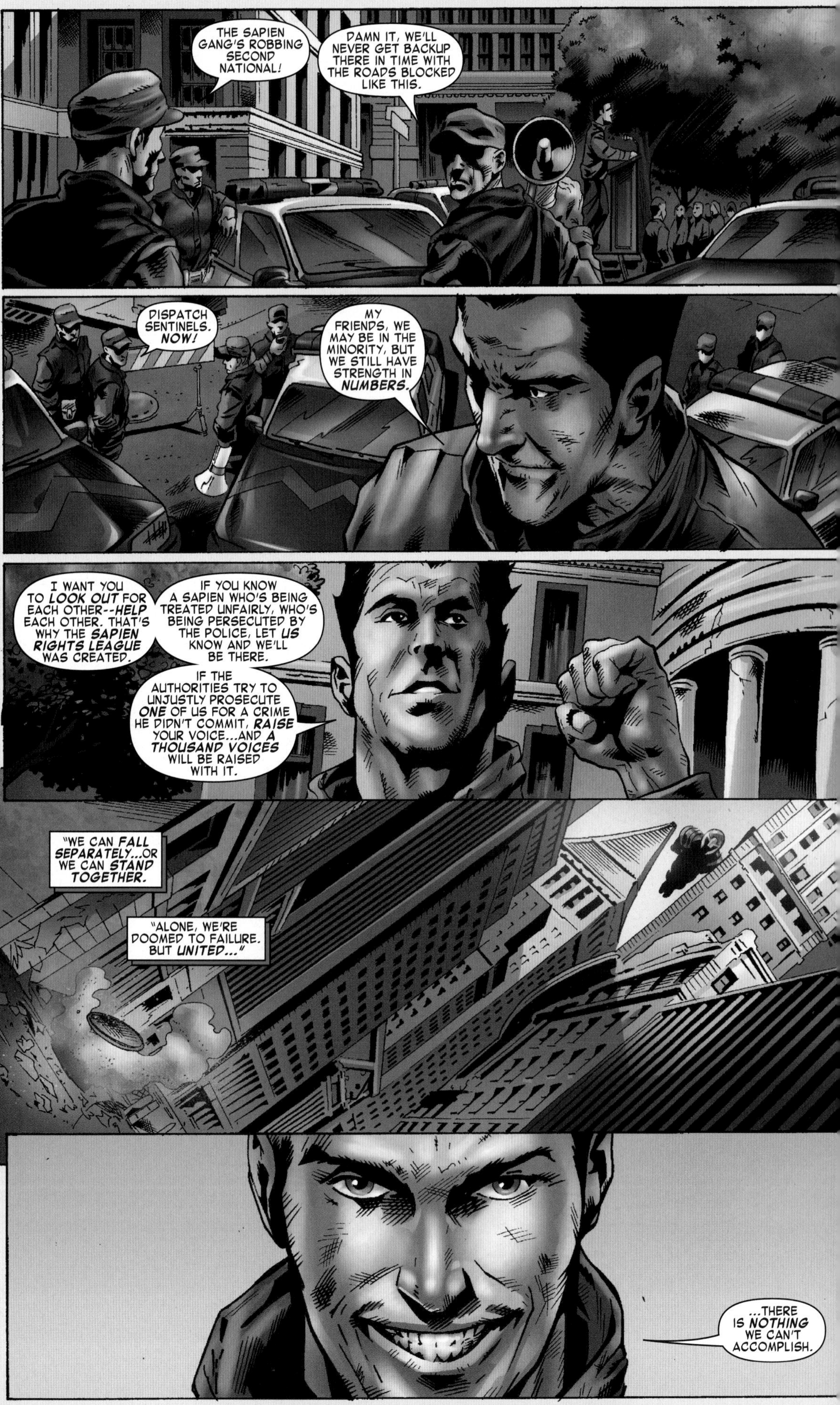
THE SAPIEN GANG'S ROBBING SECOND NATIONAL!
DAMN IT, WE'LL NEVER GET BACKUP THERE IN TIME WITH THE ROADS BLOCKED LIKE THIS.
DISPATCH SENTINELS. *NOW!*
MY FRIENDS, WE MAY BE IN THE MINORITY, BUT WE STILL HAVE STRENGTH IN *NUMBERS.*
I WANT YOU TO *LOOK OUT* FOR EACH OTHER--*HELP* EACH OTHER. THAT'S WHY THE *SAPIEN RIGHTS LEAGUE* WAS CREATED.
IF YOU KNOW A SAPIEN WHO'S BEING TREATED UNFAIRLY, WHO'S BEING PERSECUTED BY THE POLICE, LET *US* KNOW AND WE'LL BE THERE.
IF THE AUTHORITIES TRY TO UNJUSTLY PROSECUTE *ONE* OF US FOR A CRIME HE DIDN'T COMMIT, *RAISE* YOUR VOICE...AND *A THOUSAND VOICES* WILL BE RAISED WITH IT.
"WE CAN *FALL SEPARATELY*...OR WE CAN *STAND TOGETHER.*
"ALONE, WE'RE DOOMED TO FAILURE. BUT *UNITED*..."
...THERE IS *NOTHING* WE CAN'T ACCOMPLISH.

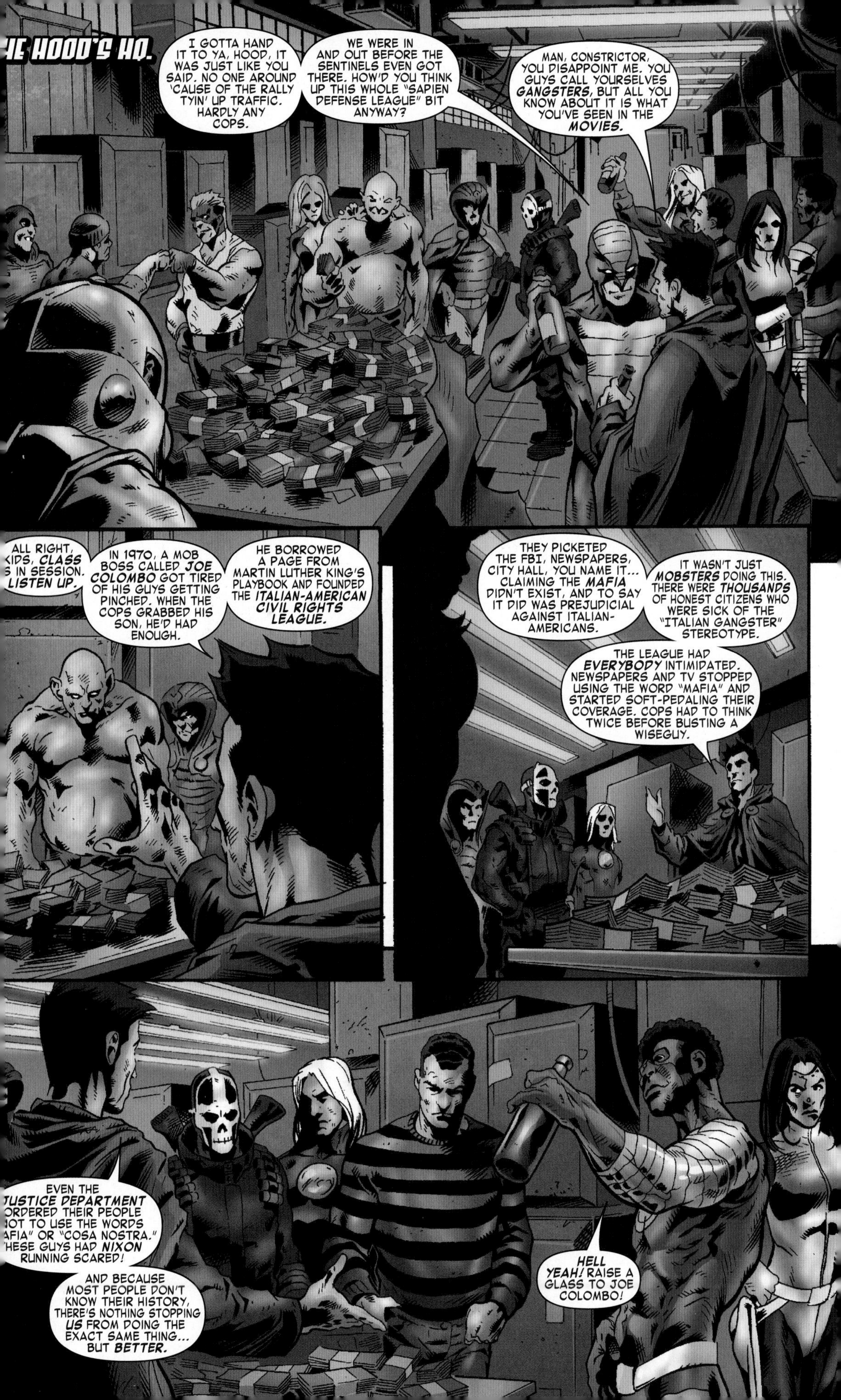
HE HOOD'S HQ.
I GOTTA HAND IT TO YA, HOOD, IT WAS JUST LIKE YOU SAID. NO ONE AROUND 'CAUSE OF THE RALLY TYIN' UP TRAFFIC. HARDLY ANY COPS.
WE WERE IN AND OUT BEFORE THE SENTINELS EVEN GOT THERE. HOW'D YOU THINK UP THIS WHOLE "SAPIEN DEFENSE LEAGUE" BIT ANYWAY?
MAN, CONSTRICTOR, YOU DISAPPOINT ME. YOU GUYS CALL YOURSELVES **GANGSTERS**, BUT ALL YOU KNOW ABOUT IT IS WHAT YOU'VE SEEN IN THE **MOVIES**.
ALL RIGHT, KIDS, **CLASS** IS IN SESSION. **LISTEN UP.**
IN 1970, A MOB BOSS CALLED **JOE COLOMBO** GOT TIRED OF HIS GUYS GETTING PINCHED. WHEN THE COPS GRABBED HIS SON, HE'D HAD ENOUGH.
HE BORROWED A PAGE FROM MARTIN LUTHER KING'S PLAYBOOK AND FOUNDED THE **ITALIAN-AMERICAN CIVIL RIGHTS LEAGUE**.
THEY PICKETED THE FBI, NEWSPAPERS, CITY HALL, YOU NAME IT... CLAIMING THE **MAFIA** DIDN'T EXIST, AND TO SAY IT DID WAS PREJUDICIAL AGAINST ITALIAN-AMERICANS.
IT WASN'T JUST **MOBSTERS** DOING THIS. THERE WERE **THOUSANDS** OF HONEST CITIZENS WHO WERE SICK OF THE "ITALIAN GANGSTER" STEREOTYPE.
THE LEAGUE HAD **EVERYBODY** INTIMIDATED. NEWSPAPERS AND TV STOPPED USING THE WORD "MAFIA" AND STARTED SOFT-PEDALING THEIR COVERAGE. COPS HAD TO THINK TWICE BEFORE BUSTING A WISEGUY.
EVEN THE **JUSTICE DEPARTMENT** ORDERED THEIR PEOPLE NOT TO USE THE WORDS "MAFIA" OR "COSA NOSTRA." THESE GUYS HAD **NIXON** RUNNING SCARED!
AND BECAUSE MOST PEOPLE DON'T KNOW THEIR HISTORY, THERE'S NOTHING STOPPING **US** FROM DOING THE EXACT SAME THING... BUT **BETTER**.
HELL YEAH! RAISE A GLASS TO JOE COLOMBO!

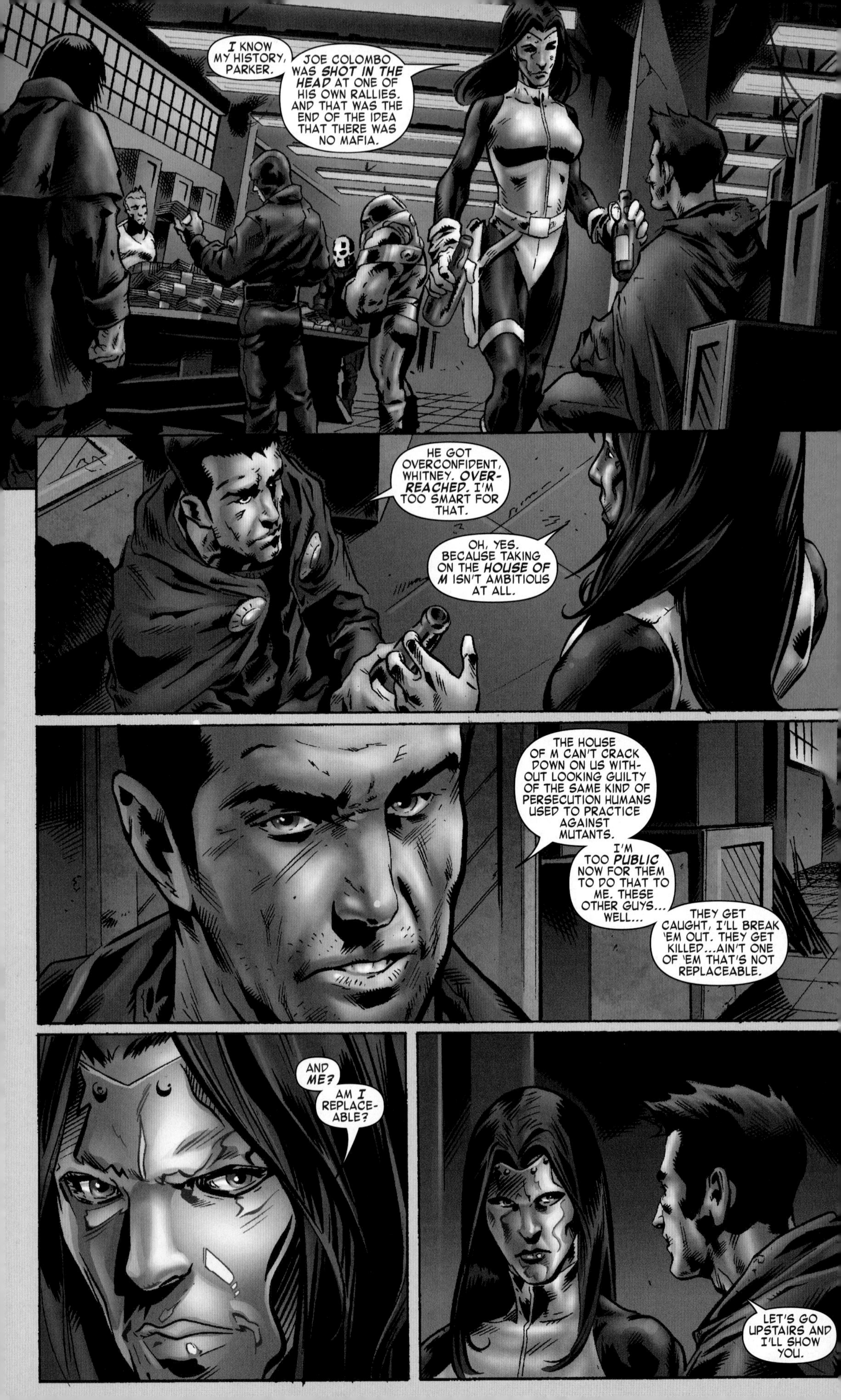
I KNOW MY HISTORY, PARKER.
JOE COLOMBO WAS SHOT IN THE HEAD AT ONE OF HIS OWN RALLIES. AND THAT WAS THE END OF THE IDEA THAT THERE WAS NO MAFIA.
HE GOT OVERCONFIDENT, WHITNEY. OVER-REACHED. I'M TOO SMART FOR THAT.
OH, YES. BECAUSE TAKING ON THE HOUSE OF M ISN'T AMBITIOUS AT ALL.
THE HOUSE OF M CAN'T CRACK DOWN ON US WITH-OUT LOOKING GUILTY OF THE SAME KIND OF PERSECUTION HUMANS USED TO PRACTICE AGAINST MUTANTS.
I'M TOO PUBLIC NOW FOR THEM TO DO THAT TO ME. THESE OTHER GUYS... WELL...
THEY GET CAUGHT, I'LL BREAK 'EM OUT. THEY GET KILLED...AIN'T ONE OF 'EM THAT'S NOT REPLACEABLE.
AND ME? AM I REPLACE-ABLE?
LET'S GO UPSTAIRS AND I'LL SHOW YOU.

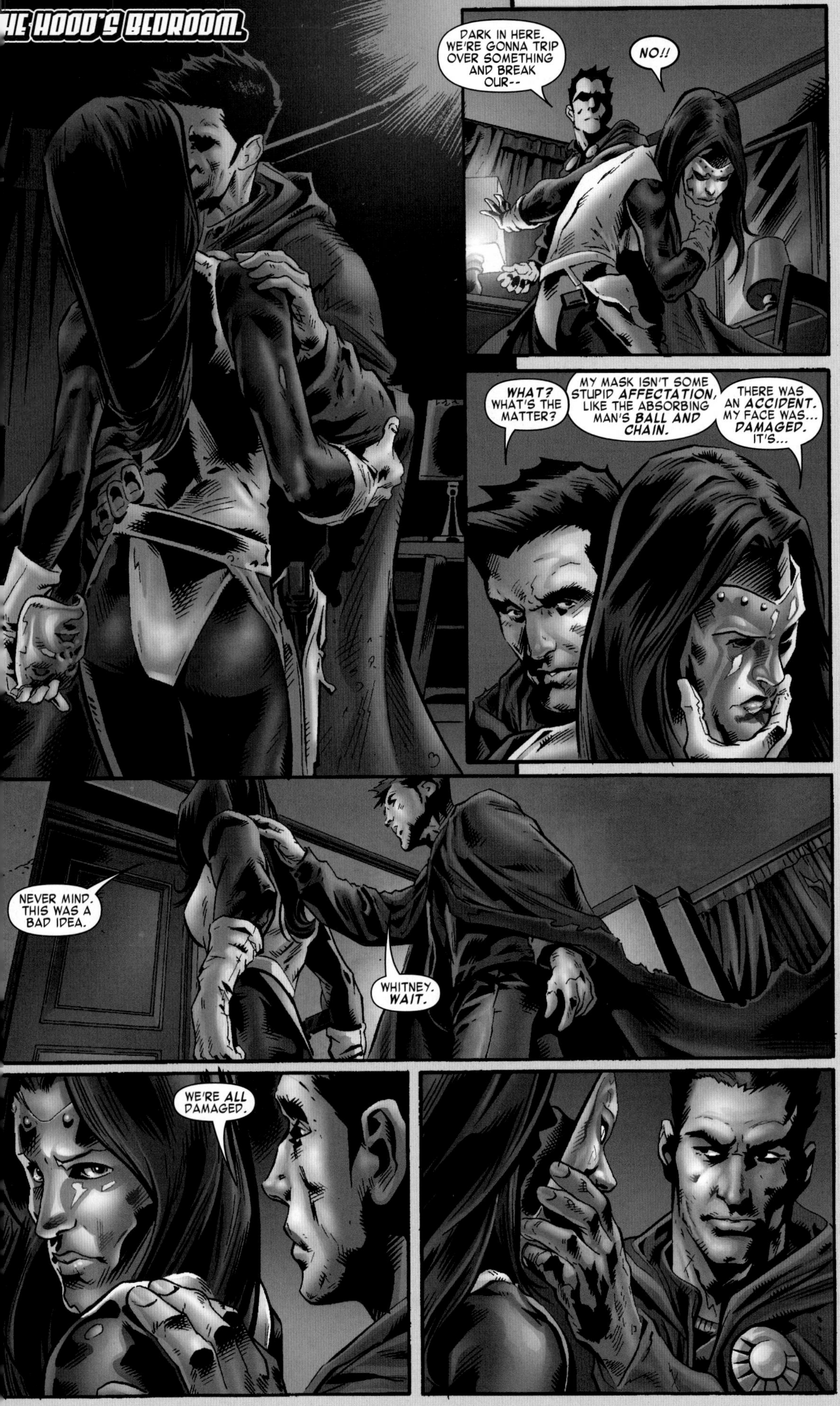

HE HOOD'S BEDROOM.
DARK IN HERE. WE'RE GONNA TRIP OVER SOMETHING AND BREAK OUR--
NO!!
WHAT? WHAT'S THE MATTER?
MY MASK ISN'T SOME STUPID AFFECTATION, LIKE THE ABSORBING MAN'S BALL AND CHAIN.
THERE WAS AN ACCIDENT. MY FACE WAS... DAMAGED. IT'S...
NEVER MIND. THIS WAS A BAD IDEA.
WHITNEY. WAIT.
WE'RE ALL DAMAGED.

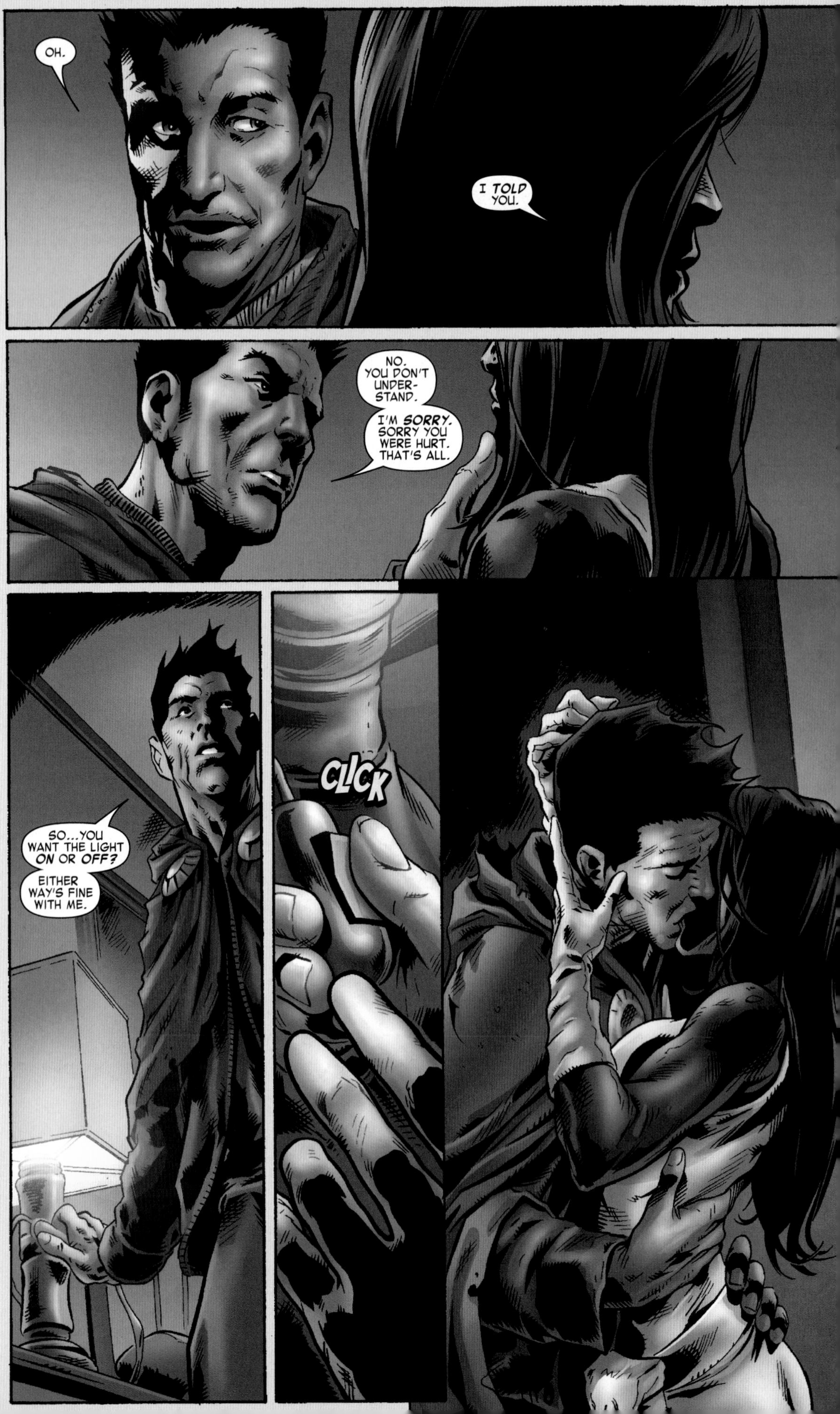
OH.
I *TOLD* YOU.
NO. YOU DON'T UNDER-STAND.
I'M ***SORRY.*** SORRY YOU WERE HURT. THAT'S ALL.
SO...YOU WANT THE LIGHT ***ON*** OR ***OFF?***
EITHER WAY'S FINE WITH ME.
CLICK

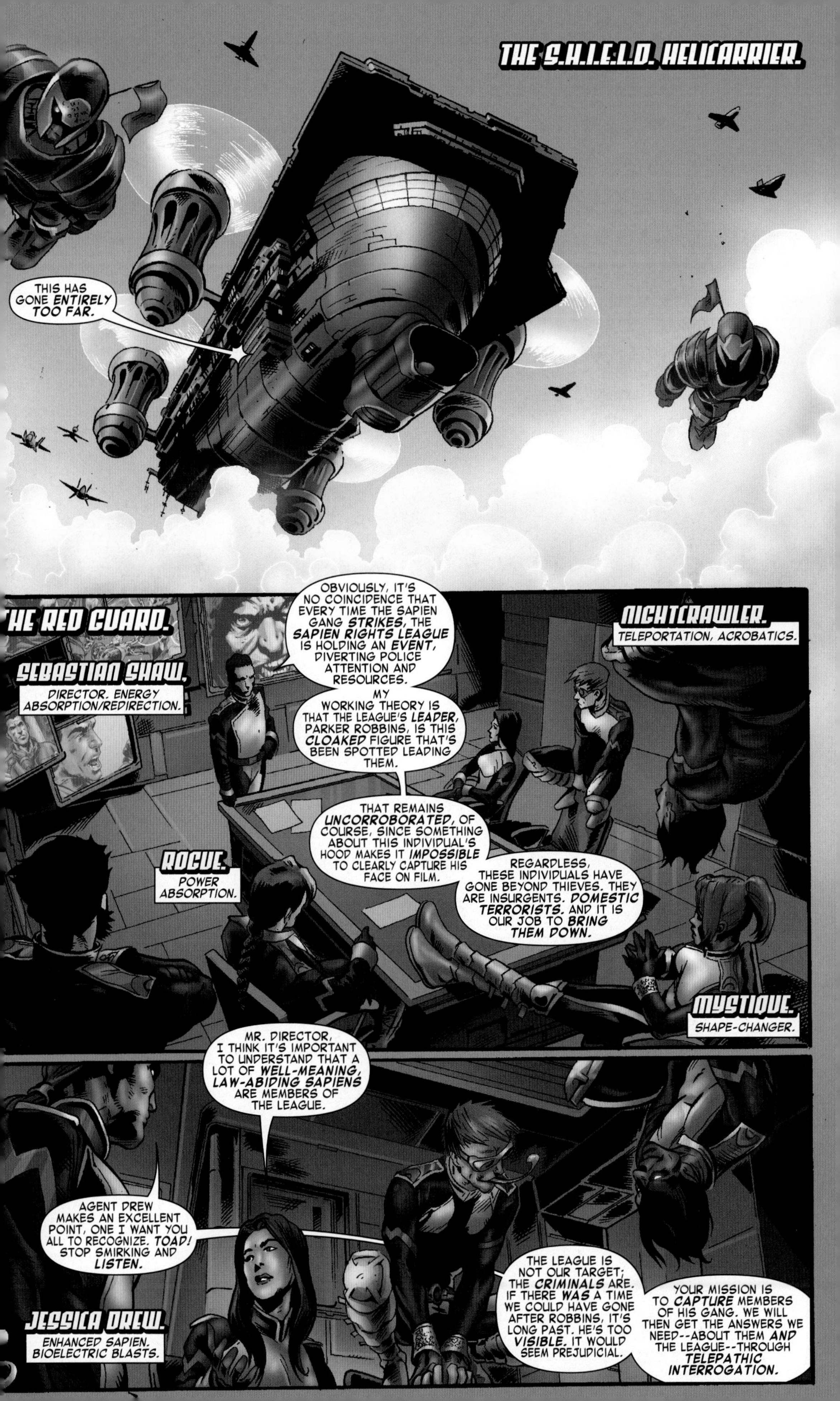

THE S.H.I.E.L.D. HELICARRIER.
THIS HAS GONE ENTIRELY TOO FAR.
HE RED GUARD.
SEBASTIAN SHAW.
DIRECTOR. ENERGY ABSORPTION/REDIRECTION.
OBVIOUSLY, IT'S NO COINCIDENCE THAT EVERY TIME THE SAPIEN GANG STRIKES, THE SAPIEN RIGHTS LEAGUE IS HOLDING AN EVENT, DIVERTING POLICE ATTENTION AND RESOURCES.
MY WORKING THEORY IS THAT THE LEAGUE'S LEADER, PARKER ROBBINS, IS THIS CLOAKED FIGURE THAT'S BEEN SPOTTED LEADING THEM.
NIGHTCRAWLER.
TELEPORTATION, ACROBATICS.
THAT REMAINS UNCORROBORATED, OF COURSE, SINCE SOMETHING ABOUT THIS INDIVIDUAL'S HOOD MAKES IT IMPOSSIBLE TO CLEARLY CAPTURE HIS FACE ON FILM.
ROGUE.
POWER ABSORPTION.
REGARDLESS, THESE INDIVIDUALS HAVE GONE BEYOND THIEVES. THEY ARE INSURGENTS. DOMESTIC TERRORISTS. AND IT IS OUR JOB TO BRING THEM DOWN.
MYSTIQUE.
SHAPE-CHANGER.
MR. DIRECTOR, I THINK IT'S IMPORTANT TO UNDERSTAND THAT A LOT OF WELL-MEANING, LAW-ABIDING SAPIENS ARE MEMBERS OF THE LEAGUE.
AGENT DREW MAKES AN EXCELLENT POINT, ONE I WANT YOU ALL TO RECOGNIZE. TOAD! STOP SMIRKING AND LISTEN.
JESSICA DREW.
ENHANCED SAPIEN. BIOELECTRIC BLASTS.
THE LEAGUE IS NOT OUR TARGET; THE CRIMINALS ARE. IF THERE WAS A TIME WE COULD HAVE GONE AFTER ROBBINS, IT'S LONG PAST. HE'S TOO VISIBLE. IT WOULD SEEM PREJUDICIAL.
YOUR MISSION IS TO CAPTURE MEMBERS OF HIS GANG. WE WILL THEN GET THE ANSWERS WE NEED--ABOUT THEM AND THE LEAGUE--THROUGH TELEPATHIC INTERROGATION.

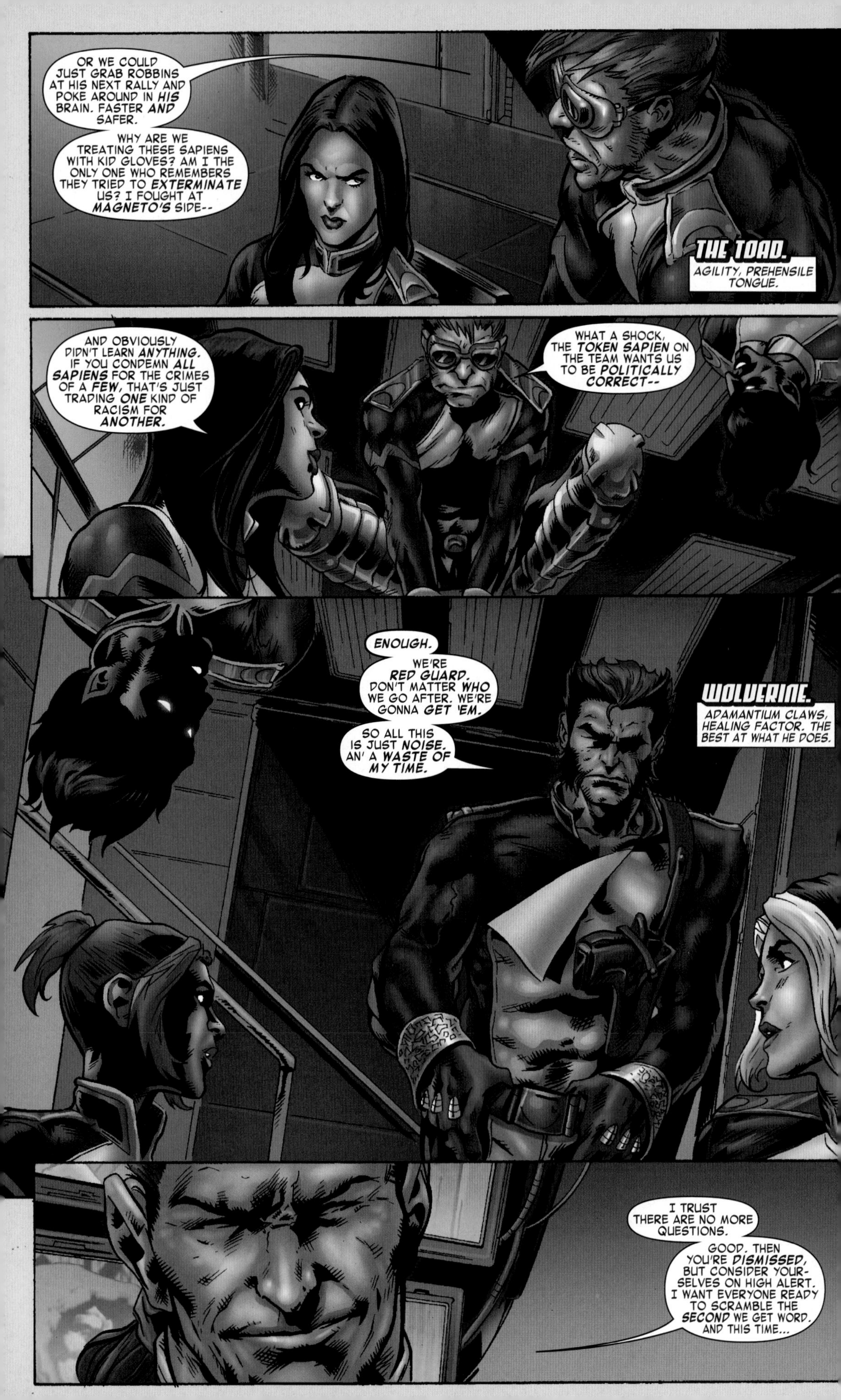

OR WE COULD JUST GRAB ROBBINS AT HIS NEXT RALLY AND POKE AROUND IN *HIS* BRAIN. FASTER *AND* SAFER.
WHY ARE WE TREATING THESE SAPIENS WITH KID GLOVES? AM I THE ONLY ONE WHO REMEMBERS THEY TRIED TO *EXTERMINATE* US? I FOUGHT AT *MAGNETO'S* SIDE--
THE TOAD.
AGILITY, PREHENSILE TONGUE.
AND OBVIOUSLY DIDN'T LEARN *ANYTHING*. IF YOU CONDEMN *ALL SAPIENS* FOR THE CRIMES OF A *FEW*, THAT'S JUST TRADING *ONE* KIND OF RACISM FOR *ANOTHER*.
WHAT A SHOCK, THE *TOKEN SAPIEN* ON THE TEAM WANTS US TO BE *POLITICALLY CORRECT*--
ENOUGH.
WE'RE *RED GUARD*. DON'T MATTER *WHO* WE GO AFTER. WE'RE GONNA *GET 'EM*.
SO ALL THIS IS JUST *NOISE*. AN' A *WASTE OF MY TIME*.
WOLVERINE.
ADAMANTIUM CLAWS, HEALING FACTOR. THE BEST AT WHAT HE DOES.
I TRUST THERE ARE NO MORE QUESTIONS.
GOOD. THEN YOU'RE *DISMISSED*, BUT CONSIDER YOUR-SELVES ON HIGH ALERT. I WANT EVERYONE READY TO SCRAMBLE THE *SECOND* WE GET WORD. AND THIS TIME...

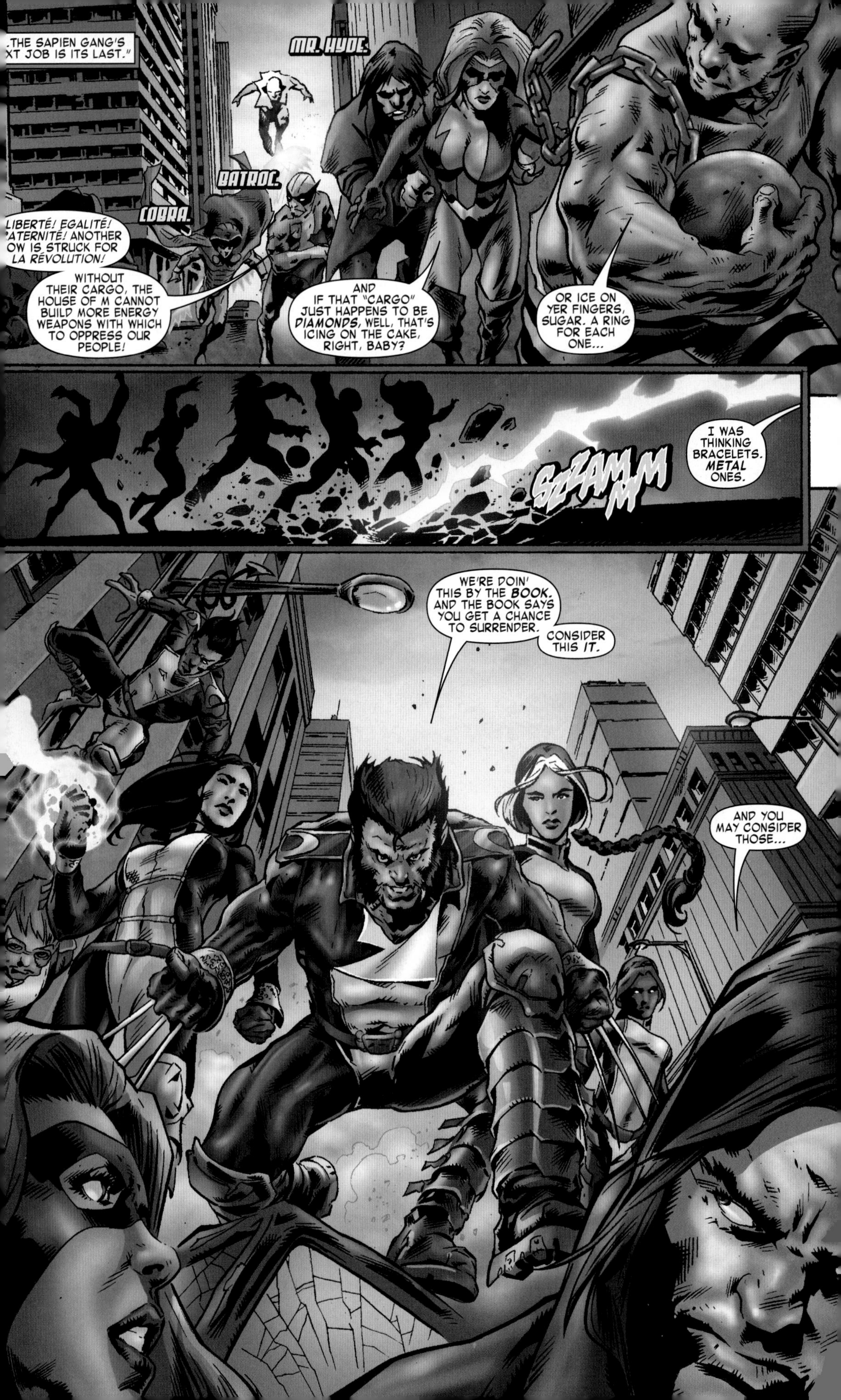

THE SAPIEN GANG'S
XT JOB IS ITS LAST."
MR. HYDE.
BATROC.
COBRA.
LIBERTÉ! EGALITÉ! ATERNITÉ! ANOTHER OW IS STRUCK FOR LA RÉVOLUTION!
WITHOUT THEIR CARGO, THE HOUSE OF M CANNOT BUILD MORE ENERGY WEAPONS WITH WHICH TO OPPRESS OUR PEOPLE!
AND IF THAT "CARGO" JUST HAPPENS TO BE DIAMONDS, WELL, THAT'S ICING ON THE CAKE, RIGHT, BABY?
OR ICE ON YER FINGERS, SUGAR. A RING FOR EACH ONE...
SZZAMMM
I WAS THINKING BRACELETS. METAL ONES.
WE'RE DOIN' THIS BY THE BOOK. AND THE BOOK SAYS YOU GET A CHANCE TO SURRENDER.
CONSIDER THIS IT.
AND YOU MAY CONSIDER THOSE...

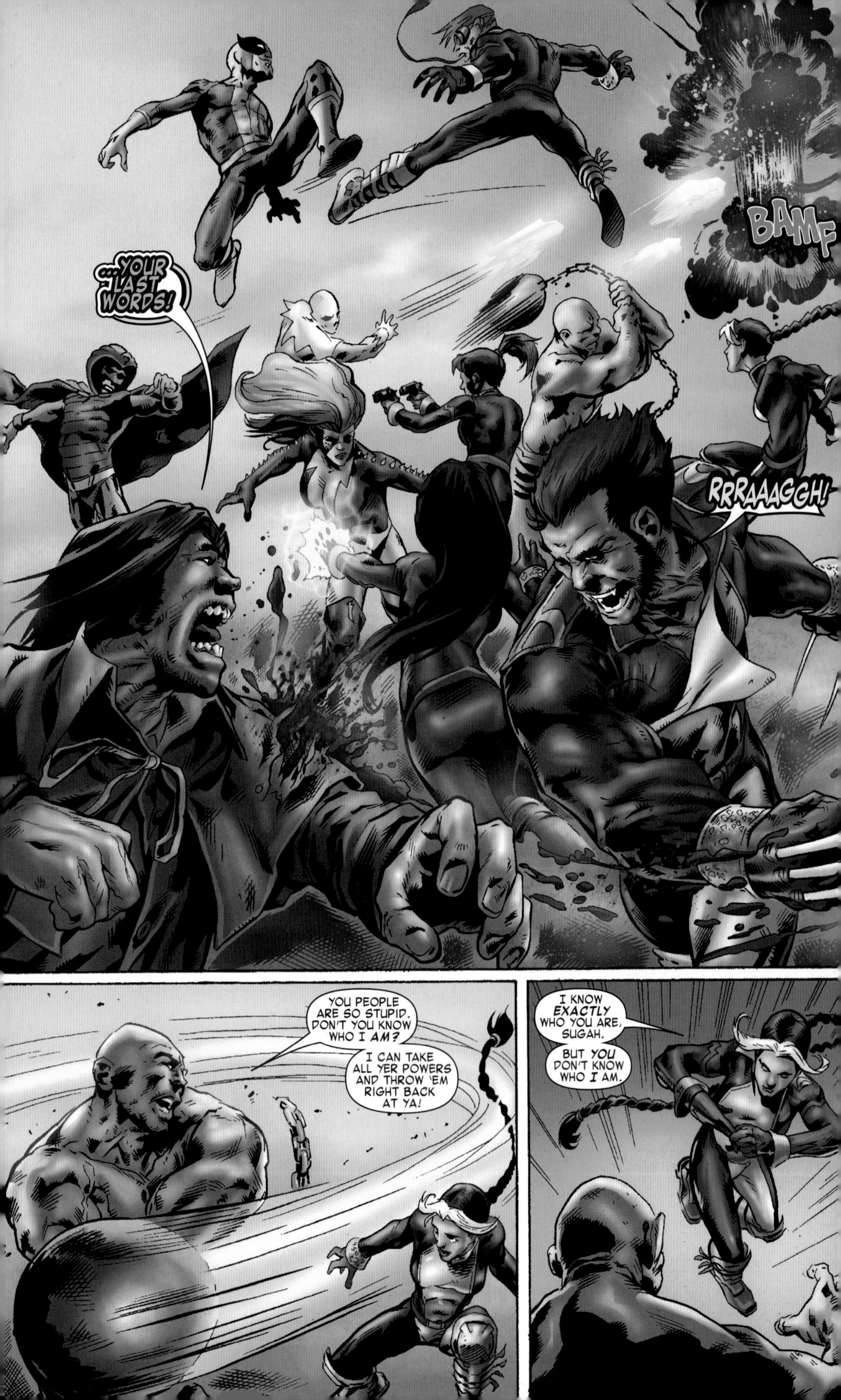
BAMF
...YOUR LAST WORDS!
RRRAAAGGH!
YOU PEOPLE ARE SO STUPID. DON'T YOU KNOW WHO I *AM?*
I CAN TAKE ALL YER POWERS AND THROW 'EM RIGHT BACK AT YA!
I KNOW *EXACTLY* WHO YOU ARE, SUGAH.
BUT *YOU* DON'T KNOW WHO *I* AM.

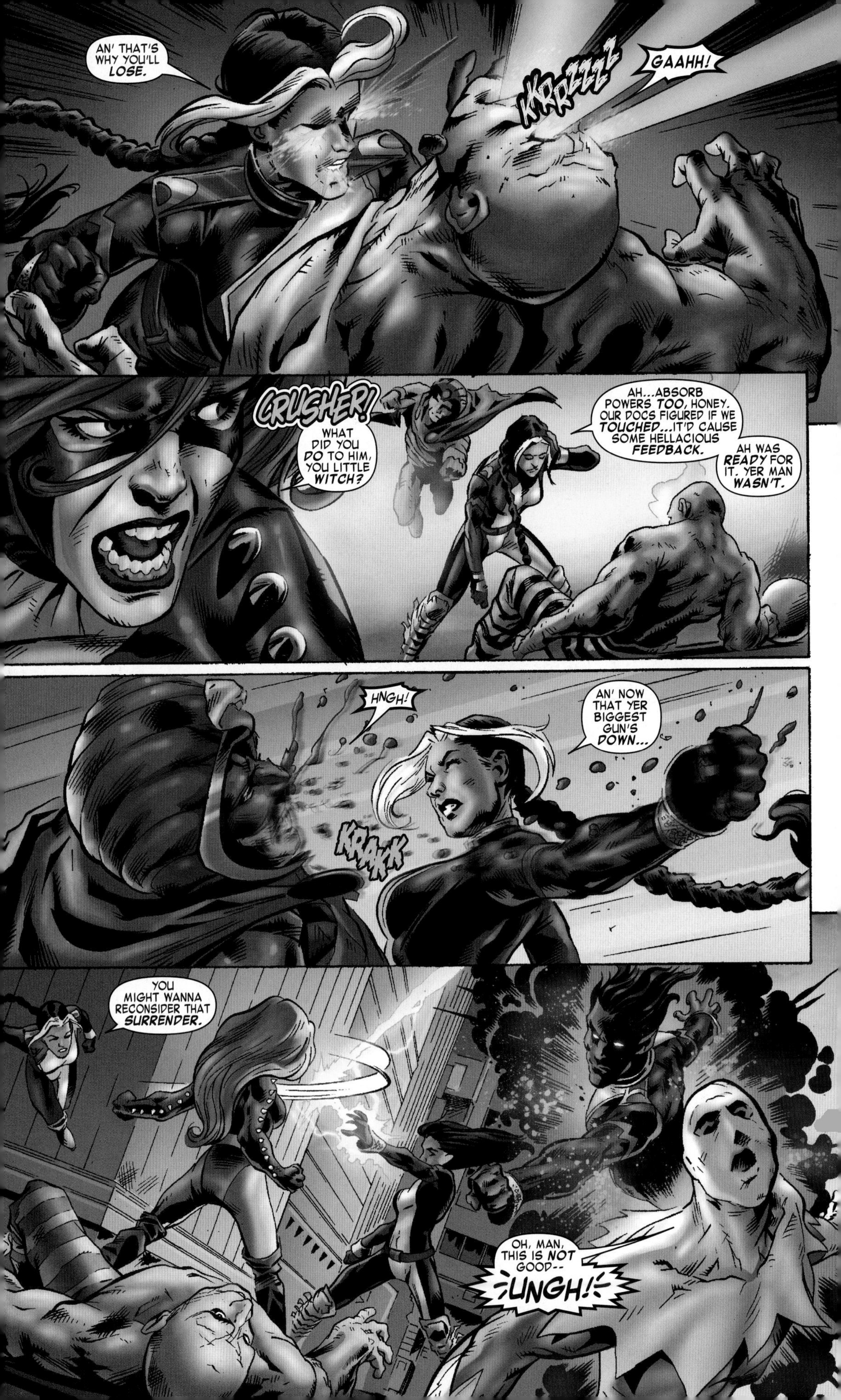

AN' THAT'S WHY YOU'LL LOSE.
KRRZZZZZ
GAAHH!
CRUSHER!
WHAT DID YOU DO TO HIM, YOU LITTLE WITCH?
AH...ABSORB POWERS TOO, HONEY. OUR DOCS FIGURED IF WE TOUCHED...IT'D CAUSE SOME HELLACIOUS FEEDBACK.
AH WAS READY FOR IT. YER MAN WASN'T.
HNGH!
AN' NOW THAT YER BIGGEST GUN'S DOWN...
KRAKK
YOU MIGHT WANNA RECONSIDER THAT SURRENDER.
OH, MAN, THIS IS NOT GOOD--
UNGH!

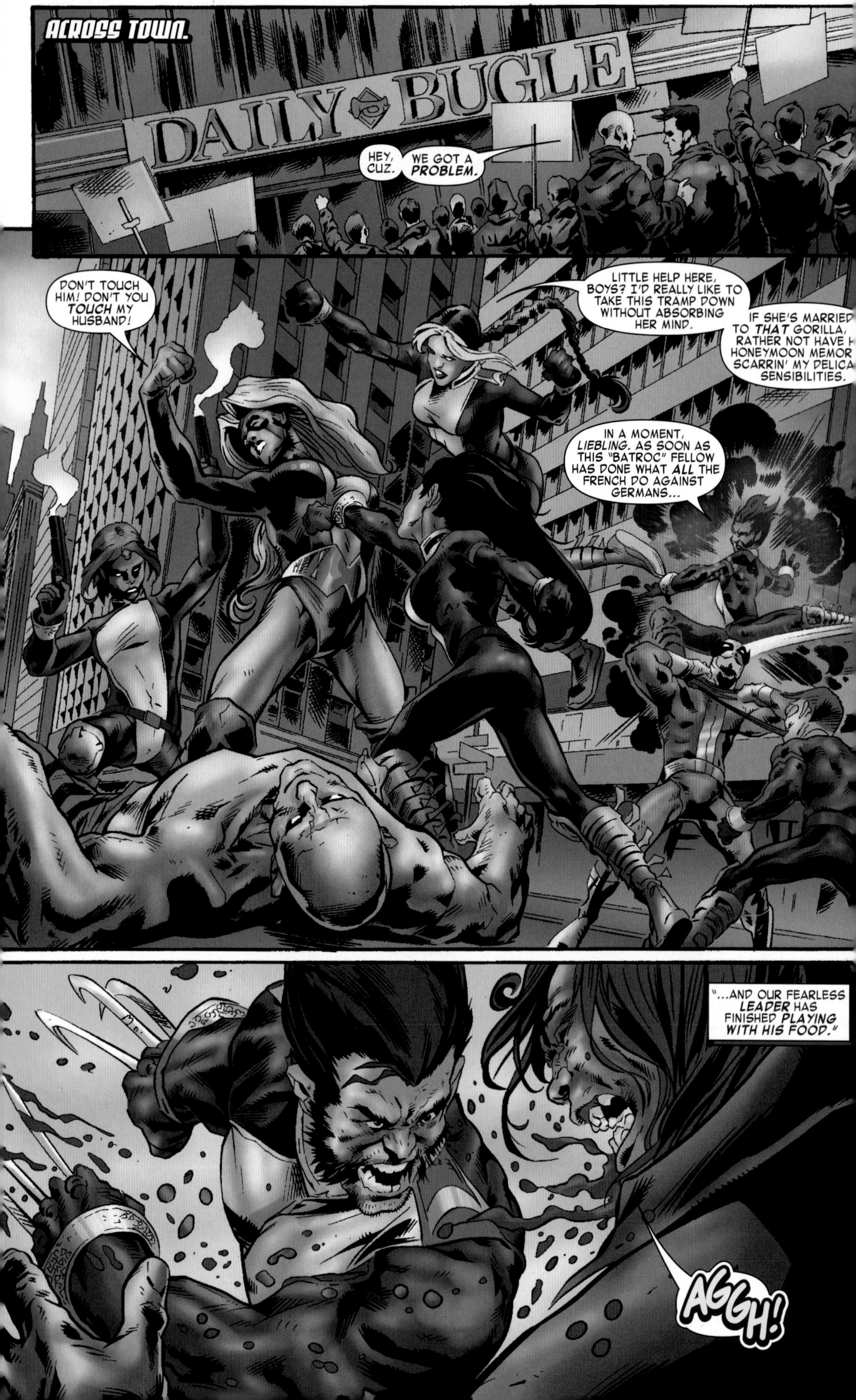
ACROSS TOWN.
DAILY BUGLE
HEY, CUZ.
WE GOT A PROBLEM.
DON'T TOUCH HIM! DON'T YOU TOUCH MY HUSBAND!
LITTLE HELP HERE, BOYS? I'D REALLY LIKE TO TAKE THIS TRAMP DOWN WITHOUT ABSORBING HER MIND.
IF SHE'S MARRIED TO THAT GORILLA, RATHER NOT HAVE
HONEYMOON MEMOR
SCARRIN' MY DELICA
SENSIBILITIES.
IN A MOMENT, LIEBLING. AS SOON AS THIS "BATROC" FELLOW HAS DONE WHAT ALL THE FRENCH DO AGAINST GERMANS...
"...AND OUR FEARLESS LEADER HAS FINISHED PLAYING WITH HIS FOOD."
AGGH!

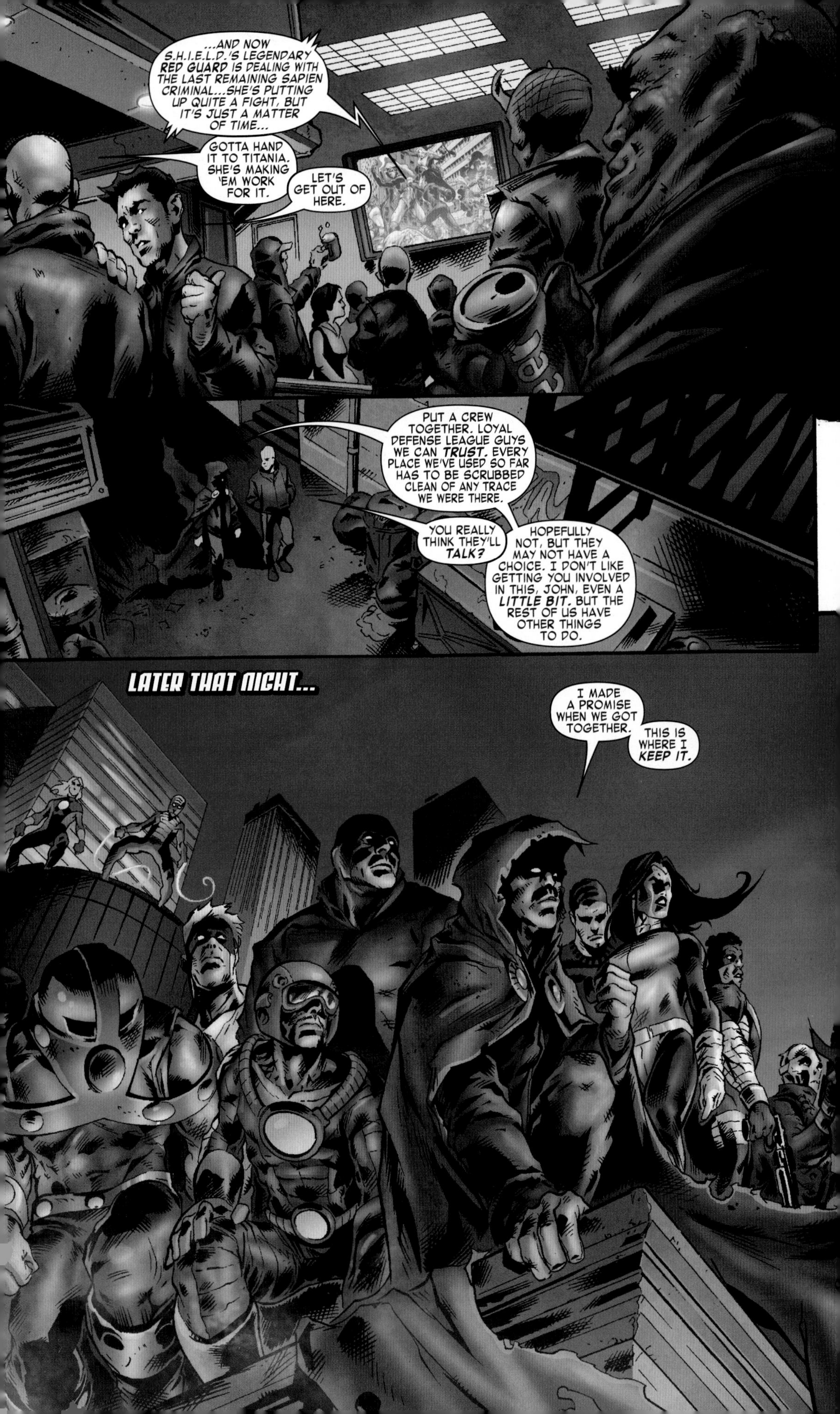
...AND NOW S.H.I.E.L.D.'S LEGENDARY **RED GUARD** IS DEALING WITH THE LAST REMAINING SAPIEN CRIMINAL...SHE'S PUTTING UP QUITE A FIGHT, BUT IT'S JUST A MATTER OF TIME...
GOTTA HAND IT TO TITANIA. SHE'S MAKING 'EM WORK FOR IT.
LET'S GET OUT OF HERE.
PUT A CREW TOGETHER. LOYAL DEFENSE LEAGUE GUYS WE CAN **TRUST.** EVERY PLACE WE'VE USED SO FAR HAS TO BE SCRUBBED CLEAN OF ANY TRACE WE WERE THERE.
YOU REALLY THINK THEY'LL ***TALK?***
HOPEFULLY NOT, BUT THEY MAY NOT HAVE A CHOICE. I DON'T LIKE GETTING YOU INVOLVED IN THIS, JOHN, EVEN A ***LITTLE BIT.*** BUT THE REST OF US HAVE OTHER THINGS TO DO.
LATER THAT NIGHT...
I MADE A PROMISE WHEN WE GOT TOGETHER.
THIS IS WHERE I ***KEEP IT.***

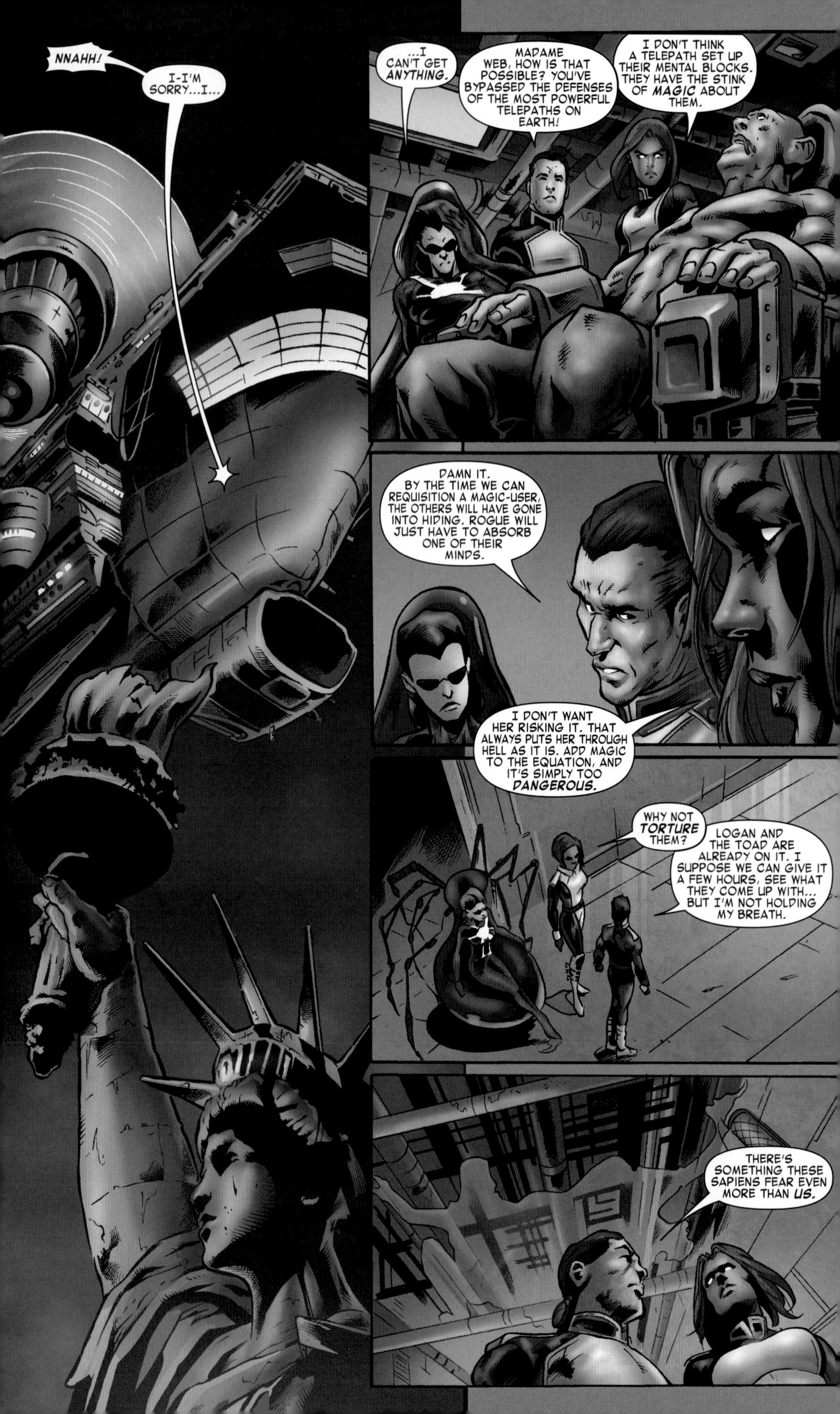
NNAHH!
I-I'M SORRY...I...
...I CAN'T GET *ANYTHING.*
MADAME WEB, HOW IS THAT POSSIBLE? YOU'VE BYPASSED THE DEFENSES OF THE MOST POWERFUL TELEPATHS ON EARTH!
I DON'T THINK A TELEPATH SET UP THEIR MENTAL BLOCKS. THEY HAVE THE STINK OF *MAGIC* ABOUT THEM.
DAMN IT. BY THE TIME WE CAN REQUISITION A MAGIC-USER, THE OTHERS WILL HAVE GONE INTO HIDING. ROGUE WILL JUST HAVE TO ABSORB ONE OF THEIR MINDS.
I DON'T WANT HER RISKING IT. THAT ALWAYS PUTS HER THROUGH HELL AS IT IS. ADD MAGIC TO THE EQUATION, AND IT'S SIMPLY TOO *DANGEROUS.*
WHY NOT *TORTURE* THEM?
LOGAN AND THE TOAD ARE ALREADY ON IT. I SUPPOSE WE CAN GIVE IT A FEW HOURS, SEE WHAT THEY COME UP WITH... BUT I'M NOT HOLDING MY BREATH.
THERE'S SOMETHING THESE SAPIENS FEAR EVEN MORE THAN *US.*

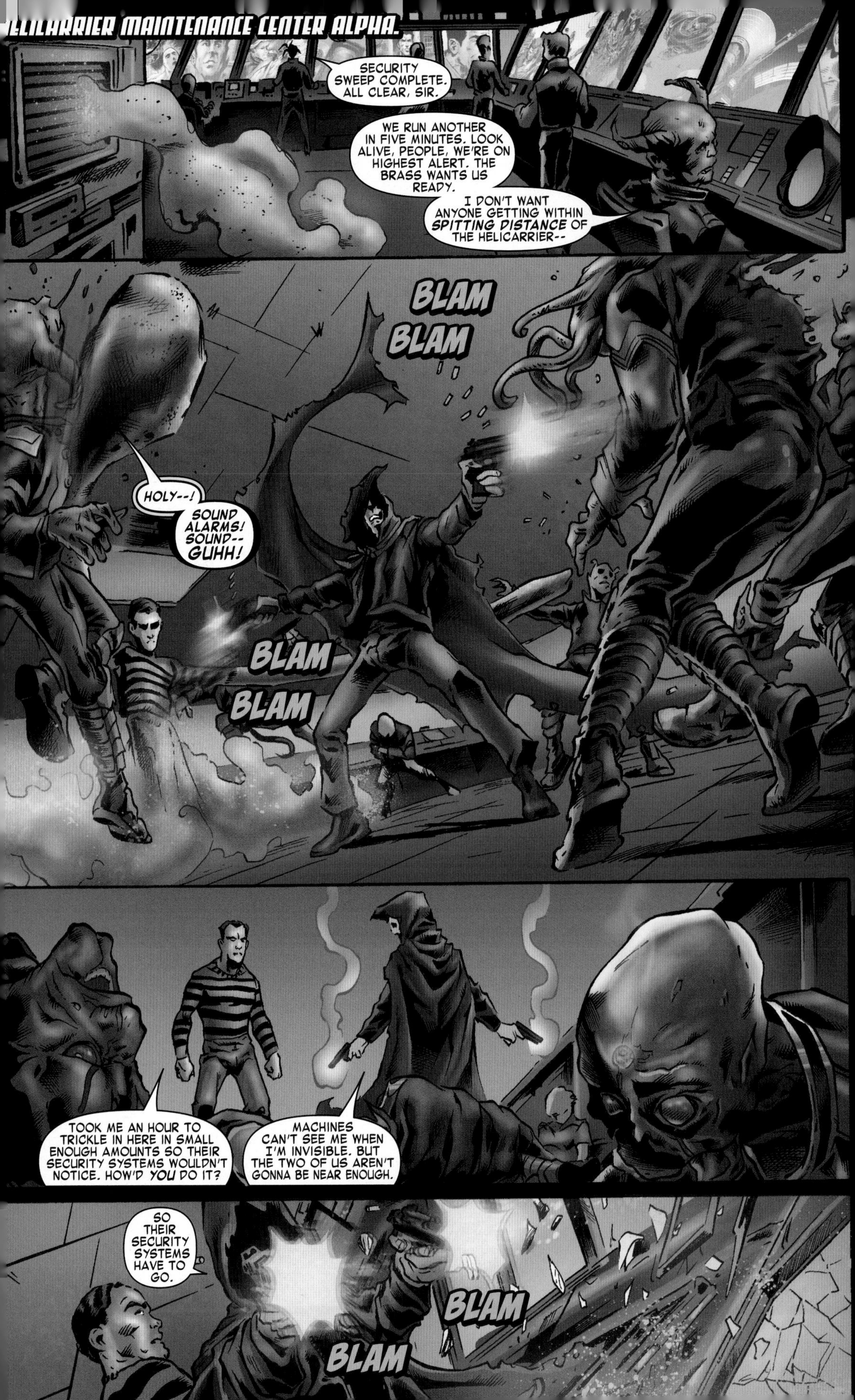
ELICARRIER MAINTENANCE CENTER ALPHA.
SECURITY SWEEP COMPLETE. ALL CLEAR, SIR.
WE RUN ANOTHER IN FIVE MINUTES. LOOK ALIVE, PEOPLE, WE'RE ON HIGHEST ALERT. THE BRASS WANTS US READY.
I DON'T WANT ANYONE GETTING WITHIN SPITTING DISTANCE OF THE HELICARRIER--
BLAM
BLAM
HOLY--!
SOUND ALARMS! SOUND-- GUHH!
BLAM
BLAM
TOOK ME AN HOUR TO TRICKLE IN HERE IN SMALL ENOUGH AMOUNTS SO THEIR SECURITY SYSTEMS WOULDN'T NOTICE. HOW'D YOU DO IT?
MACHINES CAN'T SEE ME WHEN I'M INVISIBLE. BUT THE TWO OF US AREN'T GONNA BE NEAR ENOUGH.
SO THEIR SECURITY SYSTEMS HAVE TO GO.
BLAM
BLAM

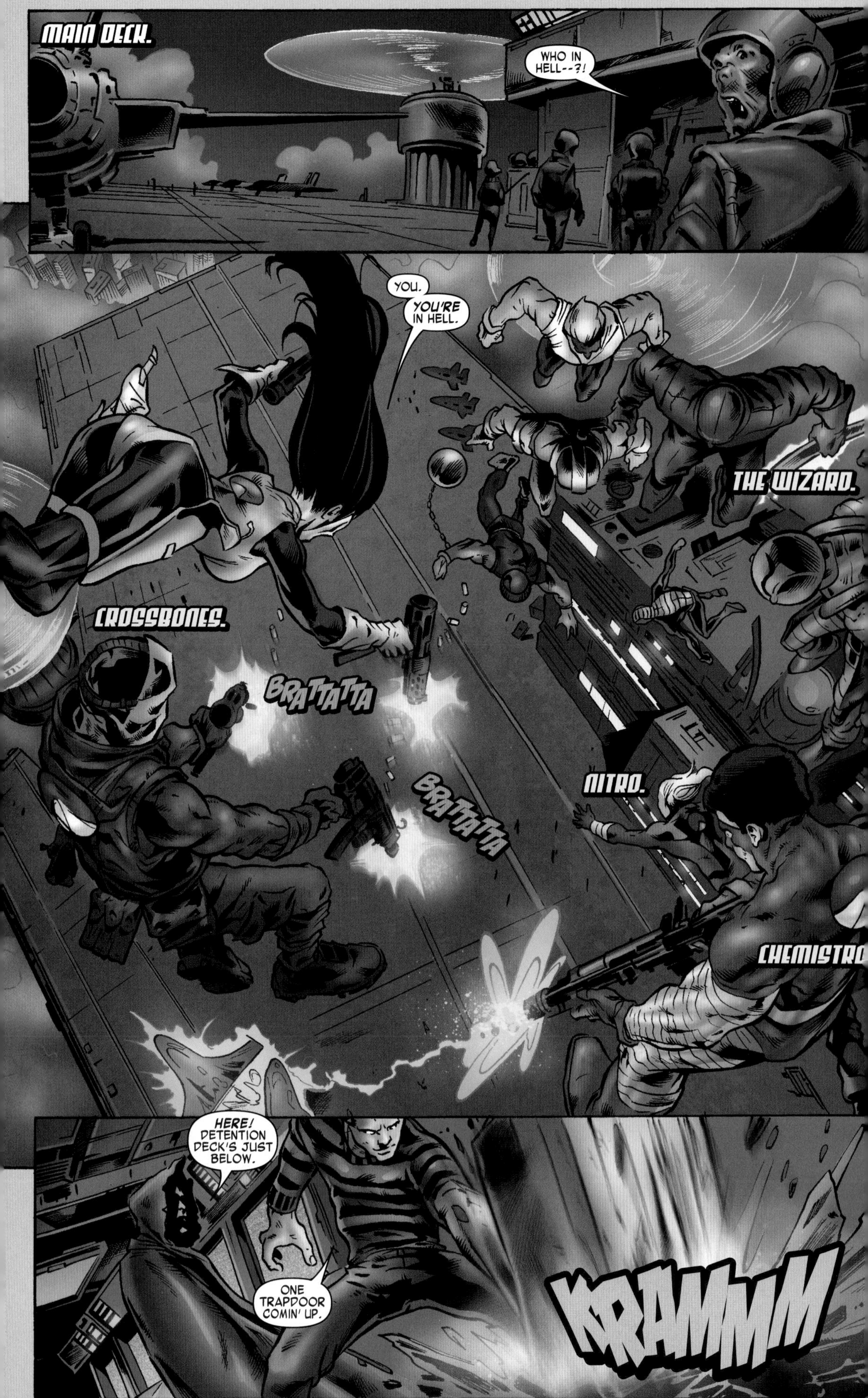
MAIN DECK.
WHO IN HELL--?!
YOU.
YOU'RE IN HELL.
THE WIZARD.
CROSSBONES.
BRATTATTA
BRATTATTA
NITRO.
CHEMISTRO
HERE! DETENTION DECK'S JUST BELOW.
ONE TRAPDOOR COMIN' UP.
KRAMMMM

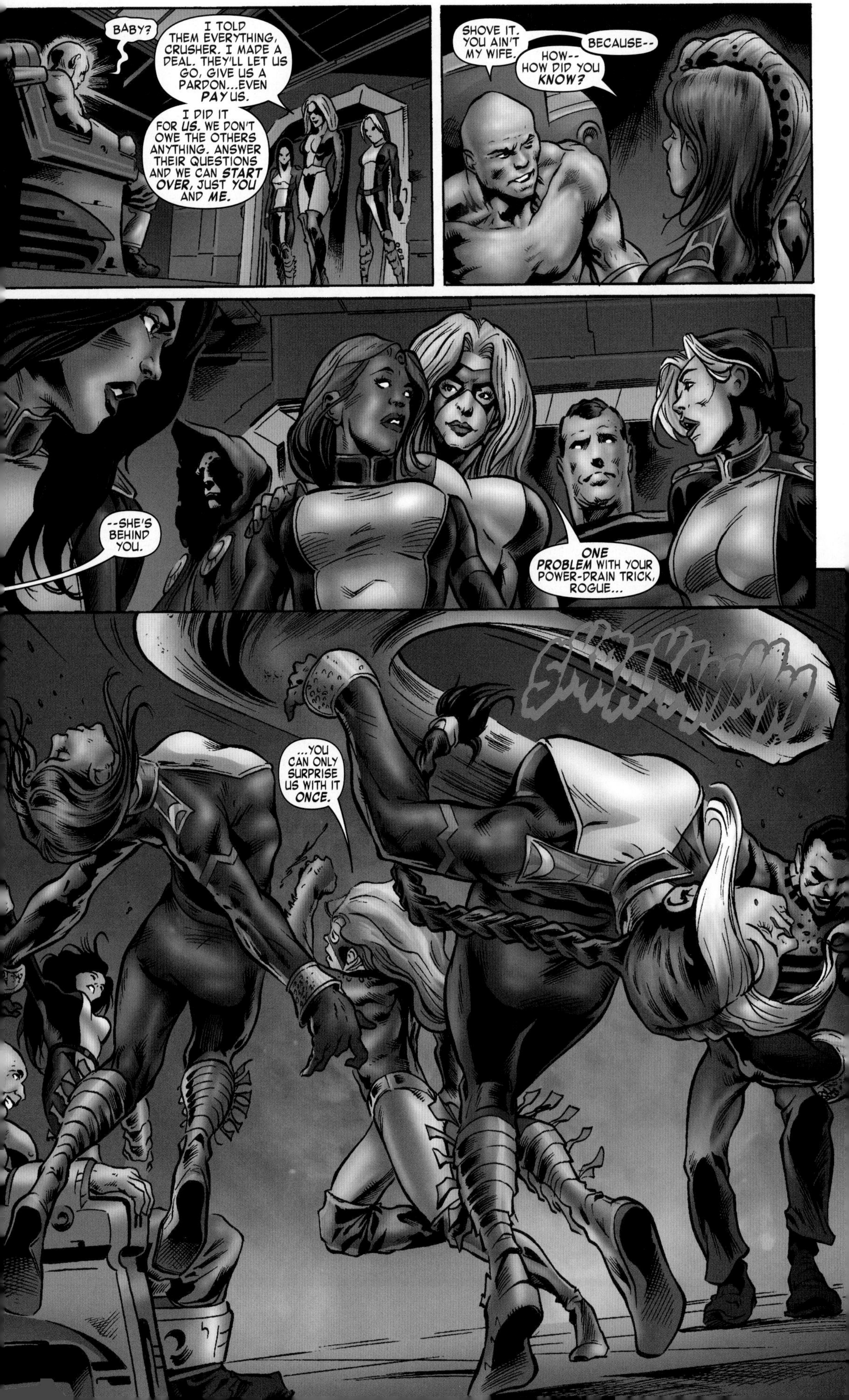
BABY?
I TOLD THEM EVERYTHING, CRUSHER. I MADE A DEAL. THEY'LL LET US GO, GIVE US A PARDON...EVEN PAY US.
I DID IT FOR US. WE DON'T OWE THE OTHERS ANYTHING. ANSWER THEIR QUESTIONS AND WE CAN START OVER, JUST YOU AND ME.
SHOVE IT. YOU AIN'T MY WIFE.
HOW-- HOW DID YOU KNOW?
BECAUSE--
--SHE'S BEHIND YOU.
ONE PROBLEM WITH YOUR POWER-DRAIN TRICK, ROGUE...
...YOU CAN ONLY SURPRISE US WITH IT ONCE.

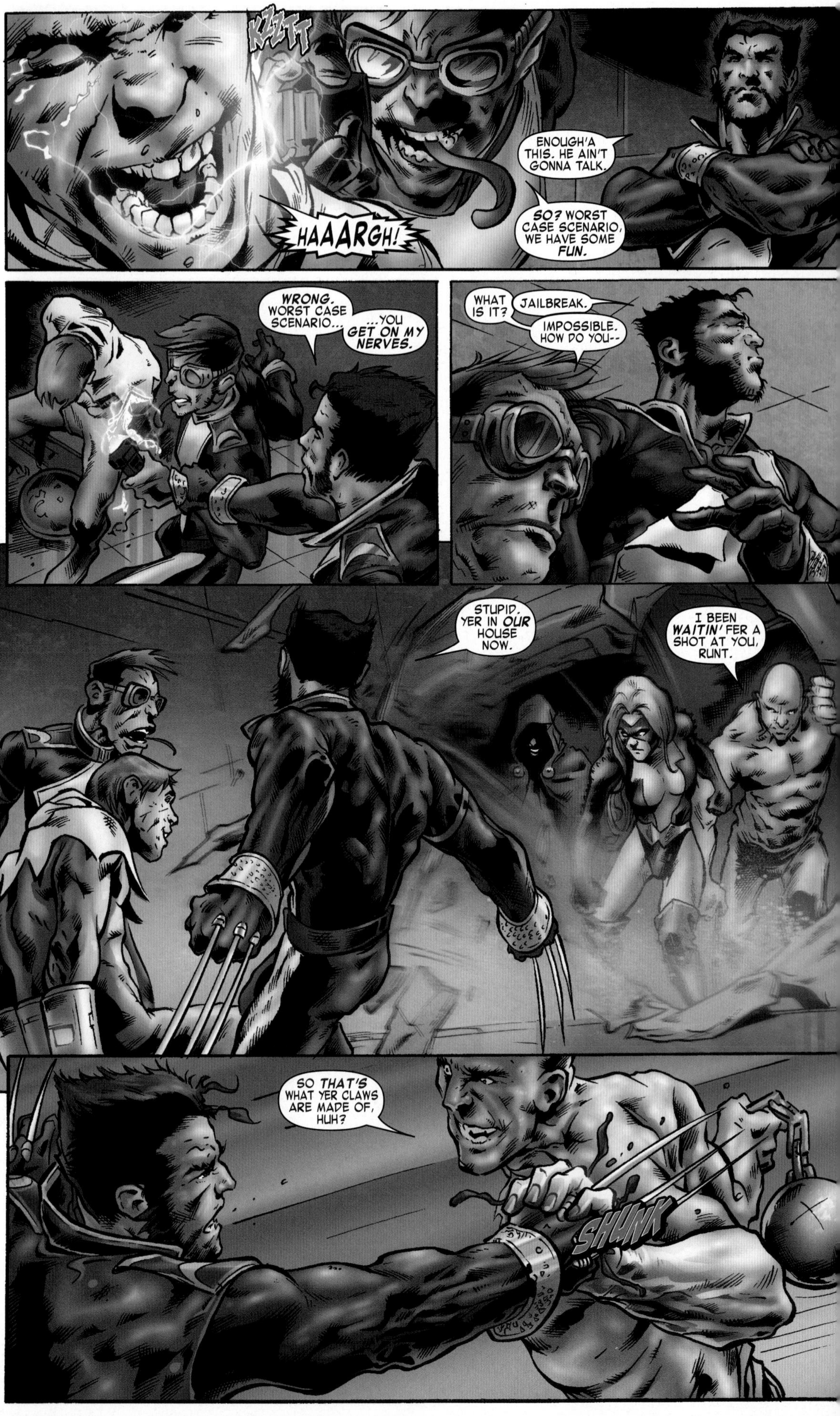
KZZTT
HAAARGH!
ENOUGH'A THIS. HE AIN'T GONNA TALK.
SO? WORST CASE SCENARIO, WE HAVE SOME FUN.
WRONG. WORST CASE SCENARIO...
...YOU GET ON MY NERVES.
WHAT IS IT?
JAILBREAK.
IMPOSSIBLE. HOW DO YOU--
STUPID. YER IN OUR HOUSE NOW.
I BEEN WAITIN' FER A SHOT AT YOU, RUNT.
SO THAT'S WHAT YER CLAWS ARE MADE OF, HUH?
SHUNK

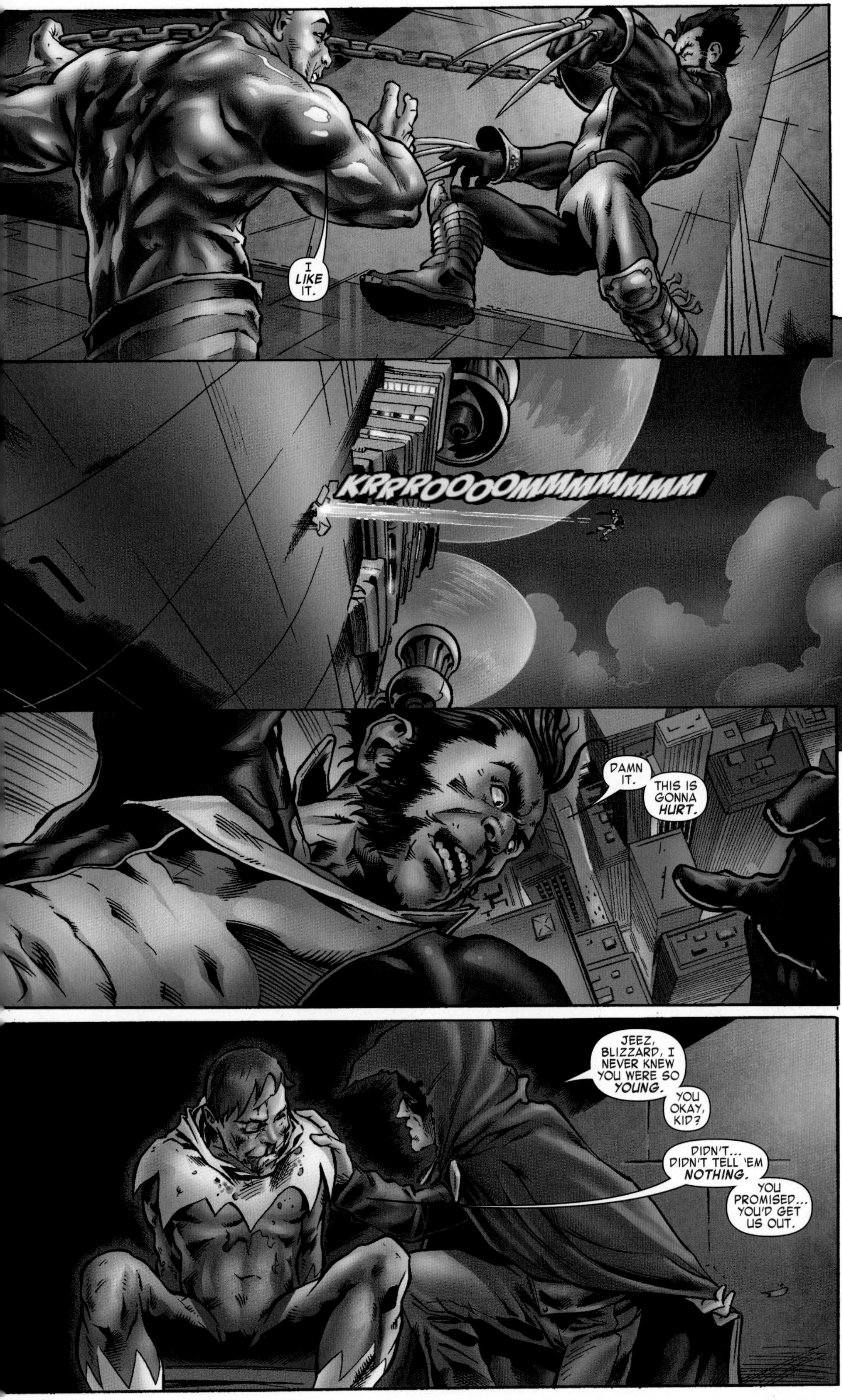

I LIKE IT.
KRRROOOOOMMMMMMMMM
DAMN IT.
THIS IS GONNA HURT.
JEEZ, BLIZZARD, I NEVER KNEW YOU WERE SO YOUNG.
YOU OKAY, KID?
DIDN'T... DIDN'T TELL 'EM NOTHING.
YOU PROMISED... YOU'D GET US OUT.

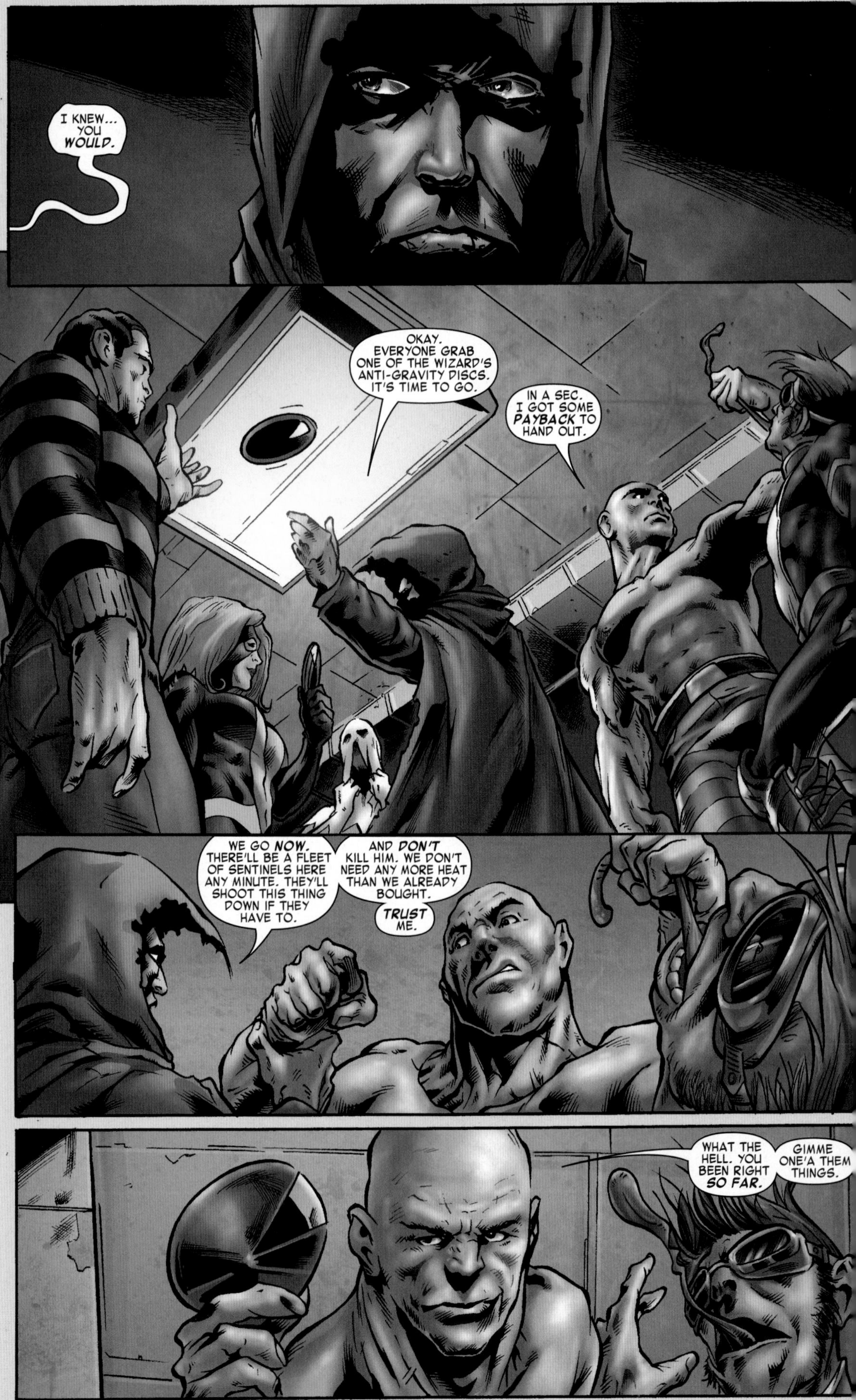
I KNEW... YOU *WOULD*.
OKAY. EVERYONE GRAB ONE OF THE WIZARD'S ANTI-GRAVITY DISCS. IT'S TIME TO GO.
IN A SEC. I GOT SOME *PAYBACK* TO HAND OUT.
WE GO *NOW*. THERE'LL BE A FLEET OF SENTINELS HERE ANY MINUTE. THEY'LL SHOOT THIS THING DOWN IF THEY HAVE TO.
AND *DON'T* KILL HIM. WE DON'T NEED ANY MORE HEAT THAN WE ALREADY BOUGHT.
TRUST ME.
WHAT THE HELL. YOU BEEN RIGHT *SO FAR*.
GIMME ONE'A THEM THINGS.

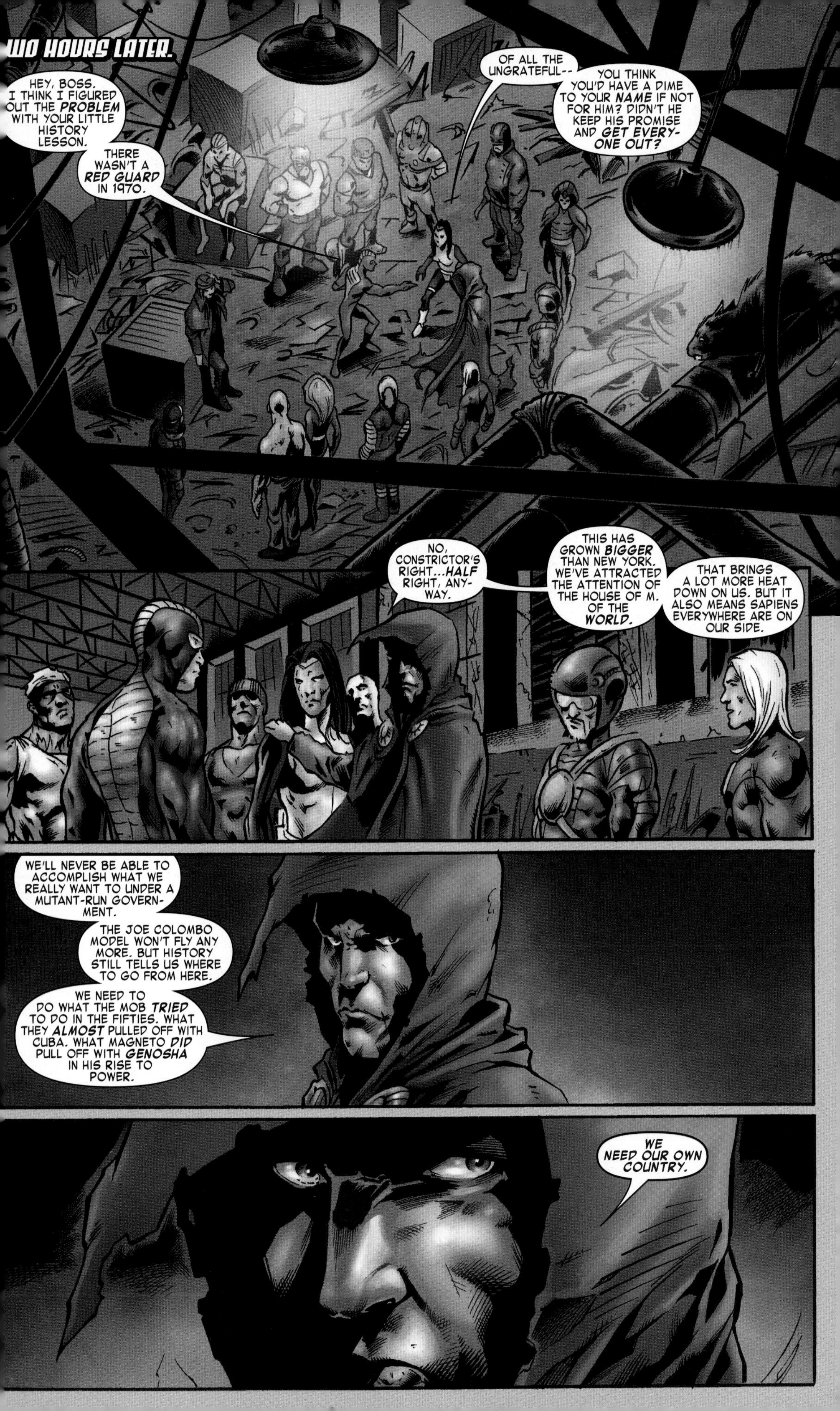
WO HOURS LATER.
HEY, BOSS. I THINK I FIGURED OUT THE ***PROBLEM*** WITH YOUR LITTLE HISTORY LESSON.
THERE WASN'T A ***RED GUARD*** IN 1970.
OF ALL THE UNGRATEFUL--
YOU THINK YOU'D HAVE A DIME TO YOUR ***NAME*** IF NOT FOR HIM? DIDN'T HE KEEP HIS PROMISE AND ***GET EVERY-ONE OUT?***
NO, CONSTRICTOR'S RIGHT... ***HALF*** RIGHT, ANY-WAY.
THIS HAS GROWN ***BIGGER*** THAN NEW YORK. WE'VE ATTRACTED THE ATTENTION OF THE HOUSE OF M. OF THE ***WORLD.***
THAT BRINGS A LOT MORE HEAT DOWN ON US. BUT IT ALSO MEANS SAPIENS EVERYWHERE ARE ON OUR SIDE.
WE'LL NEVER BE ABLE TO ACCOMPLISH WHAT WE REALLY WANT TO UNDER A MUTANT-RUN GOVERN-MENT.
THE JOE COLOMBO MODEL WON'T FLY ANY MORE. BUT HISTORY STILL TELLS US WHERE TO GO FROM HERE.
WE NEED TO DO WHAT THE MOB ***TRIED*** TO DO IN THE FIFTIES. WHAT THEY ***ALMOST*** PULLED OFF WITH CUBA. WHAT MAGNETO ***DID*** PULL OFF WITH ***GENOSHA*** IN HIS RISE TO POWER.
WE NEED OUR OWN COUNTRY.

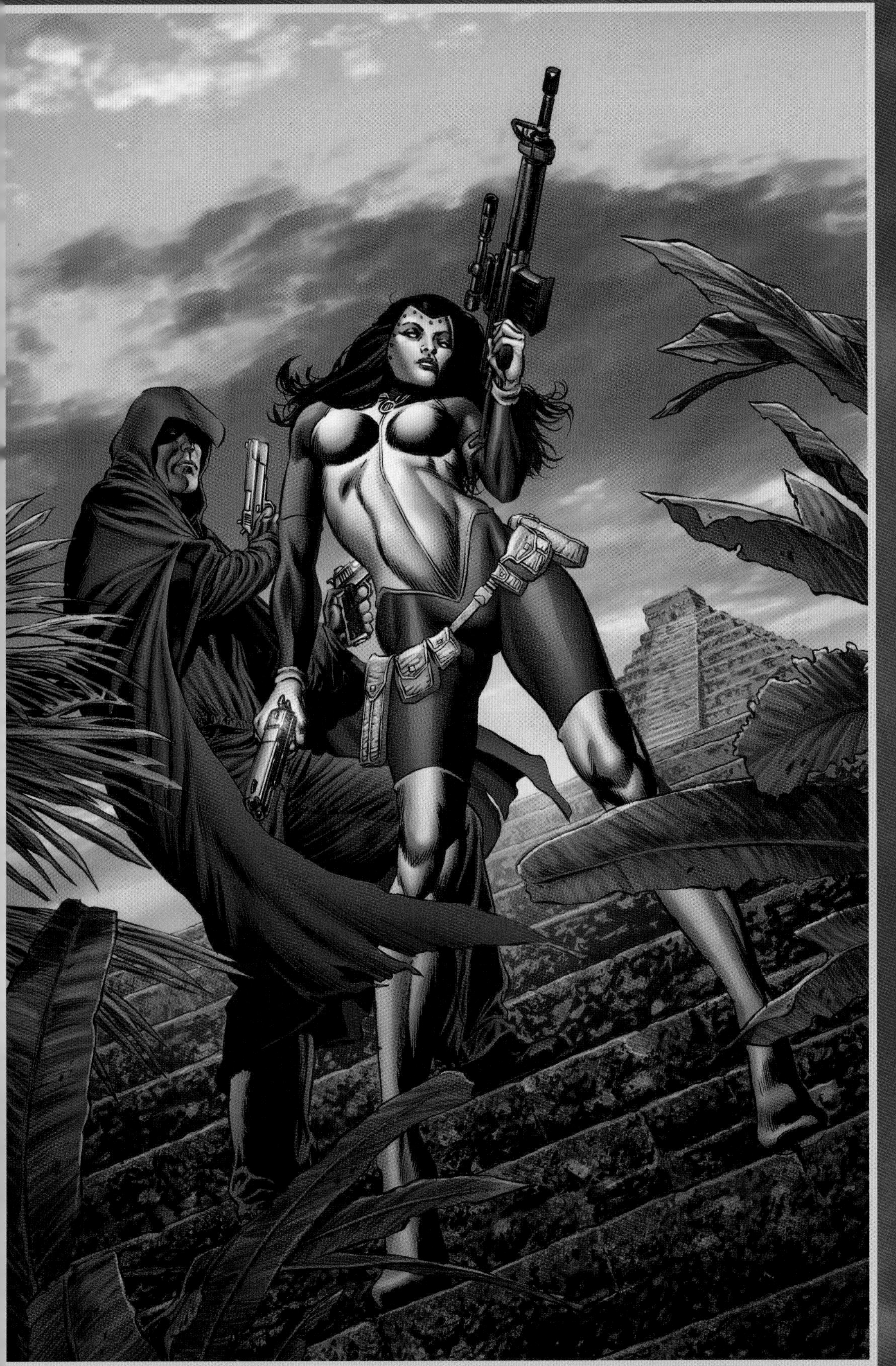

ISSUE #3: SHANGRI-LA

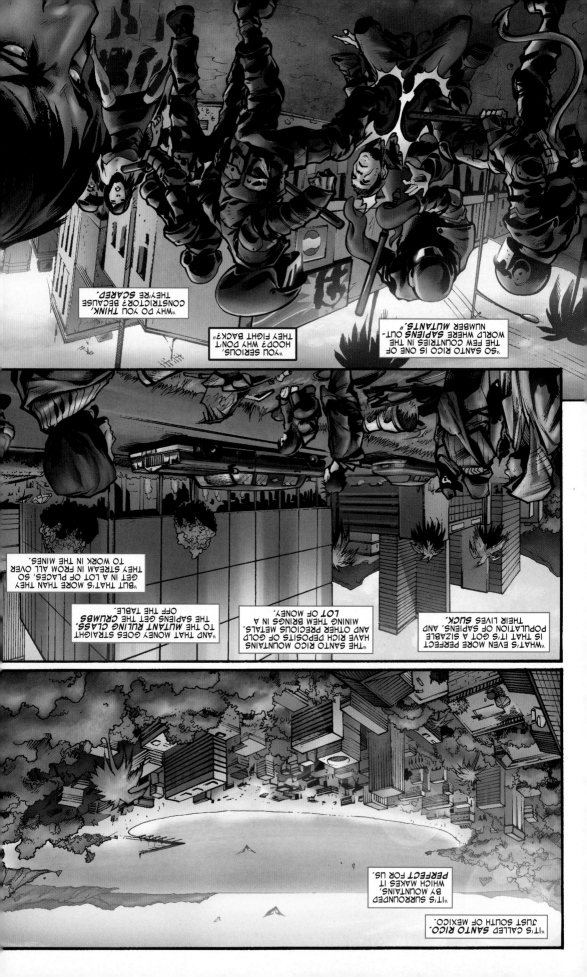

"WHY DO YOU THINK, CONSTRICTOR? BECAUSE THEY'RE SCARED."

"YOU SERIOUS, HOOD? WHY DON'T THEY FIGHT BACK?"

"SO SANTO RICO IS ONE OF THE FEW COUNTRIES IN THE WORLD WHERE SAPIENS OUT-NUMBER MUTANTS."

"BUT THAT'S MORE THAN THEY GET IN A LOT OF PLACES, SO THEY STREAM IN FROM ALL OVER TO WORK IN THE MINES."

"AND THAT MONEY GOES STRAIGHT TO THE MUTANT RULING CLASS. THE SAPIENS GET THE CRUMBS OFF THE TABLE."

"THE SANTO RICO MOUNTAINS HAVE RICH DEPOSITS OF GOLD AND OTHER PRECIOUS METALS. MINING THEM BRINGS IN A LOT OF MONEY."

"WHAT'S EVEN MORE PERFECT IS THAT IT'S GOT A SIZABLE POPULATION OF SAPIENS. AND THEIR LIVES SUCK."

"IT'S SURROUNDED BY MOUNTAINS, WHICH MAKES IT PERFECT FOR US."

"IT'S CALLED SANTO RICO. JUST SOUTH OF MEXICO."

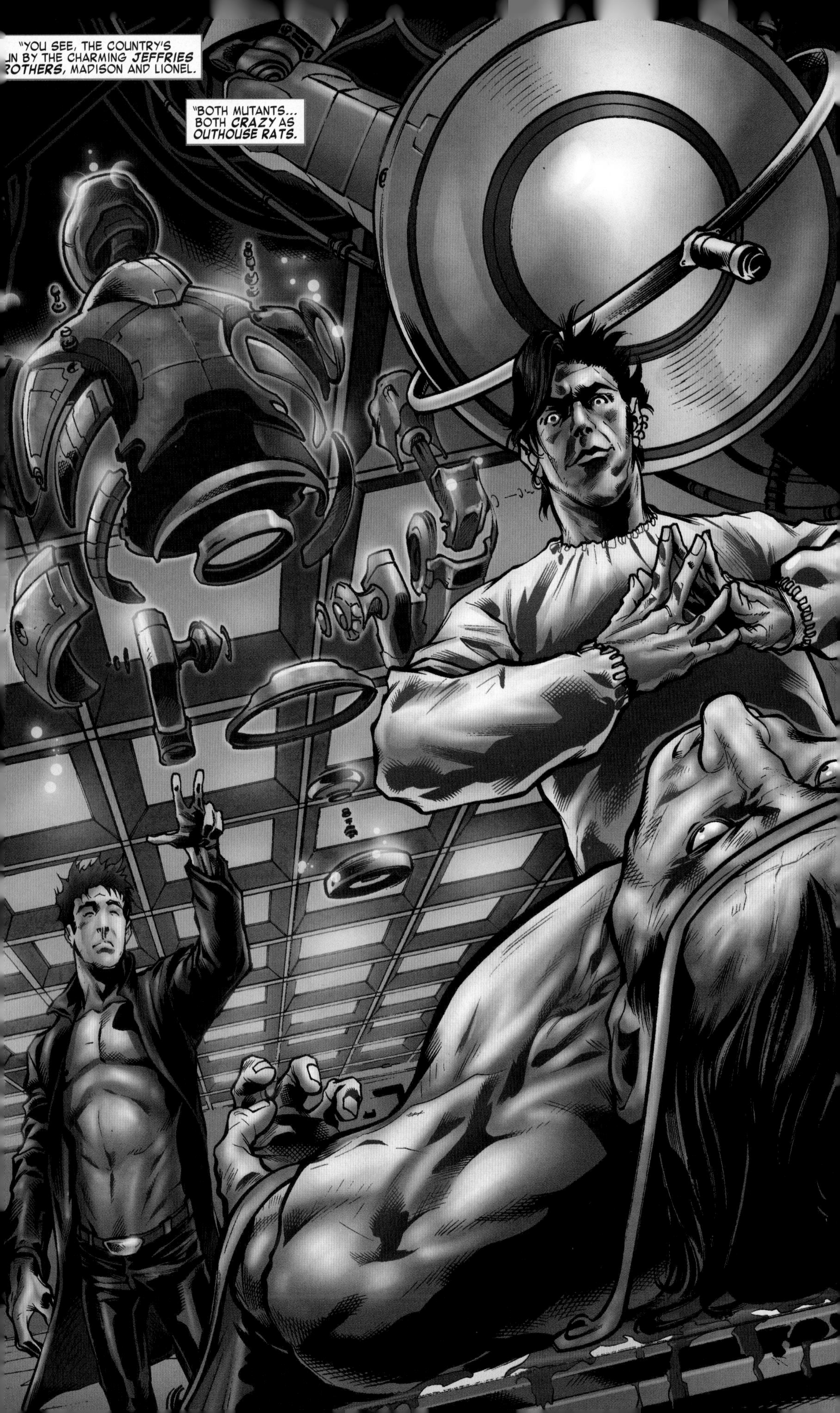
"YOU SEE, THE COUNTRY'S
UN BY THE CHARMING JEFFRIES
ROTHERS, MADISON AND LIONEL.
"BOTH MUTANTS... BOTH CRAZY AS OUTHOUSE RATS.

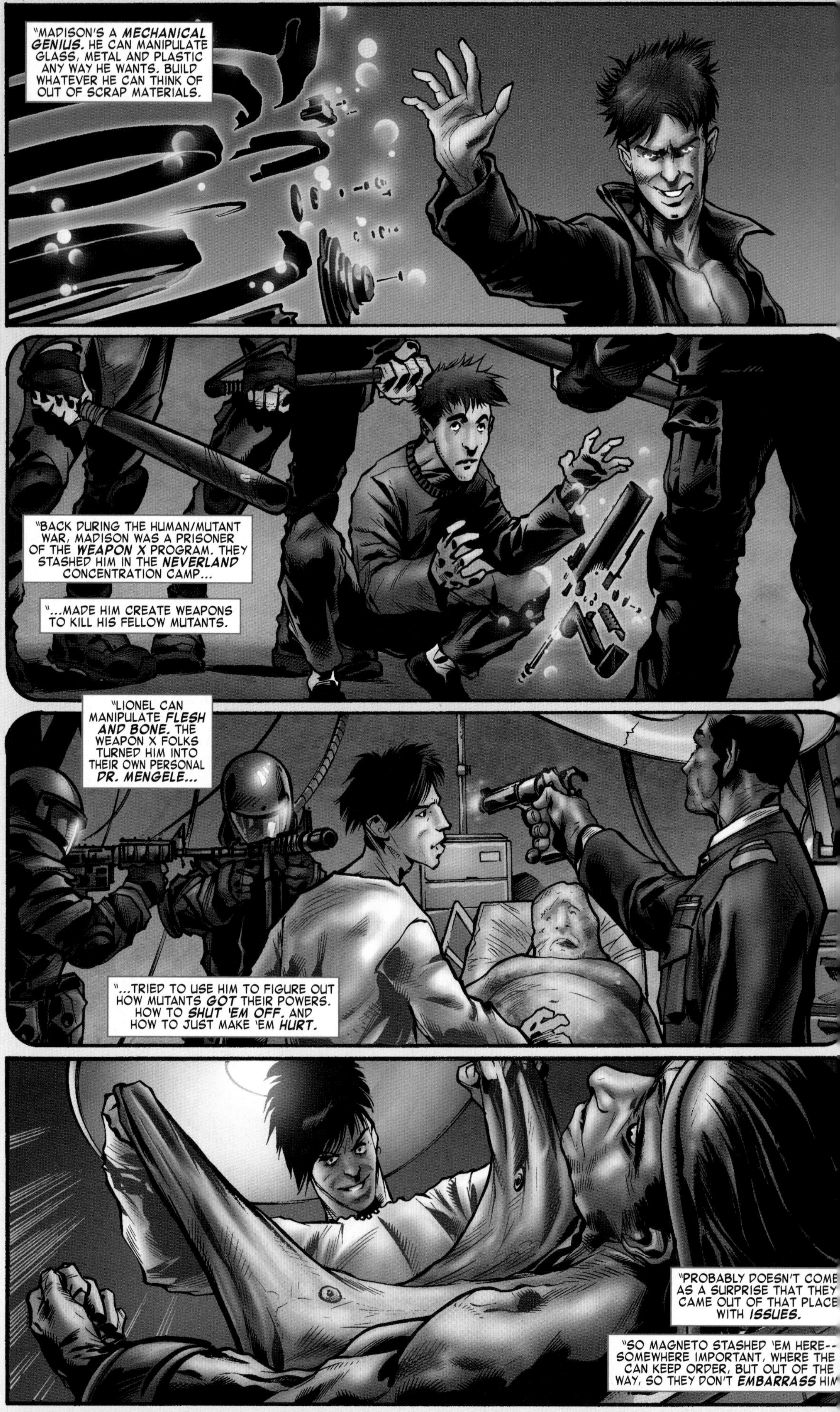
"MADISON'S A ***MECHANICAL GENIUS.*** HE CAN MANIPULATE GLASS, METAL AND PLASTIC ANY WAY HE WANTS. BUILD WHATEVER HE CAN THINK OF OUT OF SCRAP MATERIALS.
"BACK DURING THE HUMAN/MUTANT WAR, MADISON WAS A PRISONER OF THE ***WEAPON X*** PROGRAM. THEY STASHED HIM IN THE ***NEVERLAND*** CONCENTRATION CAMP...
"...MADE HIM CREATE WEAPONS TO KILL HIS FELLOW MUTANTS.
"LIONEL CAN MANIPULATE ***FLESH AND BONE.*** THE WEAPON X FOLKS TURNED HIM INTO THEIR OWN PERSONAL ***DR. MENGELE...***
"...TRIED TO USE HIM TO FIGURE OUT HOW MUTANTS ***GOT*** THEIR POWERS. HOW TO ***SHUT 'EM OFF.*** AND HOW TO JUST MAKE 'EM ***HURT.***
"PROBABLY DOESN'T COME AS A SURPRISE THAT THEY CAME OUT OF THAT PLACE WITH ***ISSUES.***
"SO MAGNETO STASHED 'EM HERE-- SOMEWHERE IMPORTANT, WHERE THE CAN KEEP ORDER, BUT OUT OF THE WAY, SO THEY DON'T ***EMBARRASS*** HIM

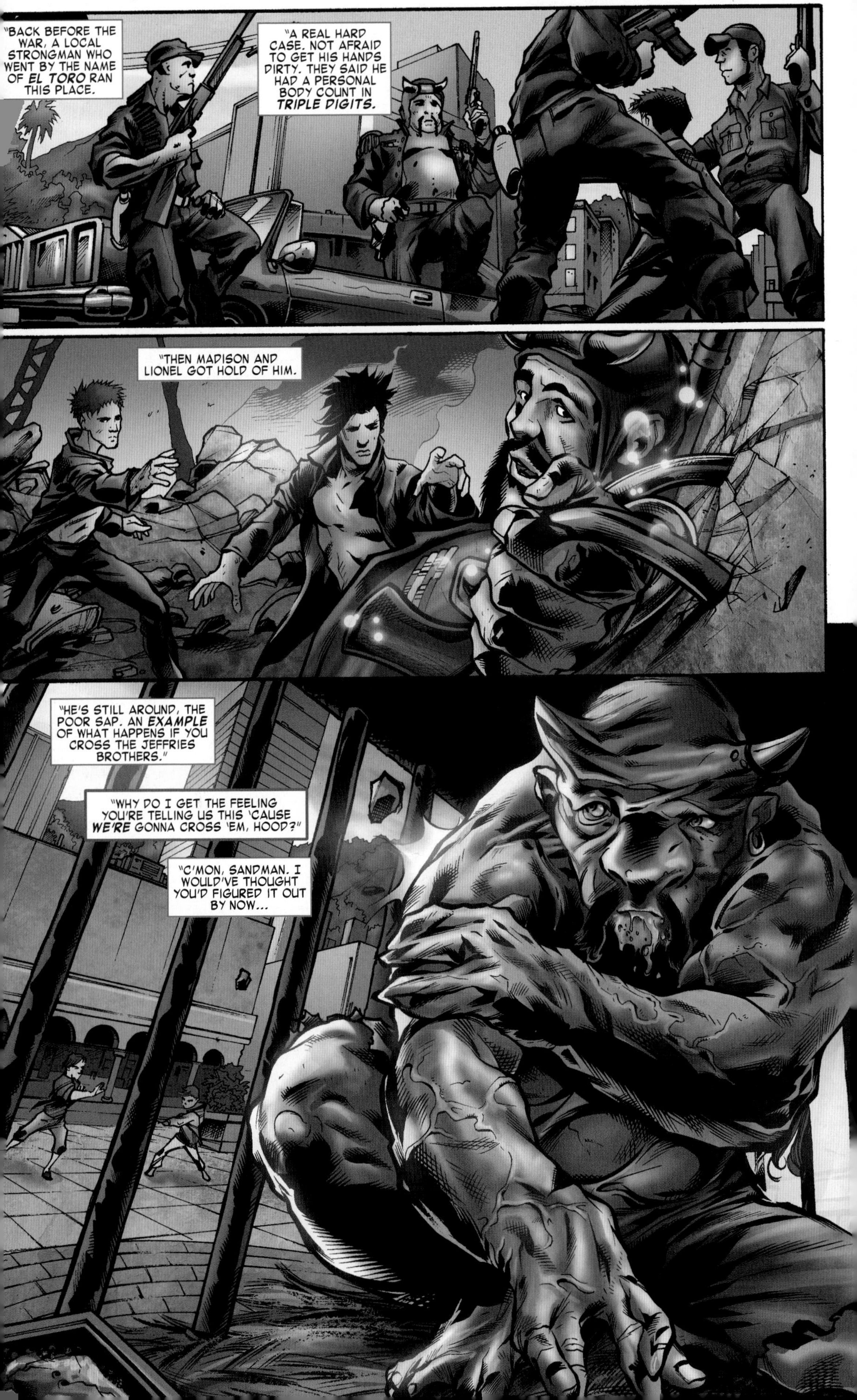
"BACK BEFORE THE WAR, A LOCAL STRONGMAN WHO WENT BY THE NAME OF *EL TORO* RAN THIS PLACE.
"A REAL HARD CASE. NOT AFRAID TO GET HIS HANDS DIRTY. THEY SAID HE HAD A PERSONAL BODY COUNT IN *TRIPLE DIGITS.*
"THEN MADISON AND LIONEL GOT HOLD OF HIM.
"HE'S STILL AROUND, THE POOR SAP. AN *EXAMPLE* OF WHAT HAPPENS IF YOU CROSS THE JEFFRIES BROTHERS."
"WHY DO I GET THE FEELING YOU'RE TELLING US THIS 'CAUSE *WE'RE* GONNA CROSS 'EM, HOOD?"
"C'MON, SANDMAN. I WOULD'VE THOUGHT YOU'D FIGURED IT OUT BY NOW...

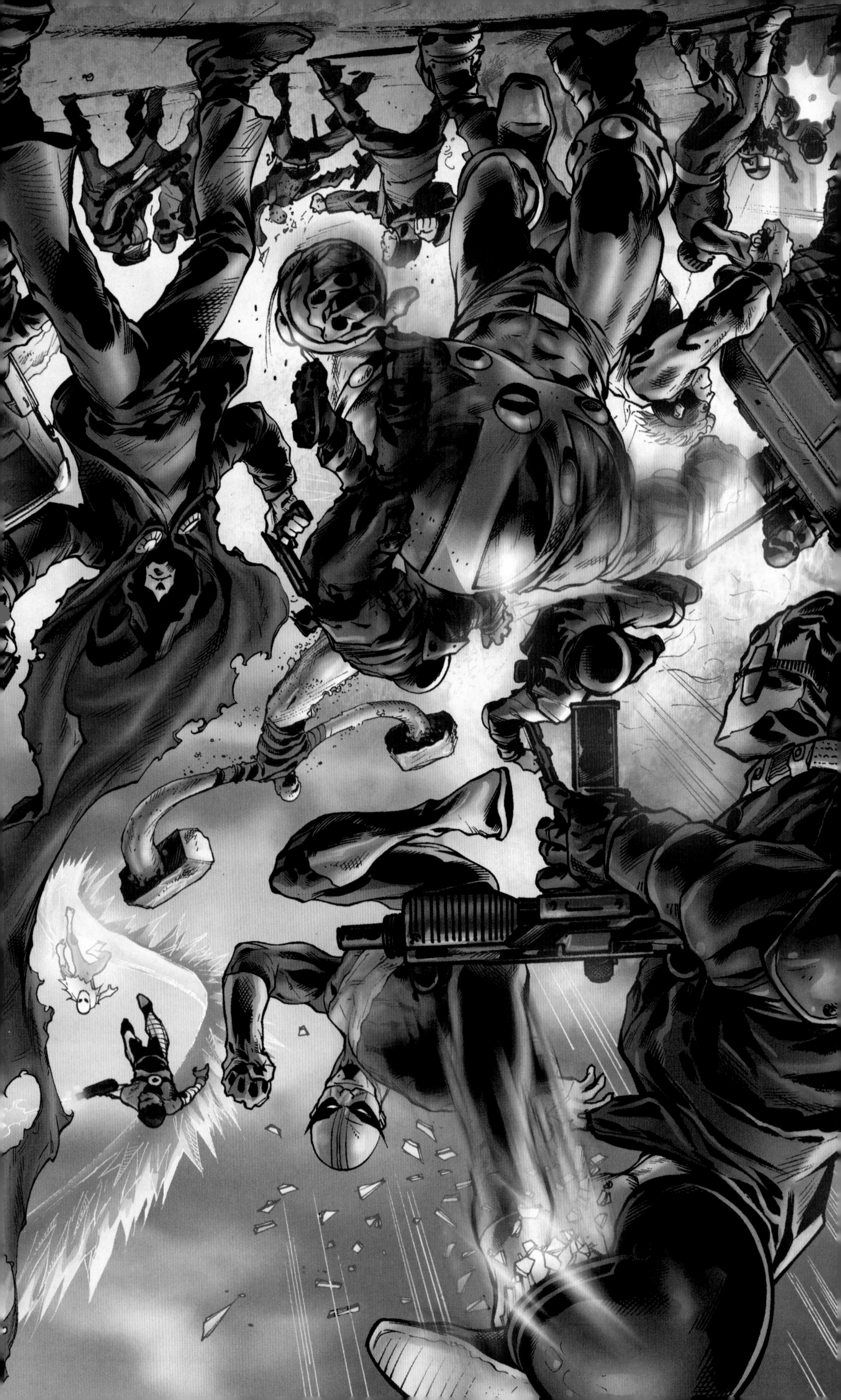

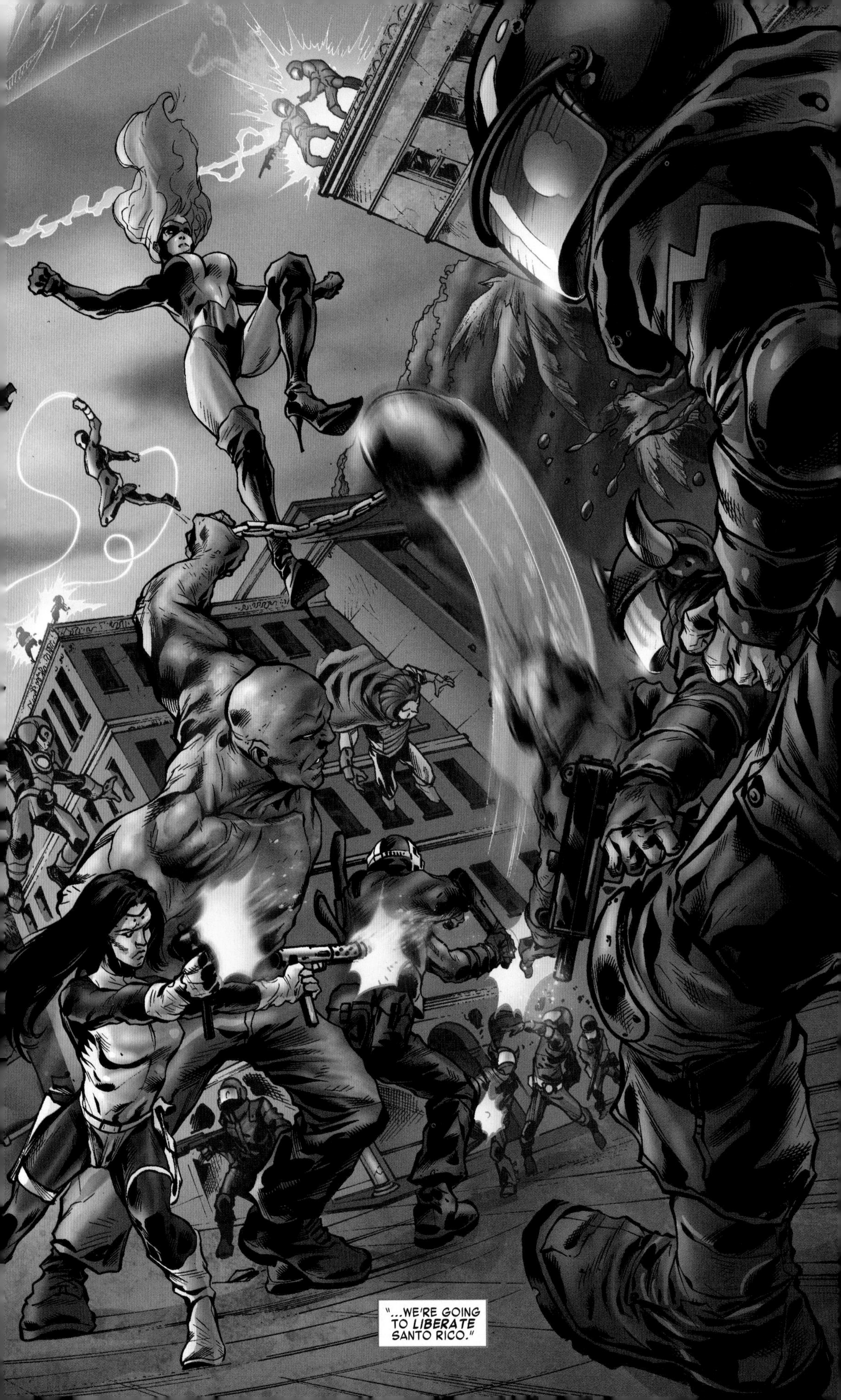
"...WE'RE GOING TO *LIBERATE* SANTO RICO."

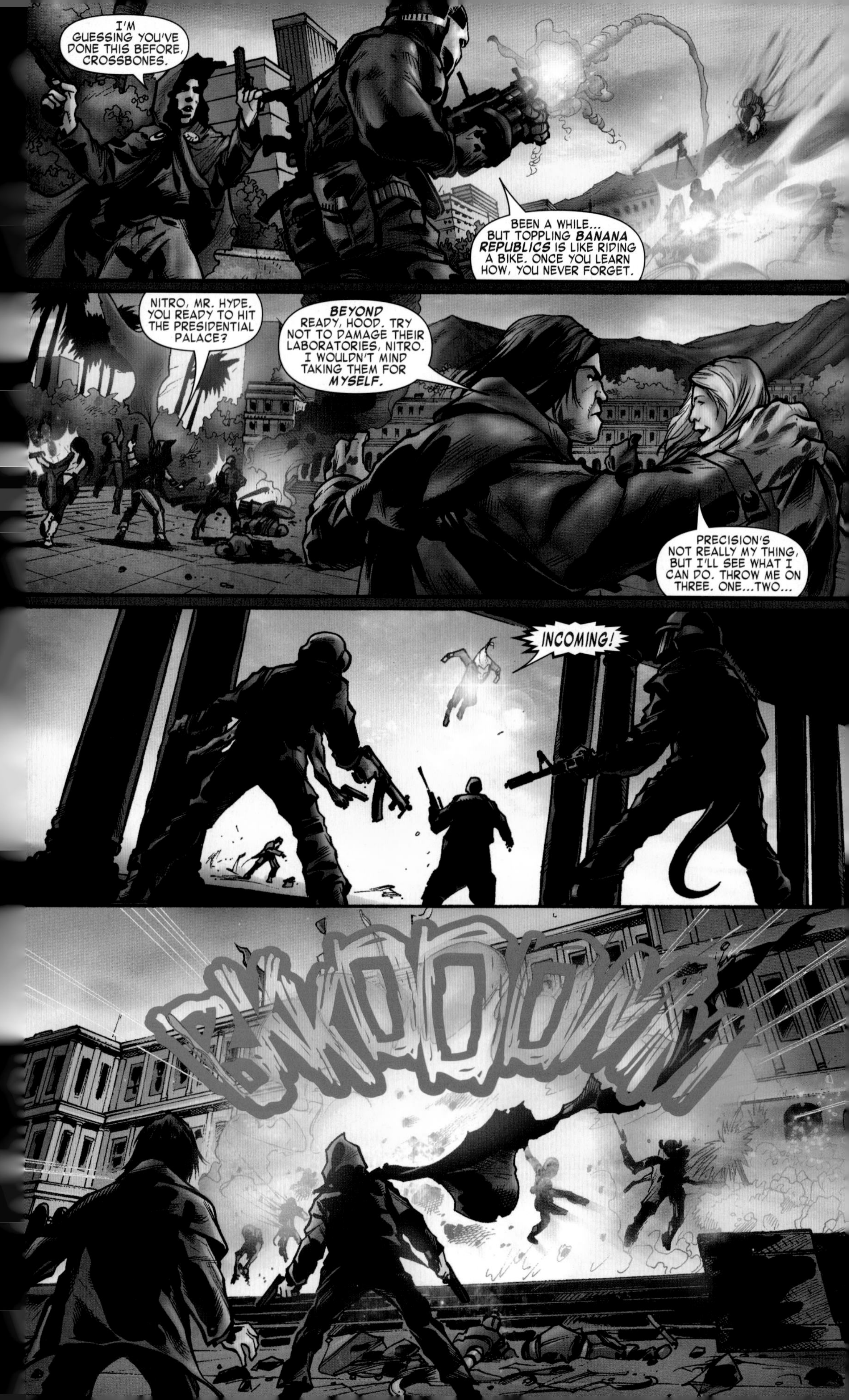
I'M GUESSING YOU'VE DONE THIS BEFORE, CROSSBONES.
BEEN A WHILE... BUT TOPPLING **BANANA REPUBLICS** IS LIKE RIDING A BIKE. ONCE YOU LEARN HOW, YOU NEVER FORGET.
NITRO, MR. HYDE. YOU READY TO HIT THE PRESIDENTIAL PALACE?
BEYOND READY, HOOD. TRY NOT TO DAMAGE THEIR LABORATORIES, NITRO. I WOULDN'T MIND TAKING THEM FOR **MYSELF**.
PRECISION'S NOT REALLY MY THING, BUT I'LL SEE WHAT I CAN DO. THROW ME ON THREE. ONE...TWO...
INCOMING!

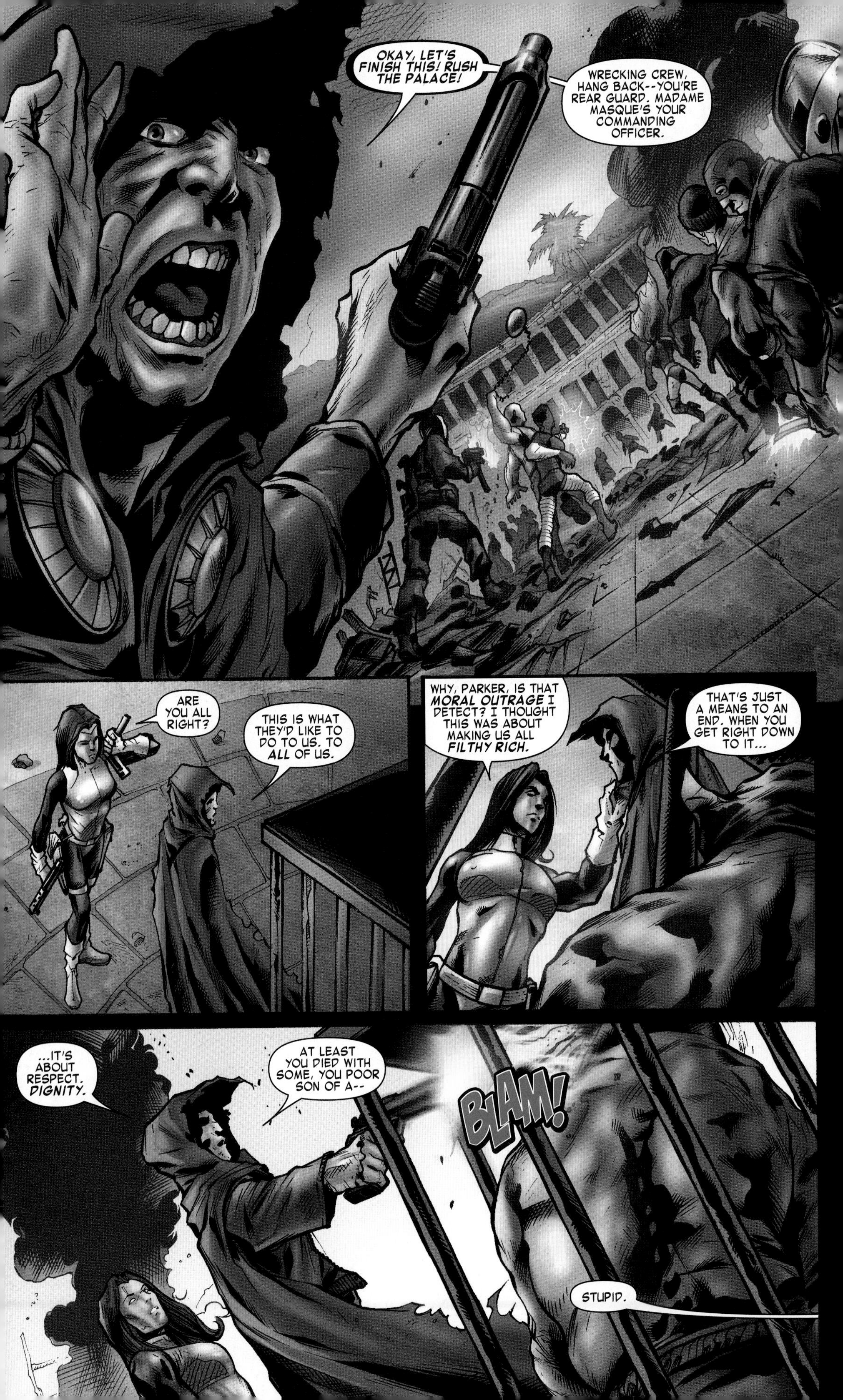
OKAY, LET'S FINISH THIS! RUSH THE PALACE!
WRECKING CREW, HANG BACK--YOU'RE REAR GUARD. MADAME MASQUE'S YOUR COMMANDING OFFICER.
ARE YOU ALL RIGHT?
THIS IS WHAT THEY'D LIKE TO DO TO US. TO ALL OF US.
WHY, PARKER, IS THAT MORAL OUTRAGE I DETECT? I THOUGHT THIS WAS ABOUT MAKING US ALL FILTHY RICH.
THAT'S JUST A MEANS TO AN END. WHEN YOU GET RIGHT DOWN TO IT...
...IT'S ABOUT RESPECT. DIGNITY.
AT LEAST YOU DIED WITH SOME, YOU POOR SON OF A--
BLAM!
STUPID.

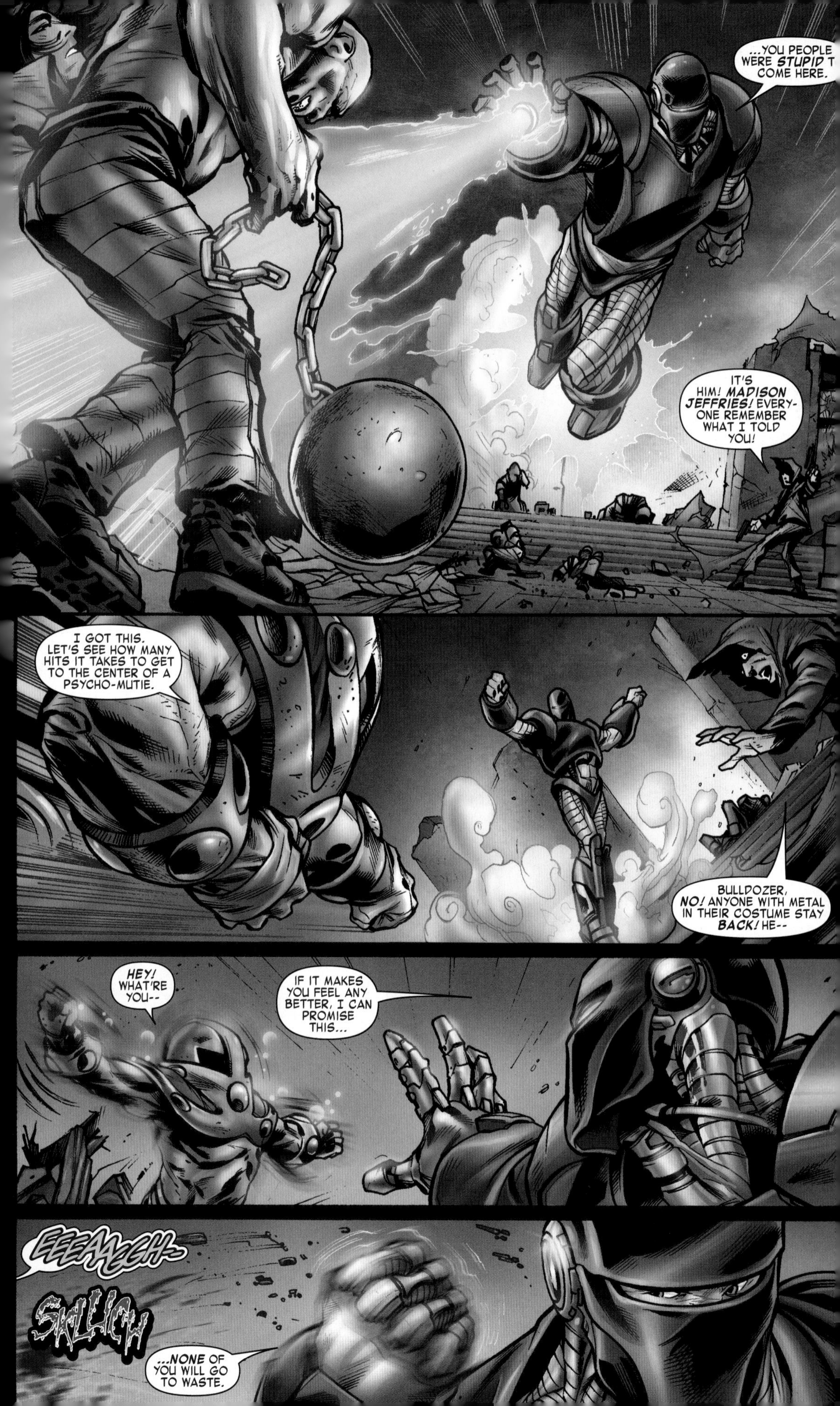
...YOU PEOPLE WERE STUPID T COME HERE.
IT'S HIM! MADISON JEFFRIES! EVERY-ONE REMEMBER WHAT I TOLD YOU!
I GOT THIS. LET'S SEE HOW MANY HITS IT TAKES TO GET TO THE CENTER OF A PSYCHO-MUTIE.
BULLDOZER, NO! ANYONE WITH METAL IN THEIR COSTUME STAY BACK! HE--
HEY! WHAT'RE YOU--
IF IT MAKES YOU FEEL ANY BETTER, I CAN PROMISE THIS...
EEEAAAGGH--
SKLLIGH
...NONE OF YOU WILL GO TO WASTE.

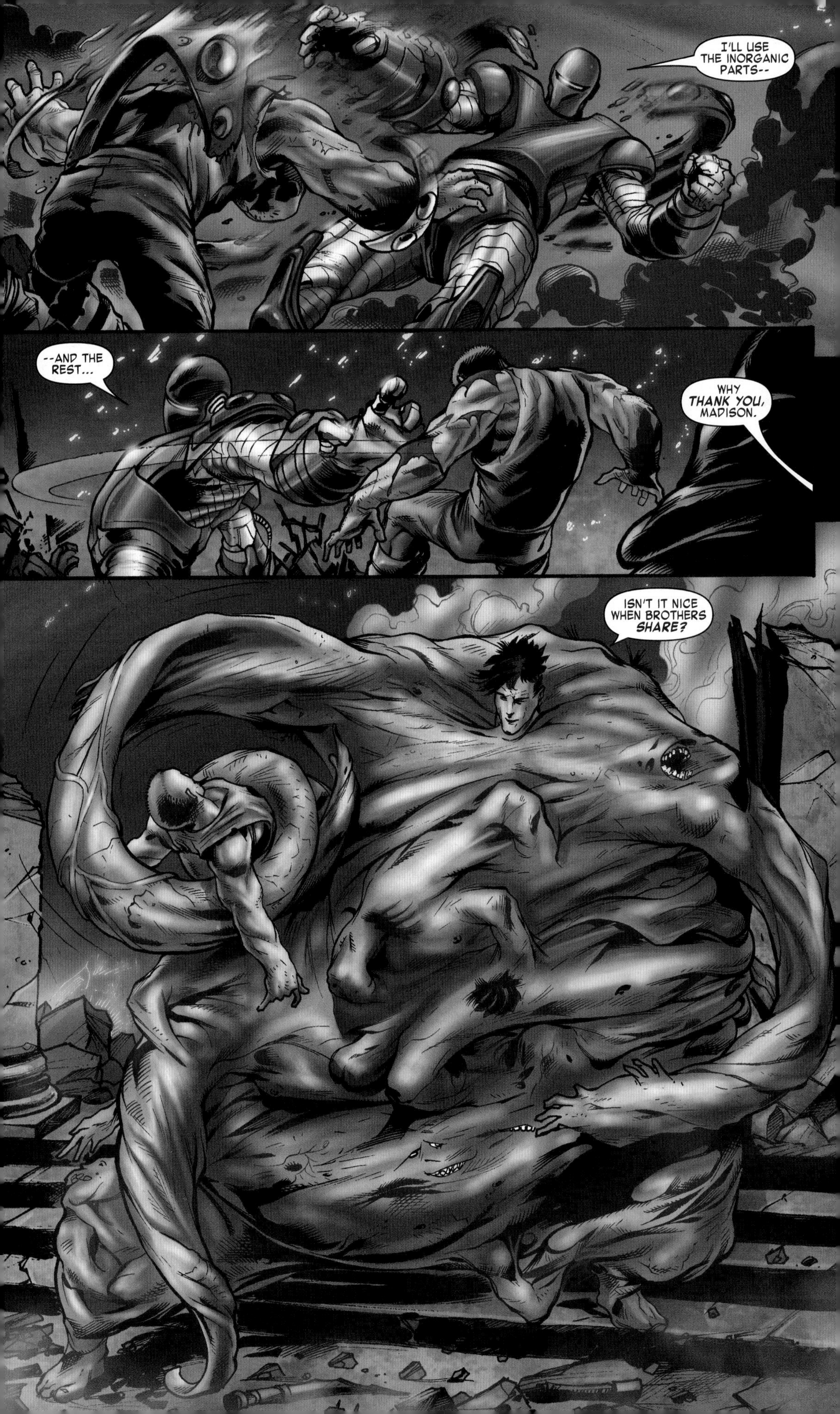
I'LL USE THE INORGANIC PARTS--
--AND THE REST...
WHY THANK YOU, MADISON.
ISN'T IT NICE WHEN BROTHERS SHARE?

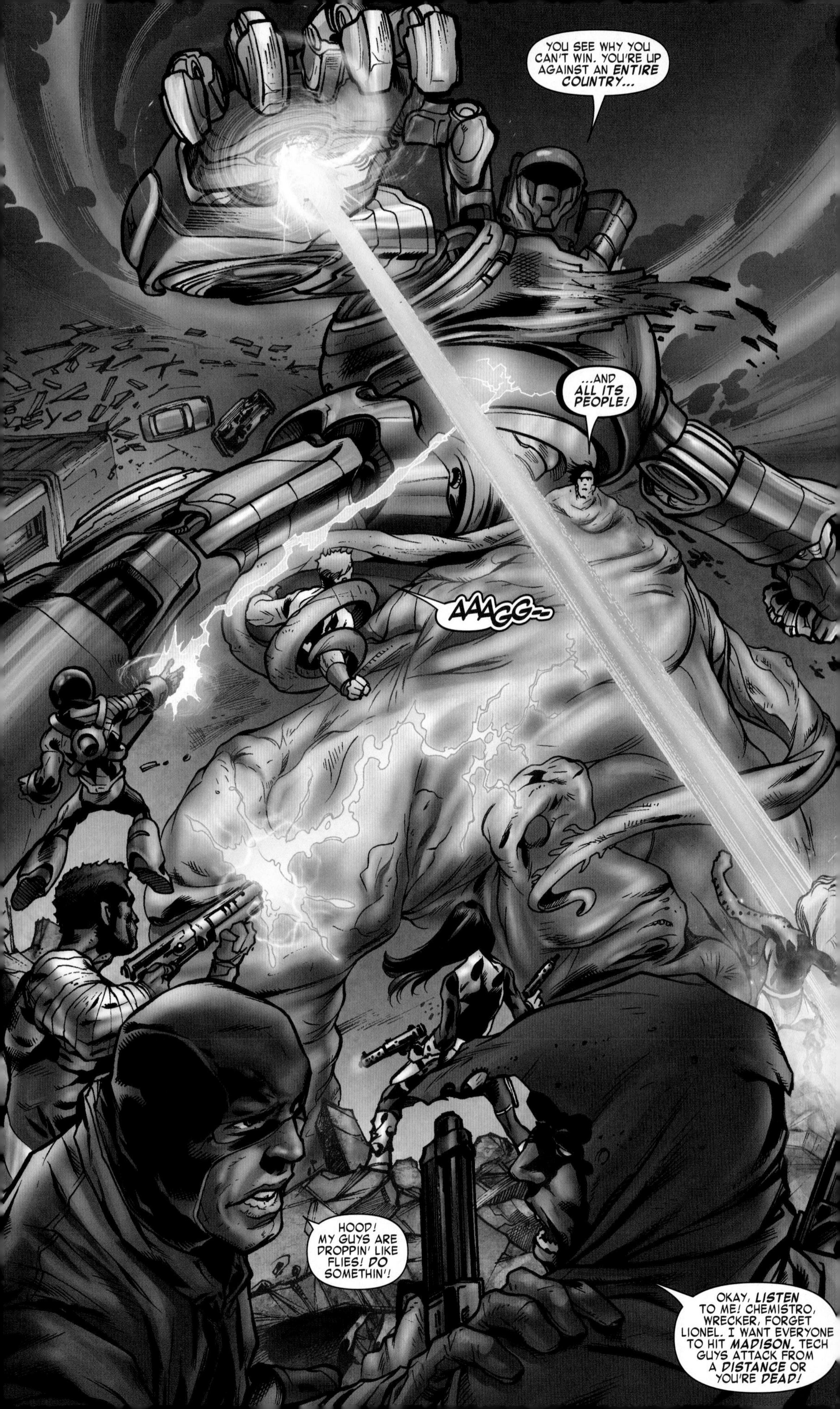
YOU SEE WHY YOU CAN'T WIN. YOU'RE UP AGAINST AN *ENTIRE COUNTRY*...
...AND *ALL ITS PEOPLE!*
AAAGG--
HOOD! MY GUYS ARE DROPPIN' LIKE FLIES! *DO* SOMETHIN'!
OKAY, *LISTEN* TO ME! CHEMISTRO, WRECKER, FORGET LIONEL. I WANT EVERYONE TO HIT *MADISON*. TECH GUYS ATTACK FROM A *DISTANCE* OR YOU'RE *DEAD!*

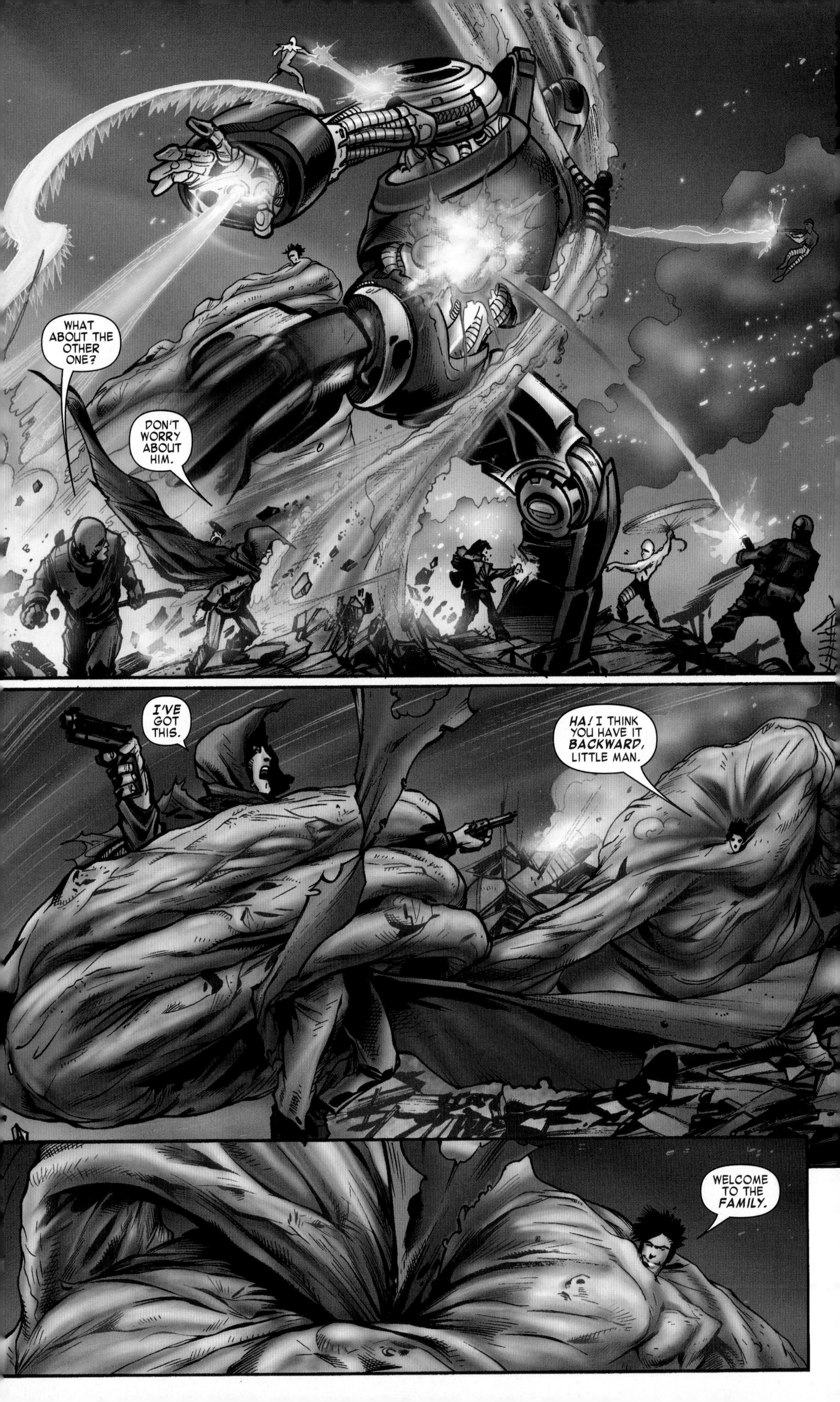
WHAT ABOUT THE OTHER ONE?
DON'T WORRY ABOUT HIM.
I'VE GOT THIS.
HA! I THINK YOU HAVE IT BACKWARD, LITTLE MAN.
WELCOME TO THE FAMILY.

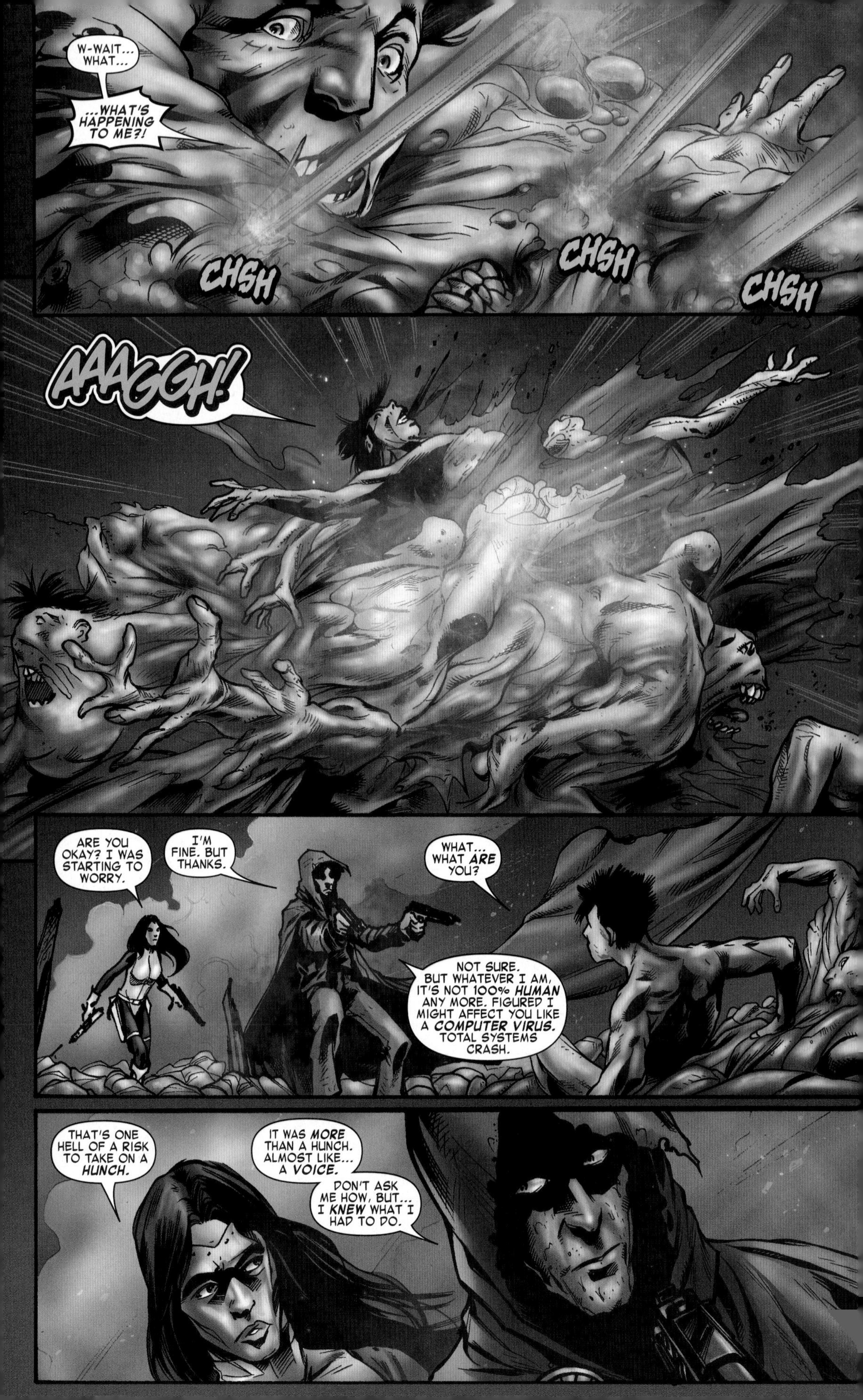
W-WAIT... WHAT...
...WHAT'S HAPPENING TO ME?!
CHSH
CHSH
CHSH
AAAGGH!
ARE YOU OKAY? I WAS STARTING TO WORRY.
I'M FINE. BUT THANKS.
WHAT... WHAT **ARE** YOU?
NOT SURE. BUT WHATEVER I AM, IT'S NOT 100% **HUMAN** ANY MORE. FIGURED I MIGHT AFFECT YOU LIKE A **COMPUTER VIRUS.** TOTAL SYSTEMS CRASH.
THAT'S ONE HELL OF A RISK TO TAKE ON A **HUNCH.**
IT WAS **MORE** THAN A HUNCH. ALMOST LIKE... A **VOICE.**
DON'T ASK ME HOW, BUT... I **KNEW** WHAT I HAD TO DO.

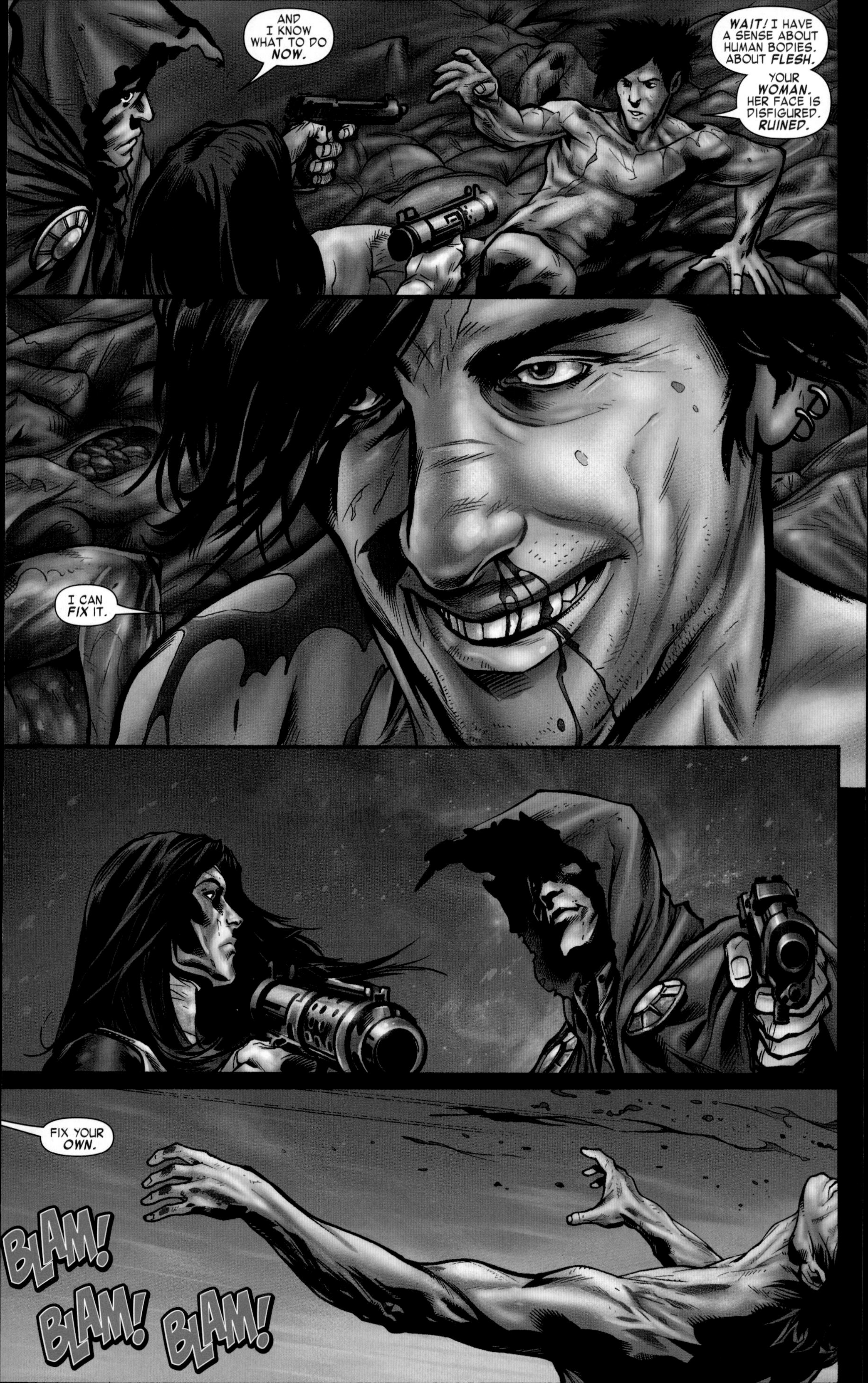
WAIT! I HAVE A SENSE ABOUT HUMAN BODIES. ABOUT FLESH.
YOUR WOMAN. HER FACE IS DISFIGURED. RUINED.
AND I KNOW WHAT TO DO NOW.
I CAN FIX IT.
FIX YOUR OWN.
BLAM! BLAM! BLAM!

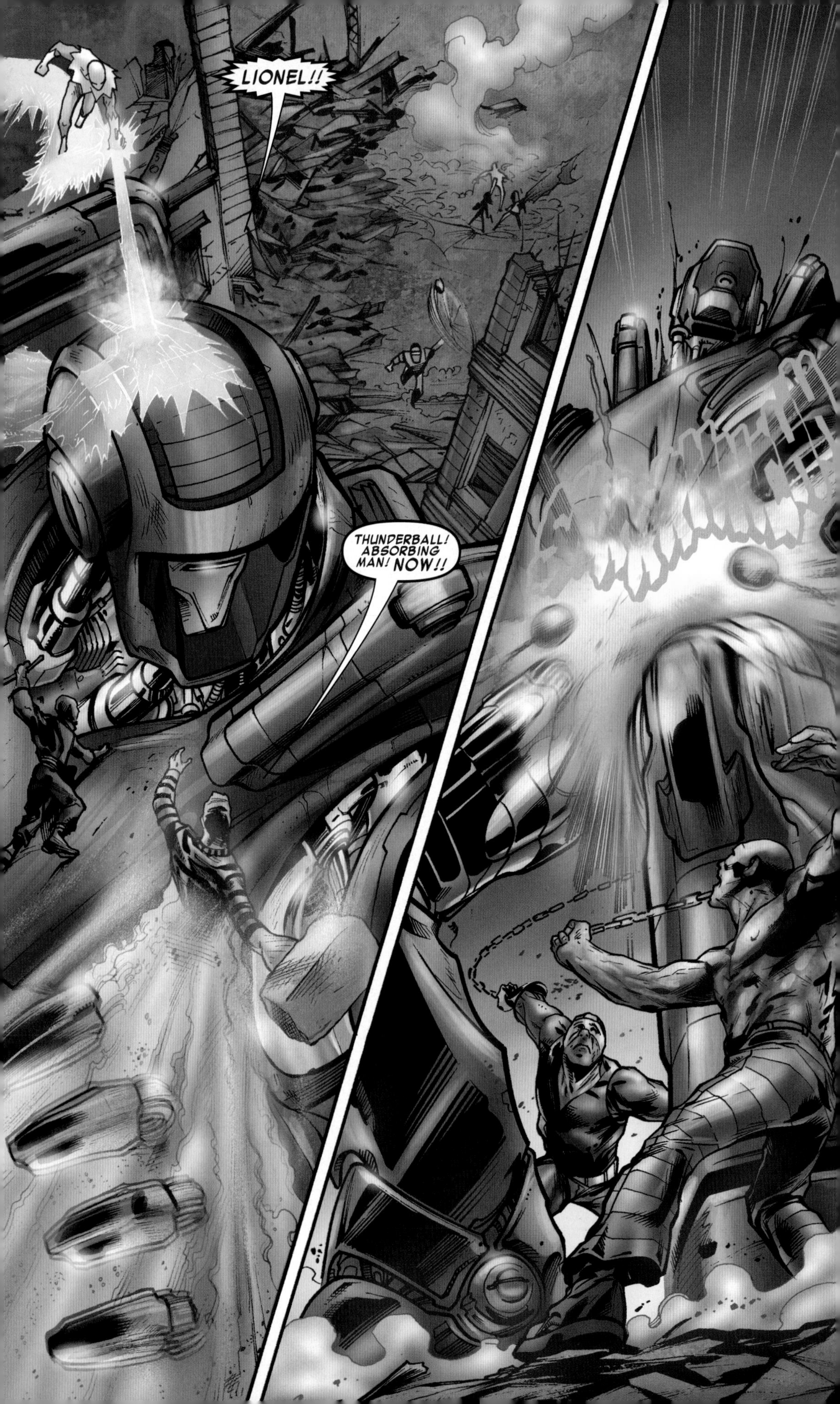
LIONEL!!
THUNDERBALL! ABSORBING MAN! NOW!!

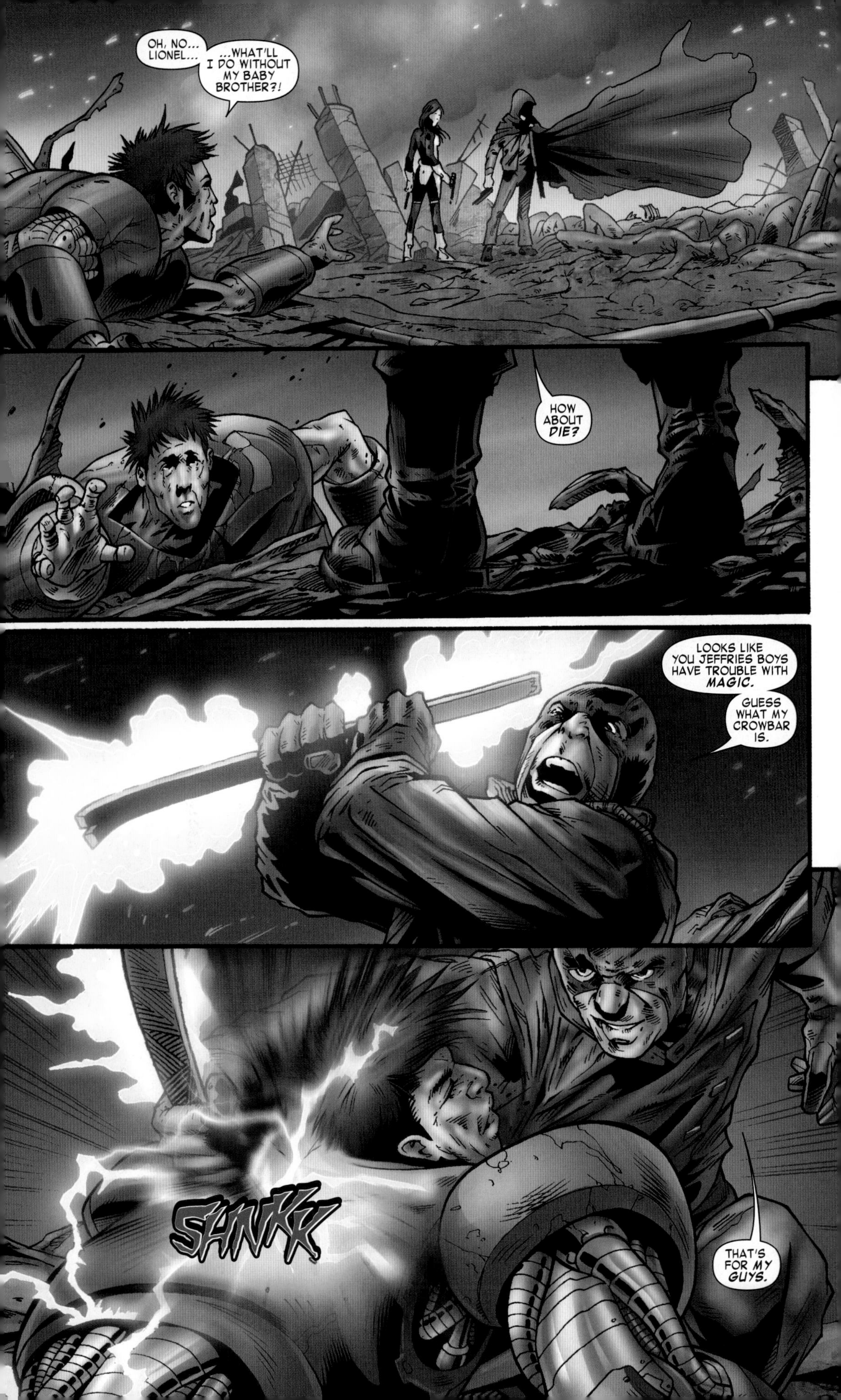
OH, NO... LIONEL...
...WHAT'LL I DO WITHOUT MY BABY BROTHER?!
HOW ABOUT *DIE*?
LOOKS LIKE YOU JEFFRIES BOYS HAVE TROUBLE WITH *MAGIC*.
GUESS WHAT MY CROWBAR IS.
SHNKK
THAT'S FOR *MY GUYS*.

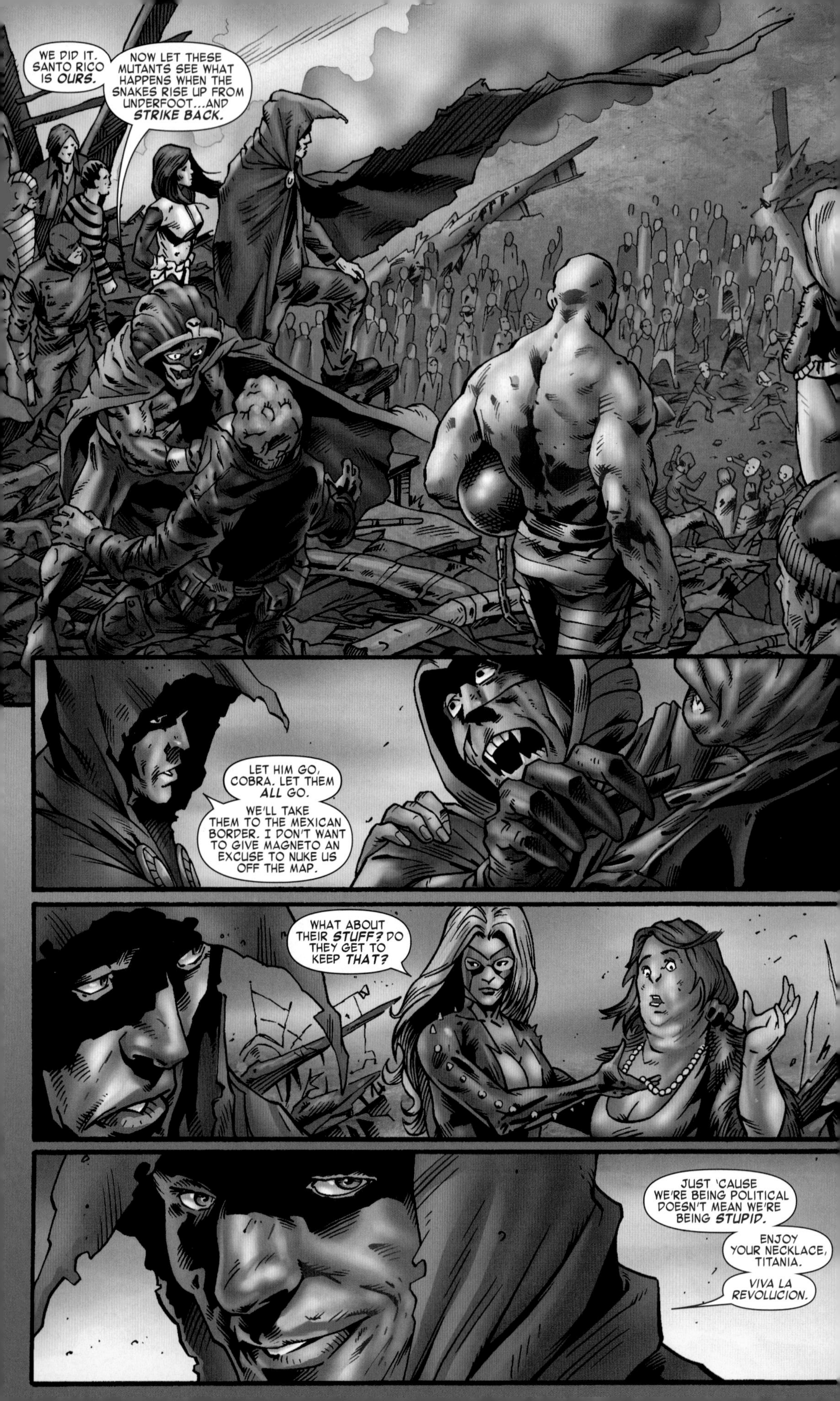

WE DID IT. SANTO RICO IS OURS.
NOW LET THESE MUTANTS SEE WHAT HAPPENS WHEN THE SNAKES RISE UP FROM UNDERFOOT...AND STRIKE BACK.
LET HIM GO, COBRA. LET THEM ALL GO.
WE'LL TAKE THEM TO THE MEXICAN BORDER. I DON'T WANT TO GIVE MAGNETO AN EXCUSE TO NUKE US OFF THE MAP.
WHAT ABOUT THEIR STUFF? DO THEY GET TO KEEP THAT?
JUST 'CAUSE WE'RE BEING POLITICAL DOESN'T MEAN WE'RE BEING STUPID.
ENJOY YOUR NECKLACE, TITANIA.
VIVA LA REVOLUCION.

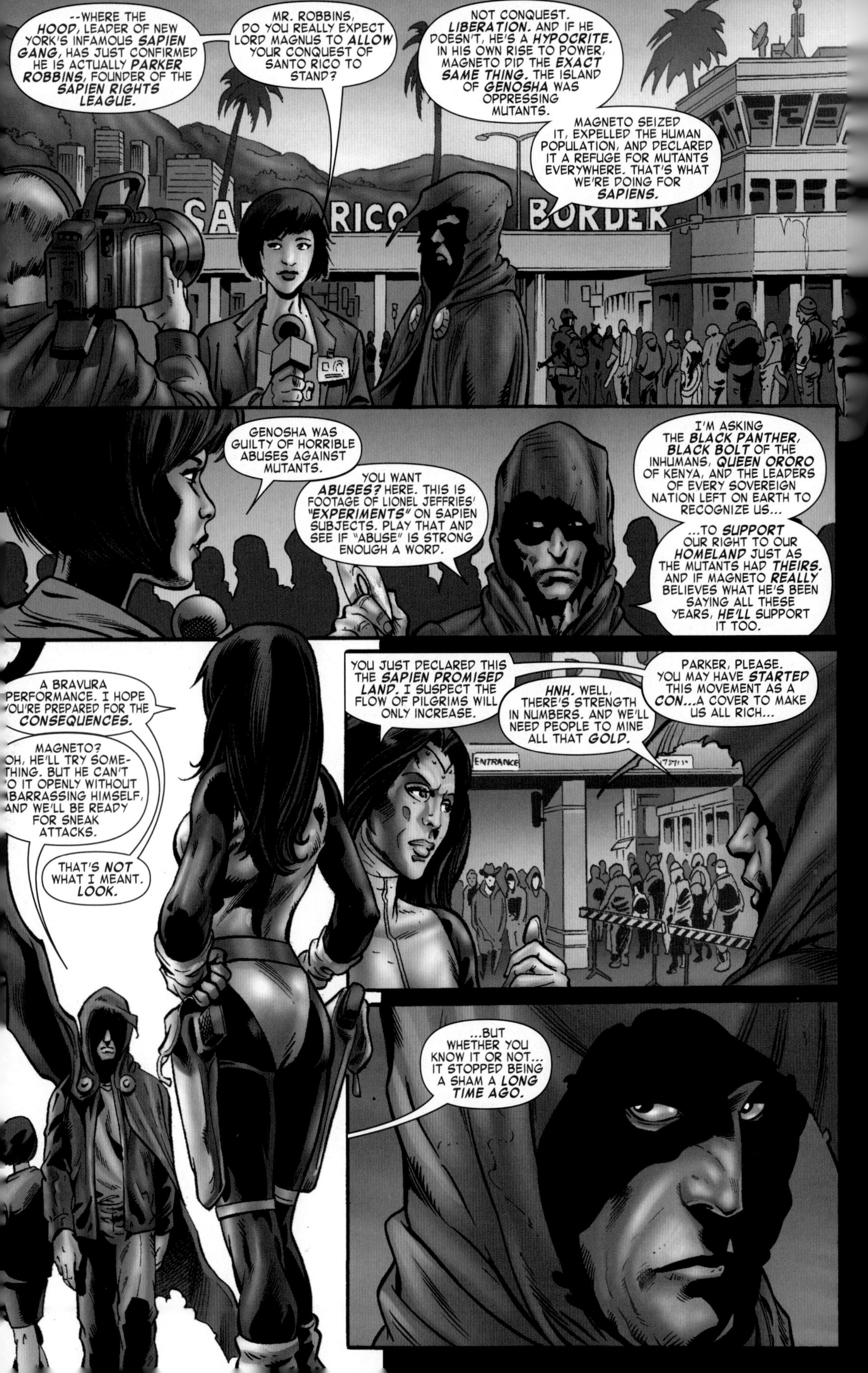
--WHERE THE HOOD, LEADER OF NEW YORK'S INFAMOUS SAPIEN GANG, HAS JUST CONFIRMED HE IS ACTUALLY PARKER ROBBINS, FOUNDER OF THE SAPIEN RIGHTS LEAGUE.
MR. ROBBINS, DO YOU REALLY EXPECT LORD MAGNUS TO ALLOW YOUR CONQUEST OF SANTO RICO TO STAND?
NOT CONQUEST. LIBERATION. AND IF HE DOESN'T, HE'S A HYPOCRITE. IN HIS OWN RISE TO POWER, MAGNETO DID THE EXACT SAME THING. THE ISLAND OF GENOSHA WAS OPPRESSING MUTANTS.
MAGNETO SEIZED IT, EXPELLED THE HUMAN POPULATION, AND DECLARED IT A REFUGE FOR MUTANTS EVERYWHERE. THAT'S WHAT WE'RE DOING FOR SAPIENS.
BORDER
GENOSHA WAS GUILTY OF HORRIBLE ABUSES AGAINST MUTANTS.
YOU WANT ABUSES? HERE. THIS IS FOOTAGE OF LIONEL JEFFRIES' "EXPERIMENTS" ON SAPIEN SUBJECTS. PLAY THAT AND SEE IF "ABUSE" IS STRONG ENOUGH A WORD.
I'M ASKING THE BLACK PANTHER, BLACK BOLT OF THE INHUMANS, QUEEN ORORO OF KENYA, AND THE LEADERS OF EVERY SOVEREIGN NATION LEFT ON EARTH TO RECOGNIZE US...
...TO SUPPORT OUR RIGHT TO OUR HOMELAND JUST AS THE MUTANTS HAD THEIRS. AND IF MAGNETO REALLY BELIEVES WHAT HE'S BEEN SAYING ALL THESE YEARS, HE'LL SUPPORT IT TOO.
A BRAVURA PERFORMANCE. I HOPE OU'RE PREPARED FOR THE CONSEQUENCES.
MAGNETO? OH, HE'LL TRY SOME- THING. BUT HE CAN'T O IT OPENLY WITHOUT BARRASSING HIMSELF, AND WE'LL BE READY FOR SNEAK ATTACKS.
THAT'S NOT WHAT I MEANT. LOOK.
YOU JUST DECLARED THIS THE SAPIEN PROMISED LAND. I SUSPECT THE FLOW OF PILGRIMS WILL ONLY INCREASE.
HNH. WELL, THERE'S STRENGTH IN NUMBERS. AND WE'LL NEED PEOPLE TO MINE ALL THAT GOLD.
PARKER, PLEASE. YOU MAY HAVE STARTED THIS MOVEMENT AS A CON...A COVER TO MAKE US ALL RICH...
ENTRANCE
...BUT WHETHER YOU KNOW IT OR NOT... IT STOPPED BEING A SHAM A LONG TIME AGO.

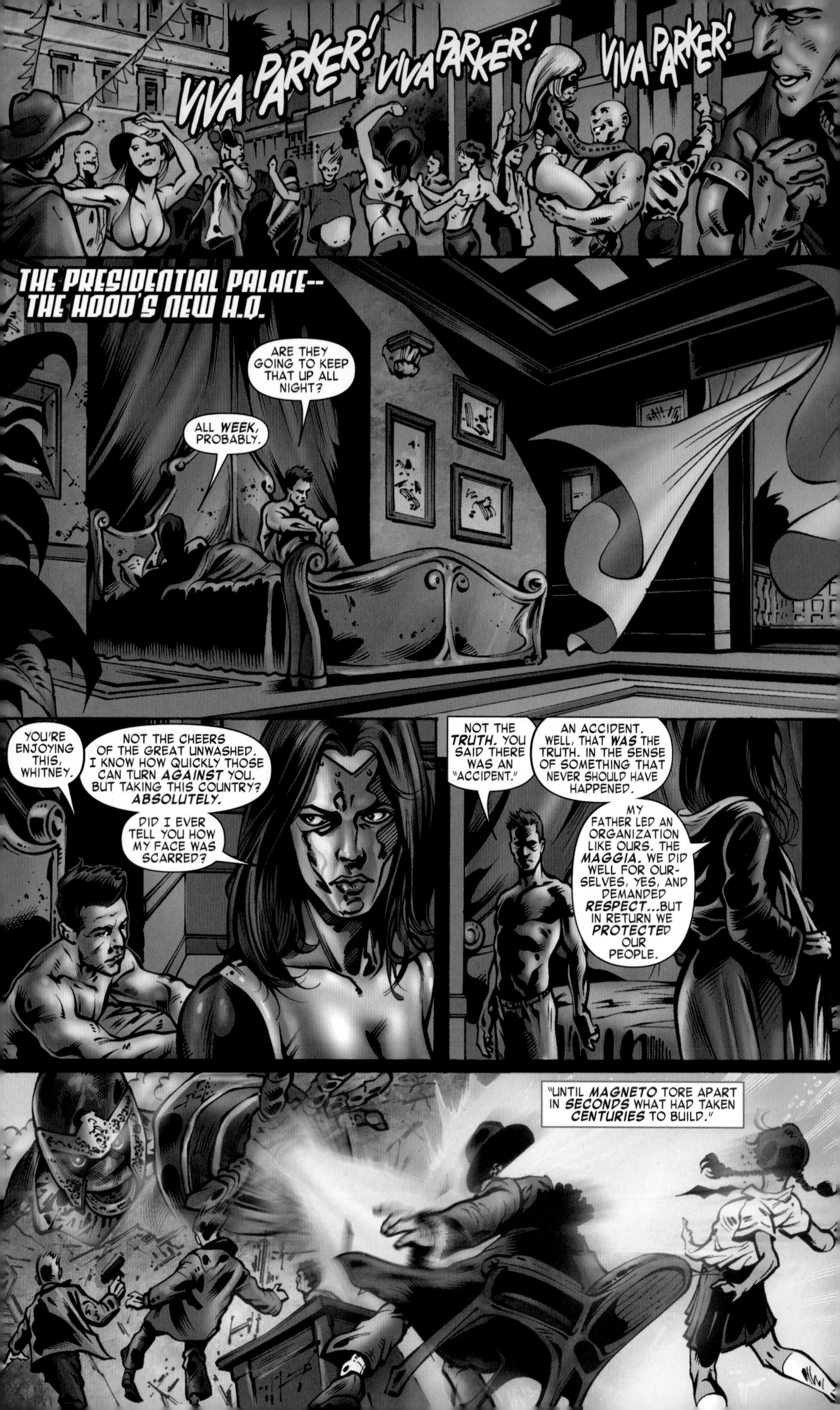
VIVA PARKER! VIVA PARKER! VIVA PARKER!
THE PRESIDENTIAL PALACE-- THE HOOD'S NEW H.Q.
ARE THEY GOING TO KEEP THAT UP ALL NIGHT?
ALL WEEK, PROBABLY.
YOU'RE ENJOYING THIS, WHITNEY.
NOT THE CHEERS OF THE GREAT UNWASHED. I KNOW HOW QUICKLY THOSE CAN TURN AGAINST YOU. BUT TAKING THIS COUNTRY? ABSOLUTELY.
DID I EVER TELL YOU HOW MY FACE WAS SCARRED?
NOT THE TRUTH. YOU SAID THERE WAS AN "ACCIDENT."
AN ACCIDENT. WELL, THAT WAS THE TRUTH. IN THE SENSE OF SOMETHING THAT NEVER SHOULD HAVE HAPPENED.
MY FATHER LED AN ORGANIZATION LIKE OURS. THE MAGGIA. WE DID WELL FOR OURSELVES, YES, AND DEMANDED RESPECT...BUT IN RETURN WE PROTECTED OUR PEOPLE.
"UNTIL MAGNETO TORE APART IN SECONDS WHAT HAD TAKEN CENTURIES TO BUILD."

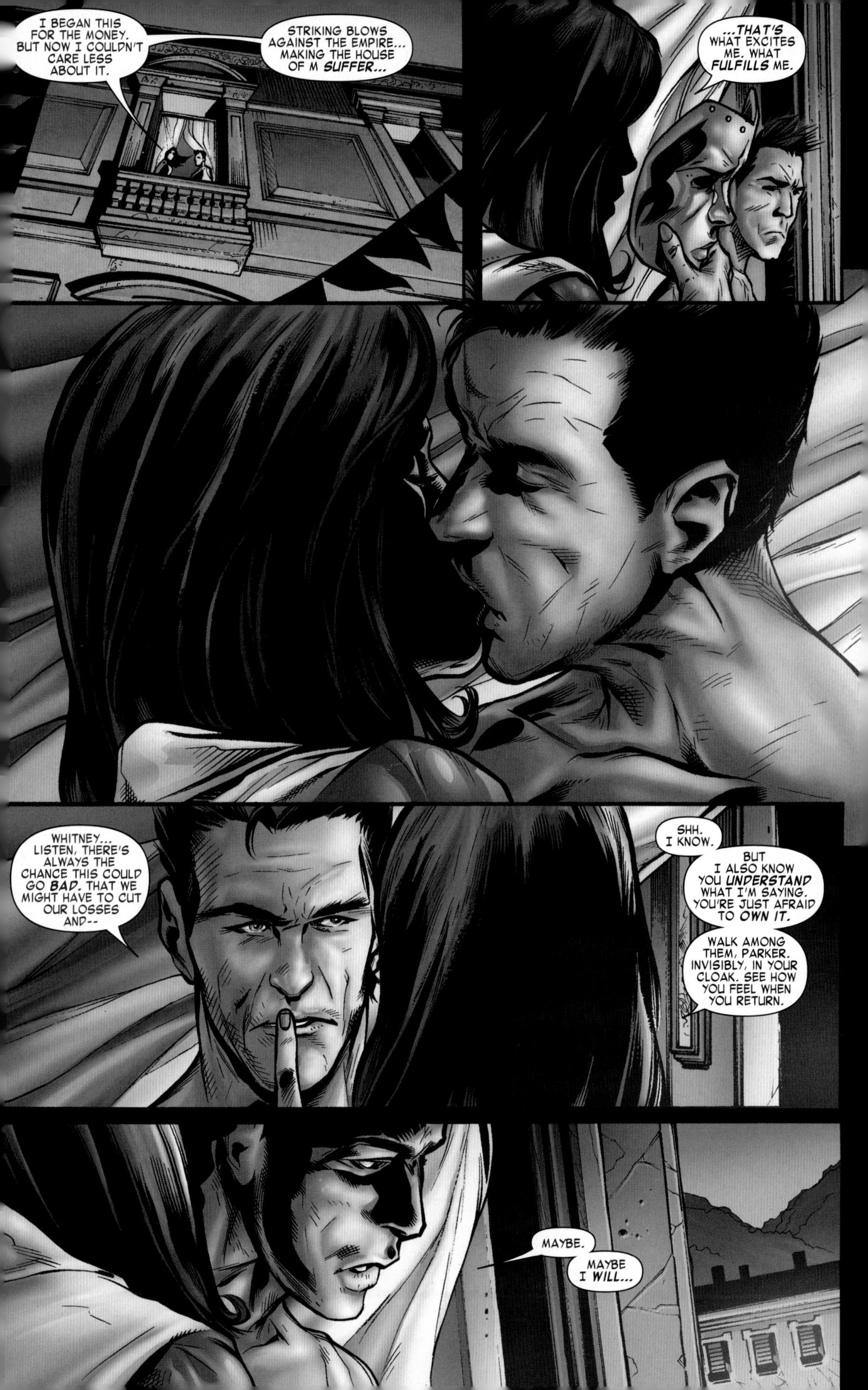
I BEGAN THIS FOR THE MONEY. BUT NOW I COULDN'T CARE LESS ABOUT IT.
STRIKING BLOWS AGAINST THE EMPIRE... MAKING THE HOUSE OF M *SUFFER*...
...*THAT'S* WHAT EXCITES ME. WHAT *FULFILLS* ME.
WHITNEY... LISTEN, THERE'S ALWAYS THE CHANCE THIS COULD GO *BAD*. THAT WE MIGHT HAVE TO CUT OUR LOSSES AND--
SHH. I KNOW.
BUT I ALSO KNOW YOU *UNDERSTAND* WHAT I'M SAYING. YOU'RE JUST AFRAID TO *OWN IT*.
WALK AMONG THEM, PARKER. INVISIBLY, IN YOUR CLOAK. SEE HOW YOU FEEL WHEN YOU RETURN.
MAYBE.
MAYBE I *WILL*...

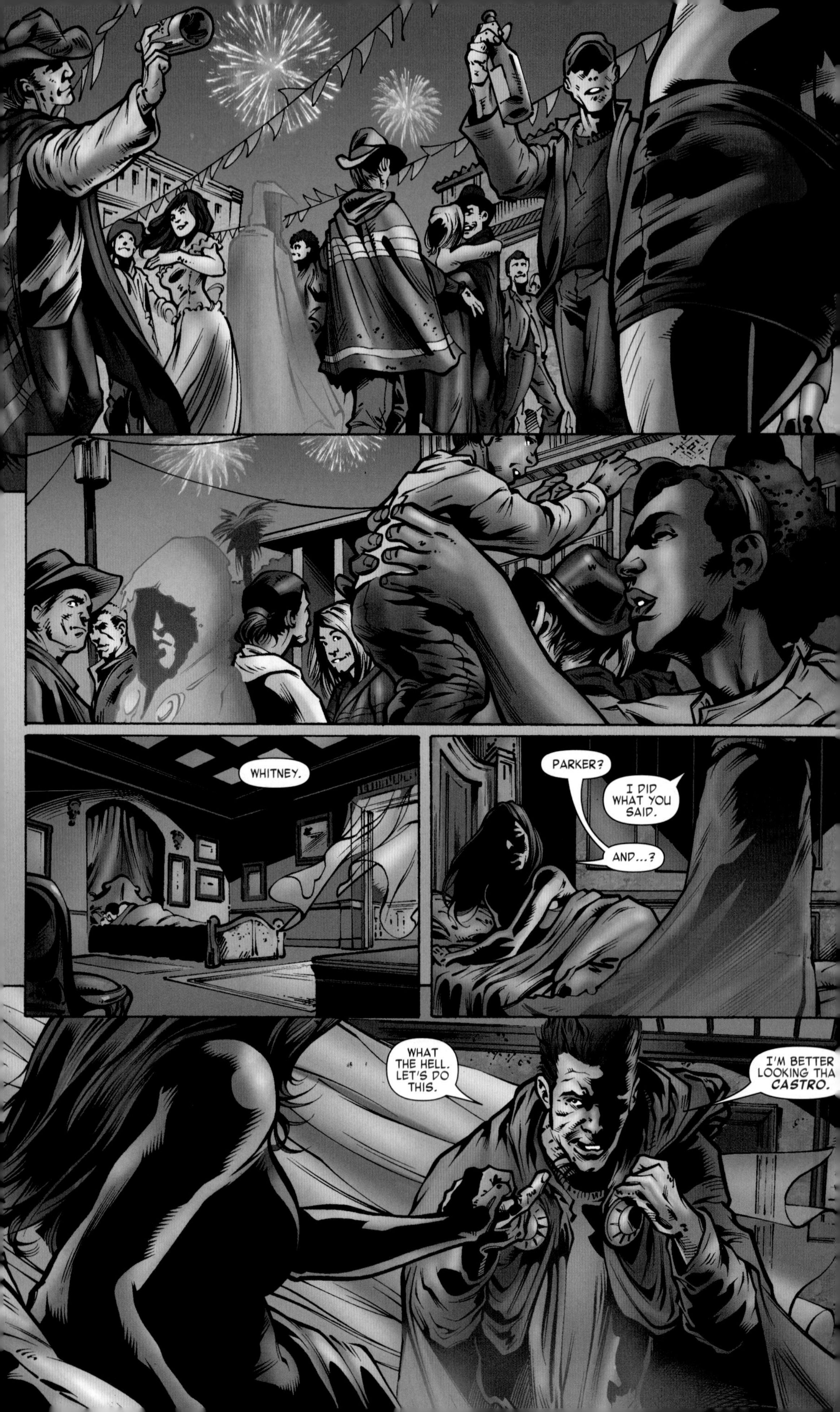
WHITNEY.
PARKER?
I DID WHAT YOU SAID.
AND...?
WHAT THE HELL. LET'S DO THIS.
I'M BETTER LOOKING THA CASTRO.

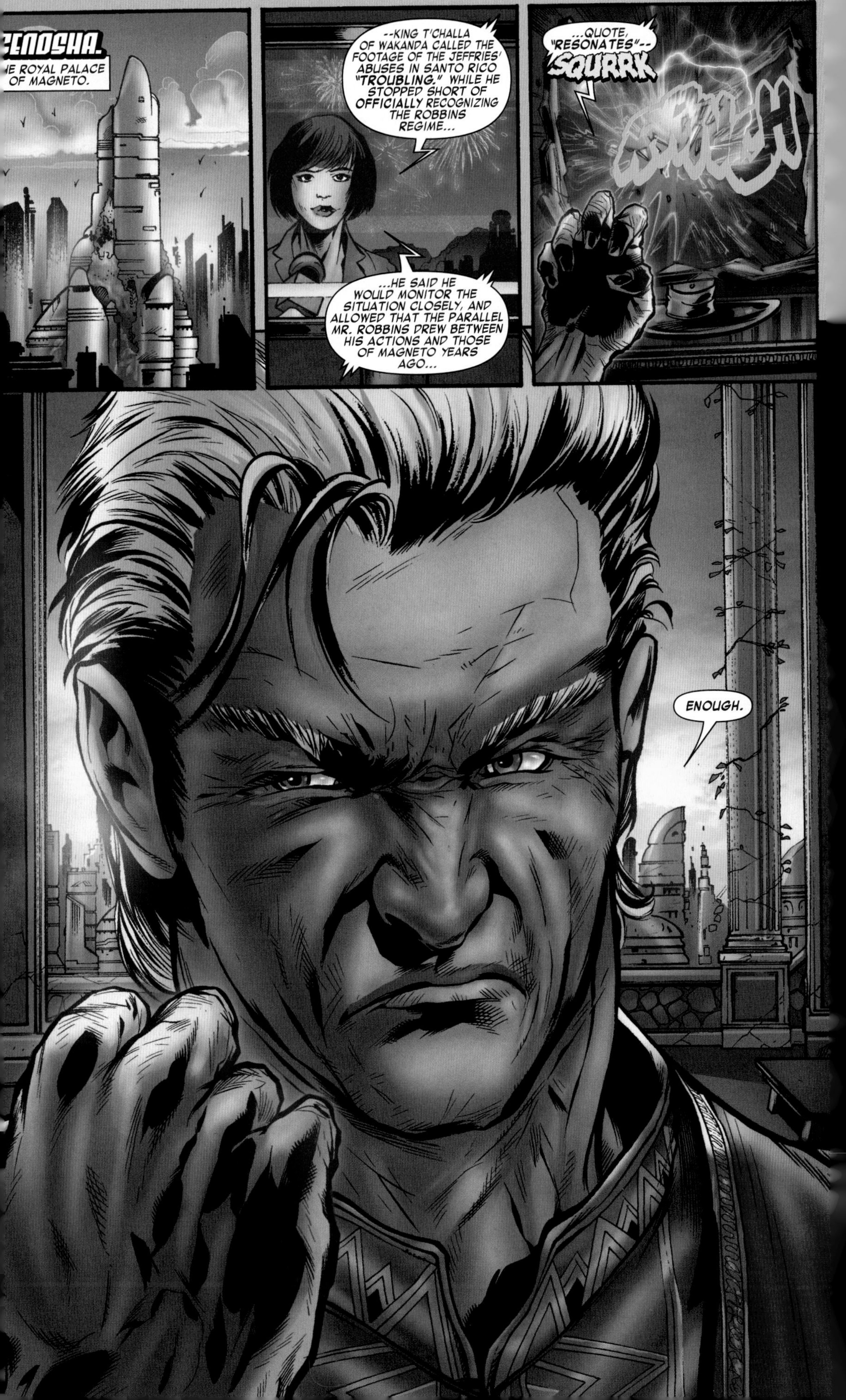

ENOSHA.
E ROYAL PALACE OF MAGNETO.
--KING T'CHALLA OF WAKANDA CALLED THE FOOTAGE OF THE JEFFRIES' ABUSES IN SANTO RICO "TROUBLING." WHILE HE STOPPED SHORT OF OFFICIALLY RECOGNIZING THE ROBBINS REGIME...
...HE SAID HE WOULD MONITOR THE SITUATION CLOSELY, AND ALLOWED THAT THE PARALLEL MR. ROBBINS DREW BETWEEN HIS ACTIONS AND THOSE OF MAGNETO YEARS AGO...
...QUOTE, "RESONATES"--
SQURRK
ENOUGH.

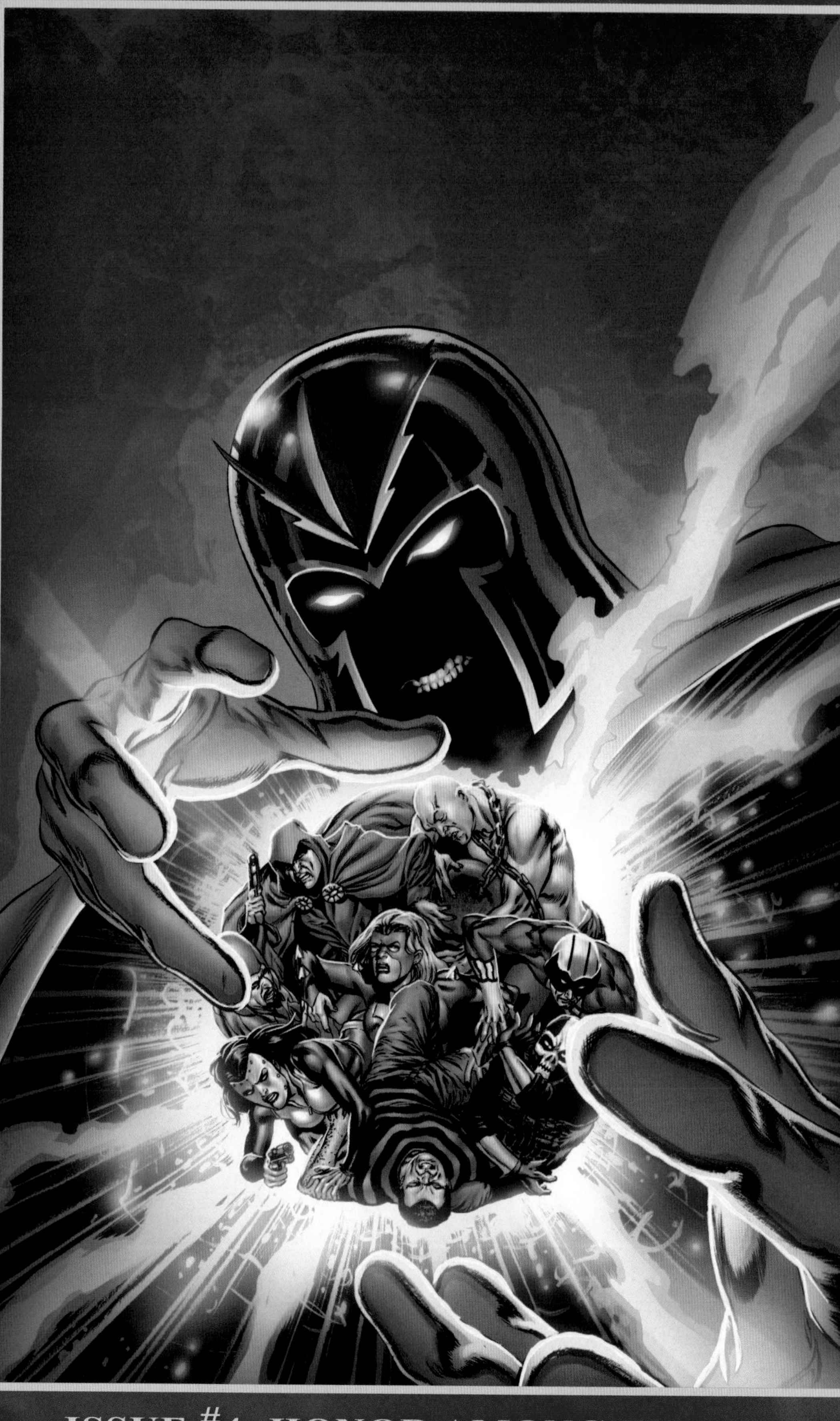

ISSUE #4: HONOR AMONG THIEVES

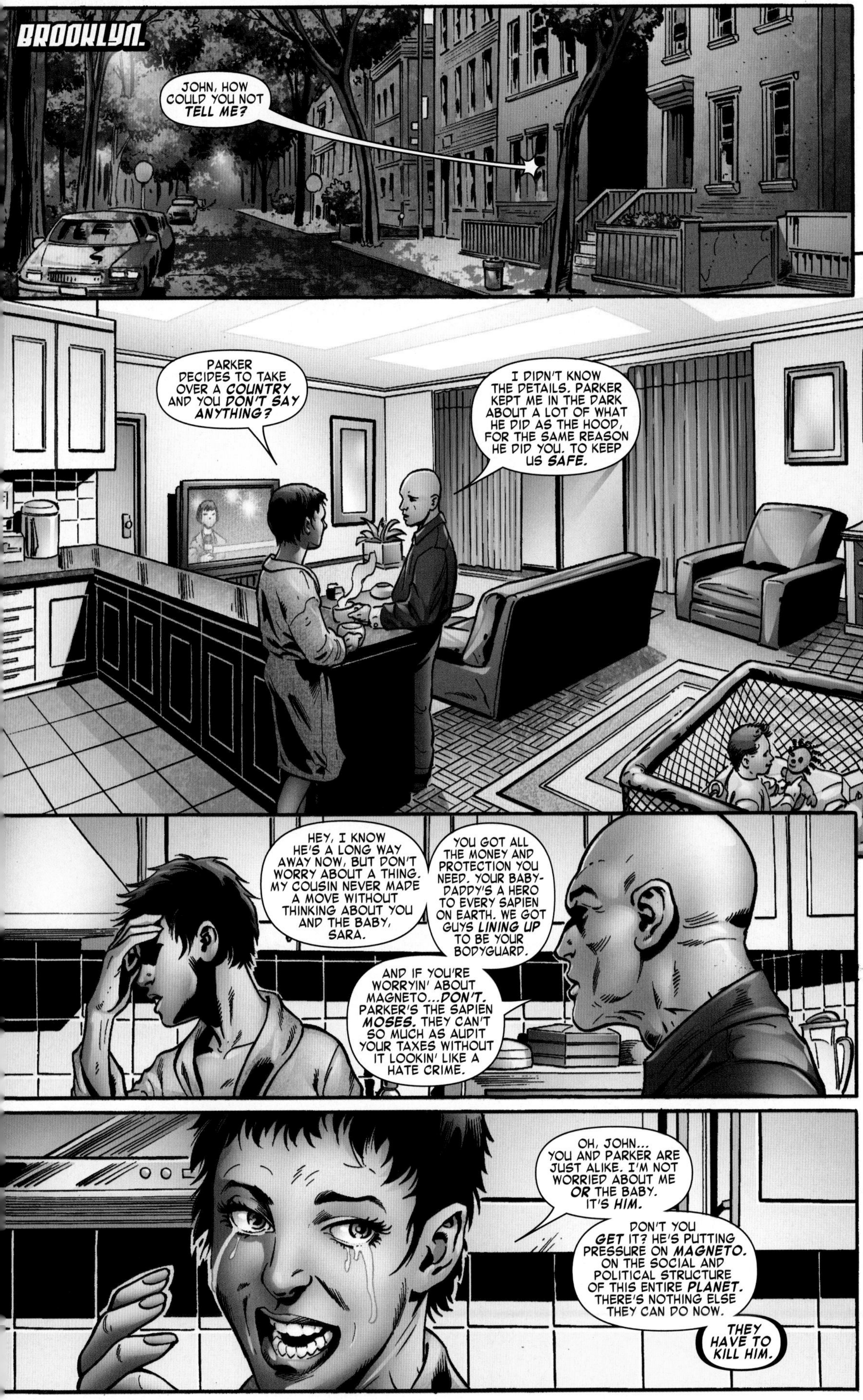
BROOKLYN.
JOHN, HOW COULD YOU NOT TELL ME?
PARKER DECIDES TO TAKE OVER A COUNTRY AND YOU DON'T SAY ANYTHING?
I DIDN'T KNOW THE DETAILS. PARKER KEPT ME IN THE DARK ABOUT A LOT OF WHAT HE DID AS THE HOOD, FOR THE SAME REASON HE DID YOU. TO KEEP US SAFE.
HEY, I KNOW HE'S A LONG WAY AWAY NOW, BUT DON'T WORRY ABOUT A THING. MY COUSIN NEVER MADE A MOVE WITHOUT THINKING ABOUT YOU AND THE BABY, SARA.
YOU GOT ALL THE MONEY AND PROTECTION YOU NEED. YOUR BABY-DADDY'S A HERO TO EVERY SAPIEN ON EARTH. WE GOT GUYS LINING UP TO BE YOUR BODYGUARD.
AND IF YOU'RE WORRYIN' ABOUT MAGNETO...DON'T. PARKER'S THE SAPIEN MOSES. THEY CAN'T SO MUCH AS AUDIT YOUR TAXES WITHOUT IT LOOKIN' LIKE A HATE CRIME.
OH, JOHN... YOU AND PARKER ARE JUST ALIKE. I'M NOT WORRIED ABOUT ME OR THE BABY. IT'S HIM.
DON'T YOU GET IT? HE'S PUTTING PRESSURE ON MAGNETO. ON THE SOCIAL AND POLITICAL STRUCTURE OF THIS ENTIRE PLANET. THERE'S NOTHING ELSE THEY CAN DO NOW.
THEY HAVE TO KILL HIM.

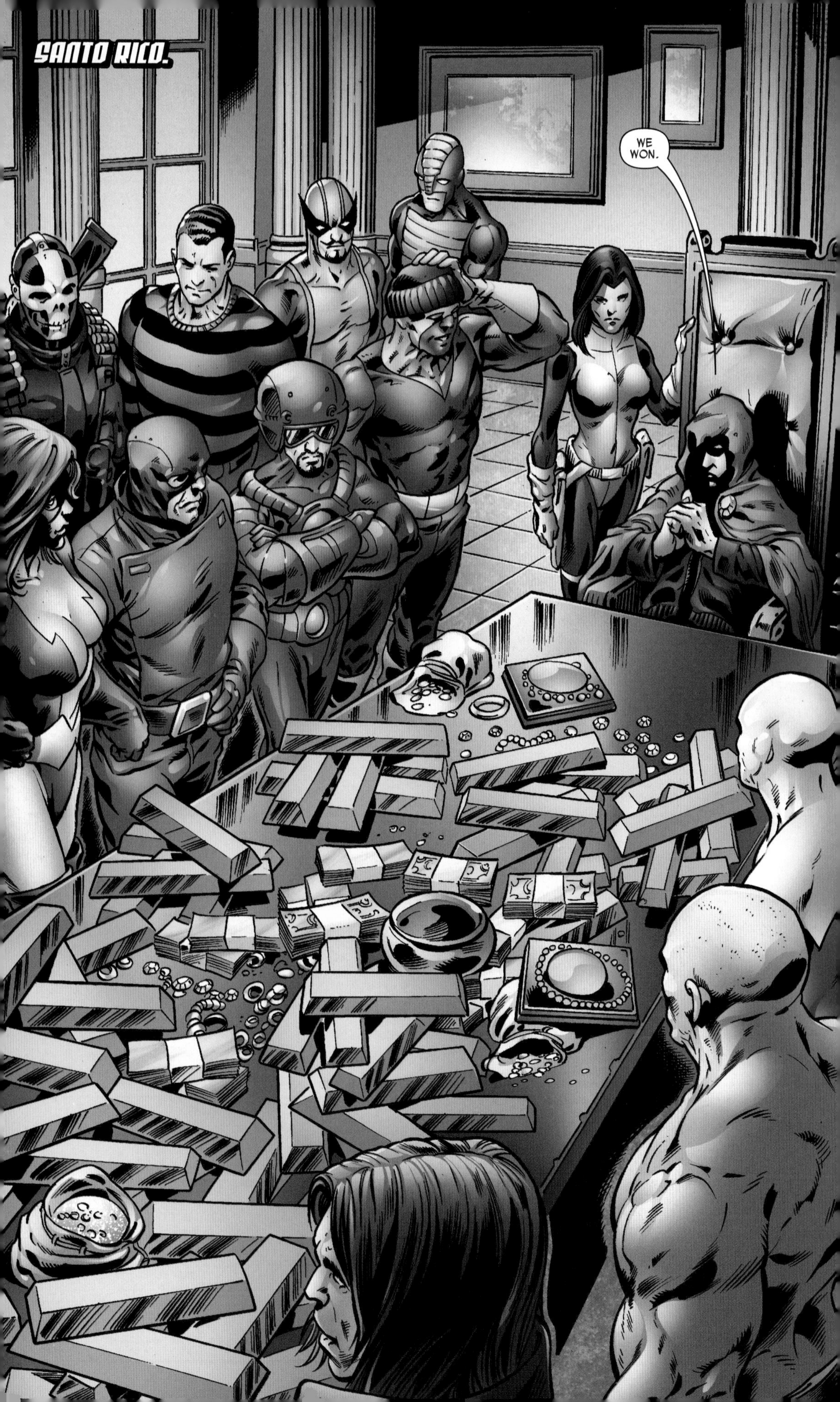
SANTO RICO.
WE WON.

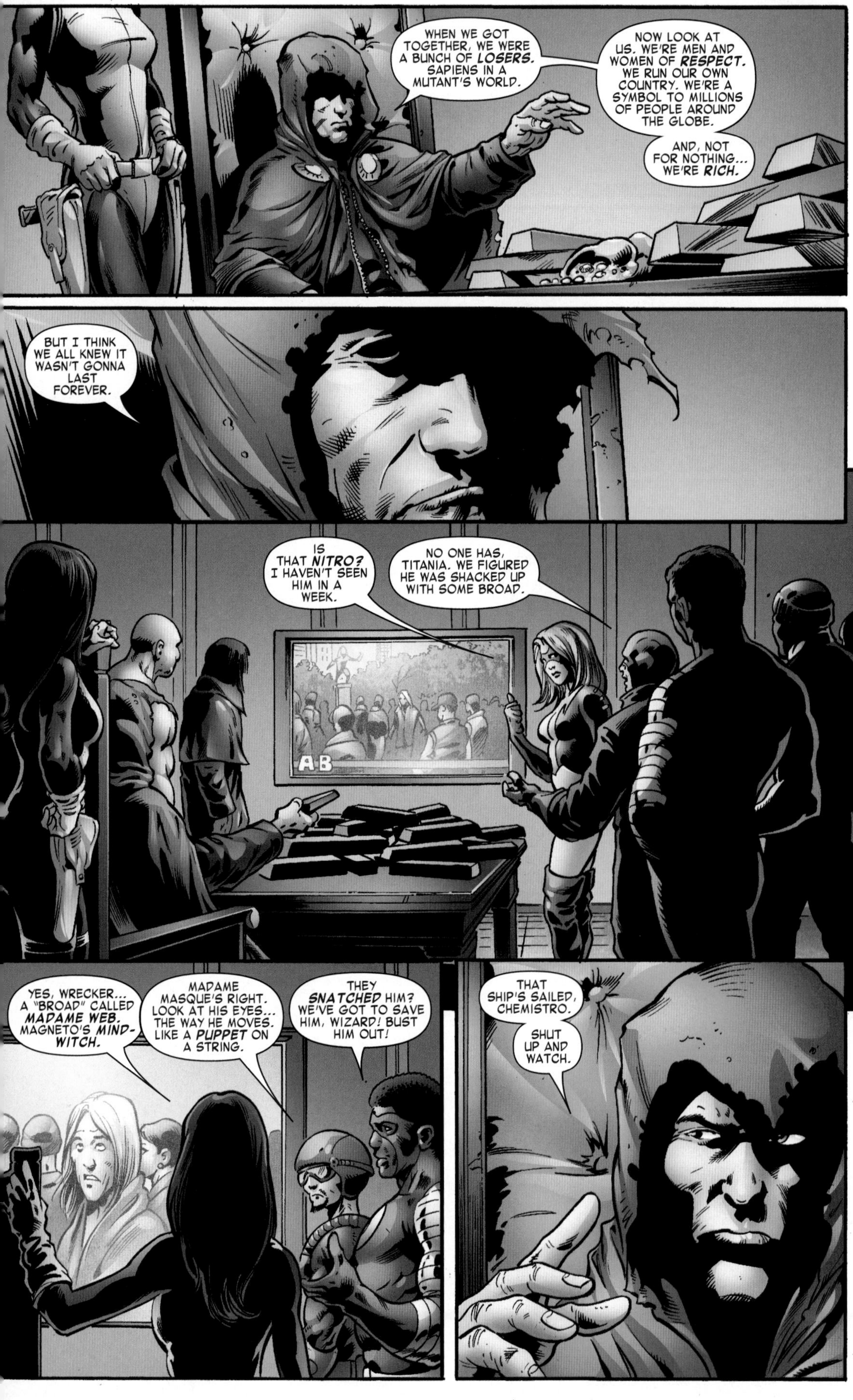

WHEN WE GOT TOGETHER, WE WERE A BUNCH OF **LOSERS.** SAPIENS IN A MUTANT'S WORLD.
NOW LOOK AT US. WE'RE MEN AND WOMEN OF **RESPECT.** WE RUN OUR OWN COUNTRY. WE'RE A SYMBOL TO MILLIONS OF PEOPLE AROUND THE GLOBE.
AND, NOT FOR NOTHING... WE'RE **RICH.**
BUT I THINK WE ALL KNEW IT WASN'T GONNA LAST FOREVER.
IS THAT **NITRO?** I HAVEN'T SEEN HIM IN A WEEK.
NO ONE HAS, TITANIA. WE FIGURED HE WAS SHACKED UP WITH SOME BROAD.
AB
YES, WRECKER... A "BROAD" CALLED **MADAME WEB.** MAGNETO'S **MIND-WITCH.**
MADAME MASQUE'S RIGHT. LOOK AT HIS EYES... THE WAY HE MOVES. LIKE A **PUPPET** ON A STRING.
THEY **SNATCHED** HIM? WE'VE GOT TO SAVE HIM, WIZARD! BUST HIM OUT!
THAT SHIP'S SAILED, CHEMISTRO.
SHUT UP AND WATCH.

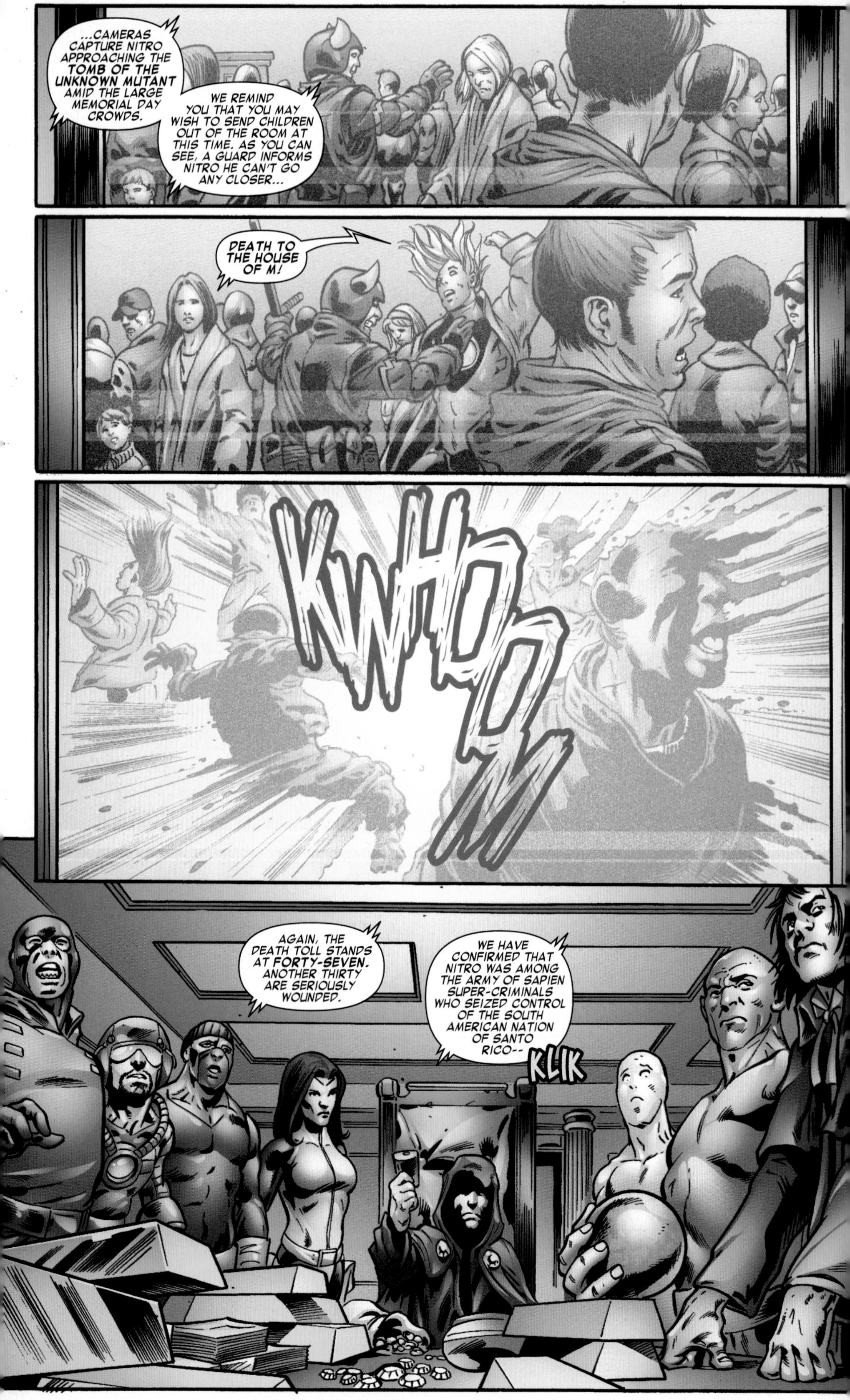
...CAMERAS CAPTURE NITRO APPROACHING THE TOMB OF THE UNKNOWN MUTANT AMID THE LARGE MEMORIAL DAY CROWDS.
WE REMIND YOU THAT YOU MAY WISH TO SEND CHILDREN OUT OF THE ROOM AT THIS TIME. AS YOU CAN SEE, A GUARD INFORMS NITRO HE CAN'T GO ANY CLOSER...
DEATH TO THE HOUSE OF M!
KWHOOM
AGAIN, THE DEATH TOLL STANDS AT FORTY-SEVEN. ANOTHER THIRTY ARE SERIOUSLY WOUNDED.
WE HAVE CONFIRMED THAT NITRO WAS AMONG THE ARMY OF SAPIEN SUPER-CRIMINALS WHO SEIZED CONTROL OF THE SOUTH AMERICAN NATION OF SANTO RICO--
KLIK

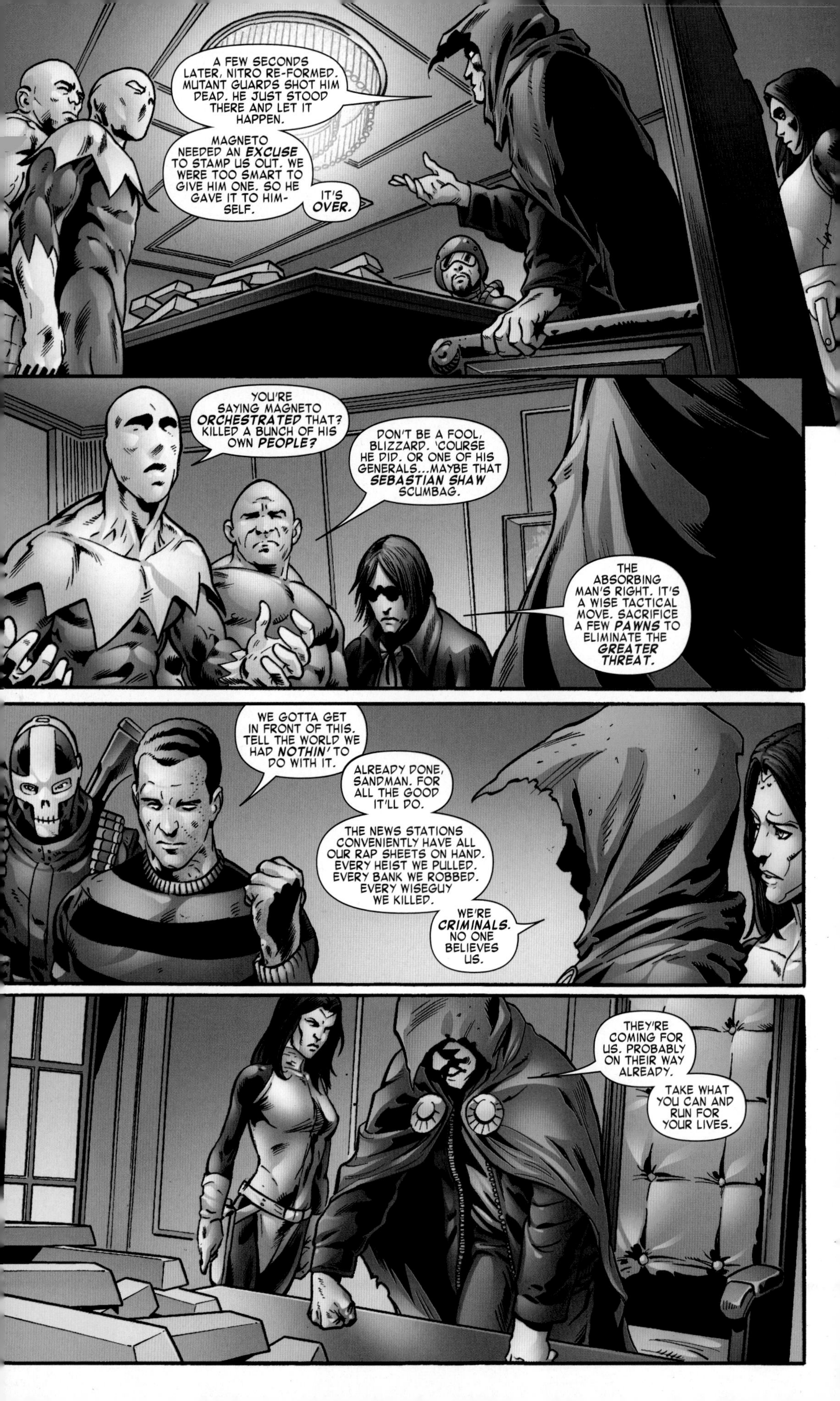

A FEW SECONDS LATER, NITRO RE-FORMED. MUTANT GUARDS SHOT HIM DEAD. HE JUST STOOD THERE AND LET IT HAPPEN.
MAGNETO NEEDED AN *EXCUSE* TO STAMP US OUT. WE WERE TOO SMART TO GIVE HIM ONE. SO HE GAVE IT TO HIM-SELF.
IT'S *OVER.*
YOU'RE SAYING MAGNETO *ORCHESTRATED* THAT? KILLED A BUNCH OF HIS OWN *PEOPLE?*
DON'T BE A FOOL, BLIZZARD. 'COURSE HE DID. OR ONE OF HIS GENERALS...MAYBE THAT *SEBASTIAN SHAW* SCUMBAG.
THE ABSORBING MAN'S RIGHT. IT'S A WISE TACTICAL MOVE. SACRIFICE A FEW *PAWNS* TO ELIMINATE THE *GREATER THREAT.*
WE GOTTA GET IN FRONT OF THIS. TELL THE WORLD WE HAD *NOTHIN'* TO DO WITH IT.
ALREADY DONE, SANDMAN. FOR ALL THE GOOD IT'LL DO.
THE NEWS STATIONS CONVENIENTLY HAVE ALL OUR RAP SHEETS ON HAND. EVERY HEIST WE PULLED. EVERY BANK WE ROBBED. EVERY WISEGUY WE KILLED.
WE'RE *CRIMINALS.* NO ONE BELIEVES US.
THEY'RE COMING FOR US. PROBABLY ON THEIR WAY ALREADY.
TAKE WHAT YOU CAN AND RUN FOR YOUR LIVES.

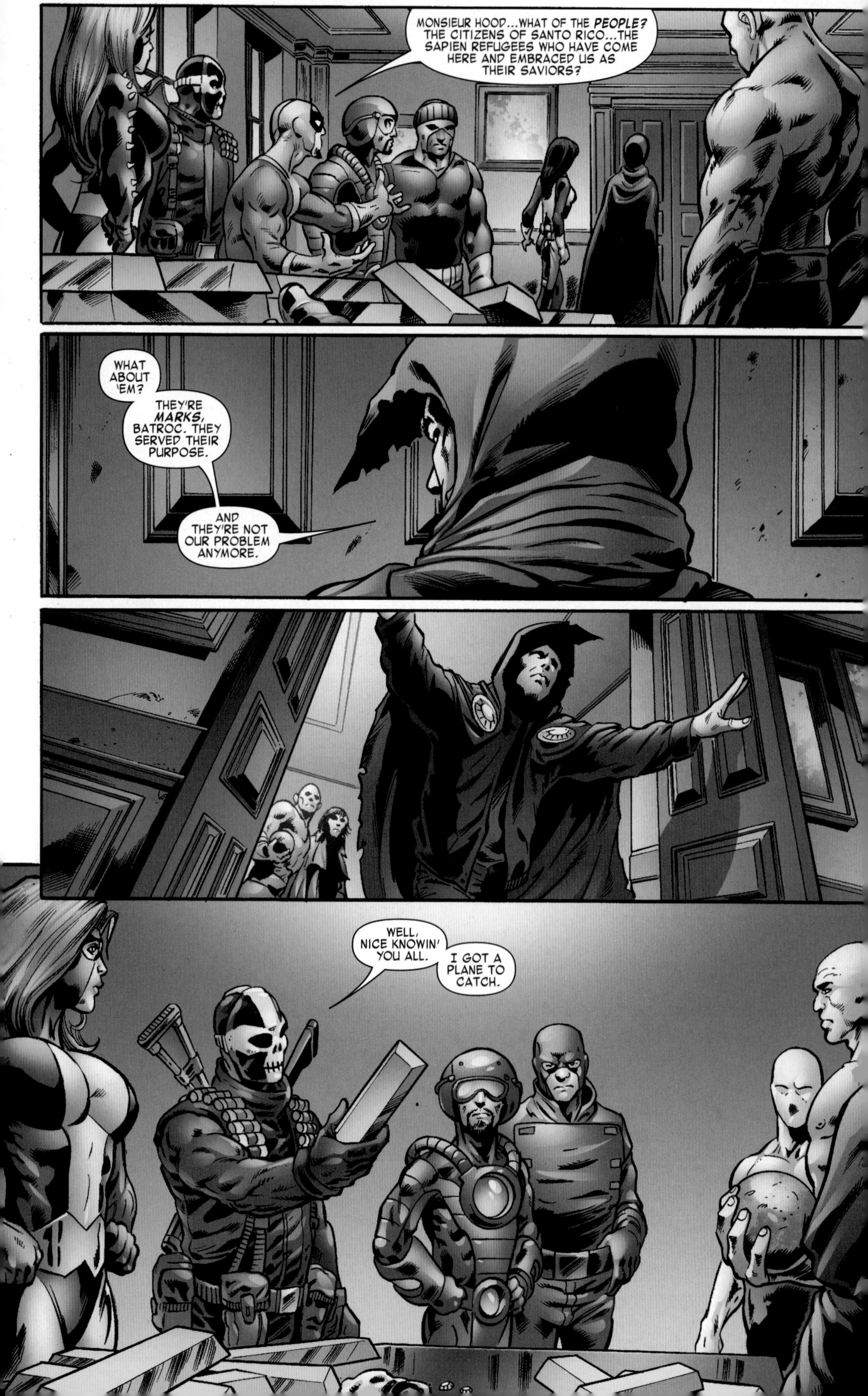
MONSIEUR HOOD...WHAT OF THE PEOPLE? THE CITIZENS OF SANTO RICO...THE SAPIEN REFUGEES WHO HAVE COME HERE AND EMBRACED US AS THEIR SAVIORS?
WHAT ABOUT 'EM?
THEY'RE MARKS, BATROC. THEY SERVED THEIR PURPOSE.
AND THEY'RE NOT OUR PROBLEM ANYMORE.
WELL, NICE KNOWIN' YOU ALL.
I GOT A PLANE TO CATCH.

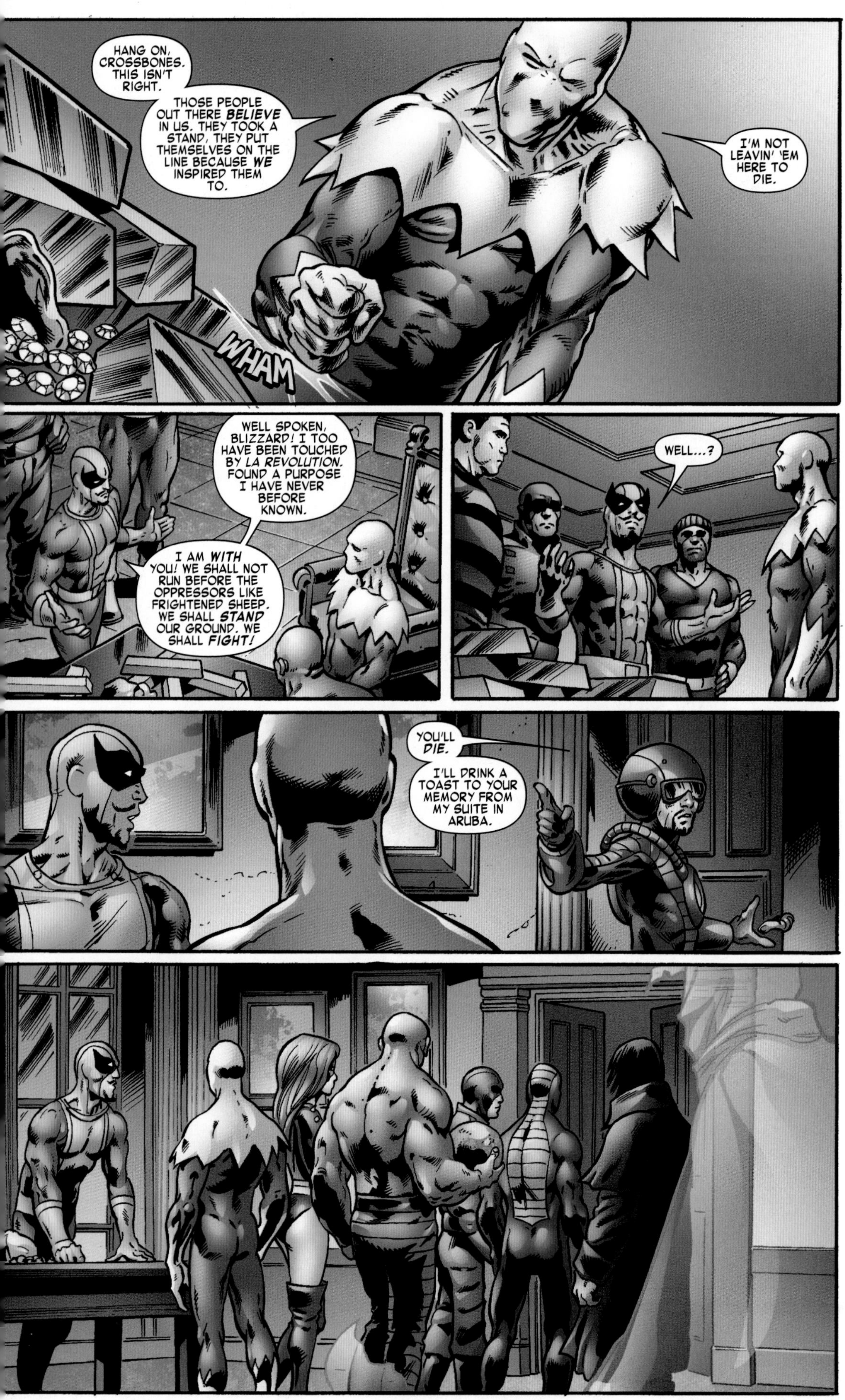
HANG ON, CROSSBONES. THIS ISN'T RIGHT.
THOSE PEOPLE OUT THERE *BELIEVE* IN US. THEY TOOK A STAND, THEY PUT THEMSELVES ON THE LINE BECAUSE *WE* INSPIRED THEM TO.
I'M NOT LEAVIN' 'EM HERE TO DIE.
WHAM
WELL SPOKEN, BLIZZARD! I TOO HAVE BEEN TOUCHED BY *LA REVOLUTION*. FOUND A PURPOSE I HAVE NEVER BEFORE KNOWN.
I AM *WITH* YOU! WE SHALL NOT RUN BEFORE THE OPPRESSORS LIKE FRIGHTENED SHEEP. WE SHALL *STAND* OUR GROUND. WE SHALL *FIGHT!*
WELL...?
YOU'LL *DIE*.
I'LL DRINK A TOAST TO YOUR MEMORY FROM MY SUITE IN ARUBA.

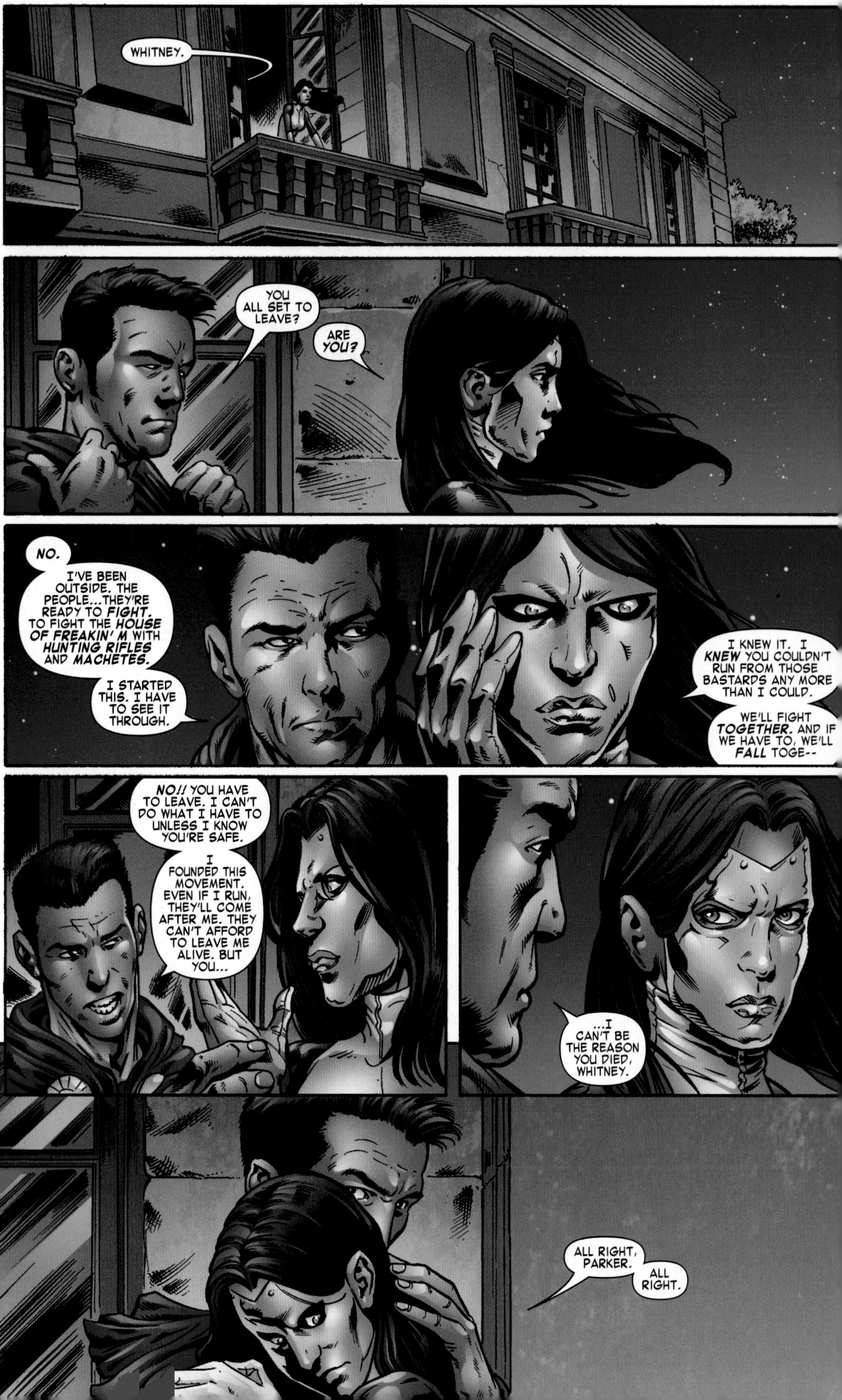
WHITNEY.
YOU ALL SET TO LEAVE?
ARE ***YOU?***
NO.
I'VE BEEN OUTSIDE. THE PEOPLE...THEY'RE READY TO ***FIGHT.*** TO FIGHT THE ***HOUSE OF FREAKIN' M*** WITH ***HUNTING RIFLES*** AND ***MACHETES.***
I STARTED THIS. I HAVE TO SEE IT THROUGH.
I KNEW IT. I ***KNEW*** YOU COULDN'T RUN FROM THOSE BASTARDS ANY MORE THAN I COULD.
WE'LL FIGHT ***TOGETHER.*** AND IF WE HAVE TO, WE'LL ***FALL*** TOGE--
NO!! YOU HAVE TO LEAVE. I CAN'T DO WHAT I HAVE TO UNLESS I KNOW YOU'RE SAFE.
I FOUNDED THIS MOVEMENT. EVEN IF I RUN, THEY'LL COME AFTER ME. THEY CAN'T AFFORD TO LEAVE ME ALIVE. BUT YOU...
...I CAN'T BE THE REASON YOU DIED, WHITNEY.
ALL RIGHT, PARKER.
ALL RIGHT.

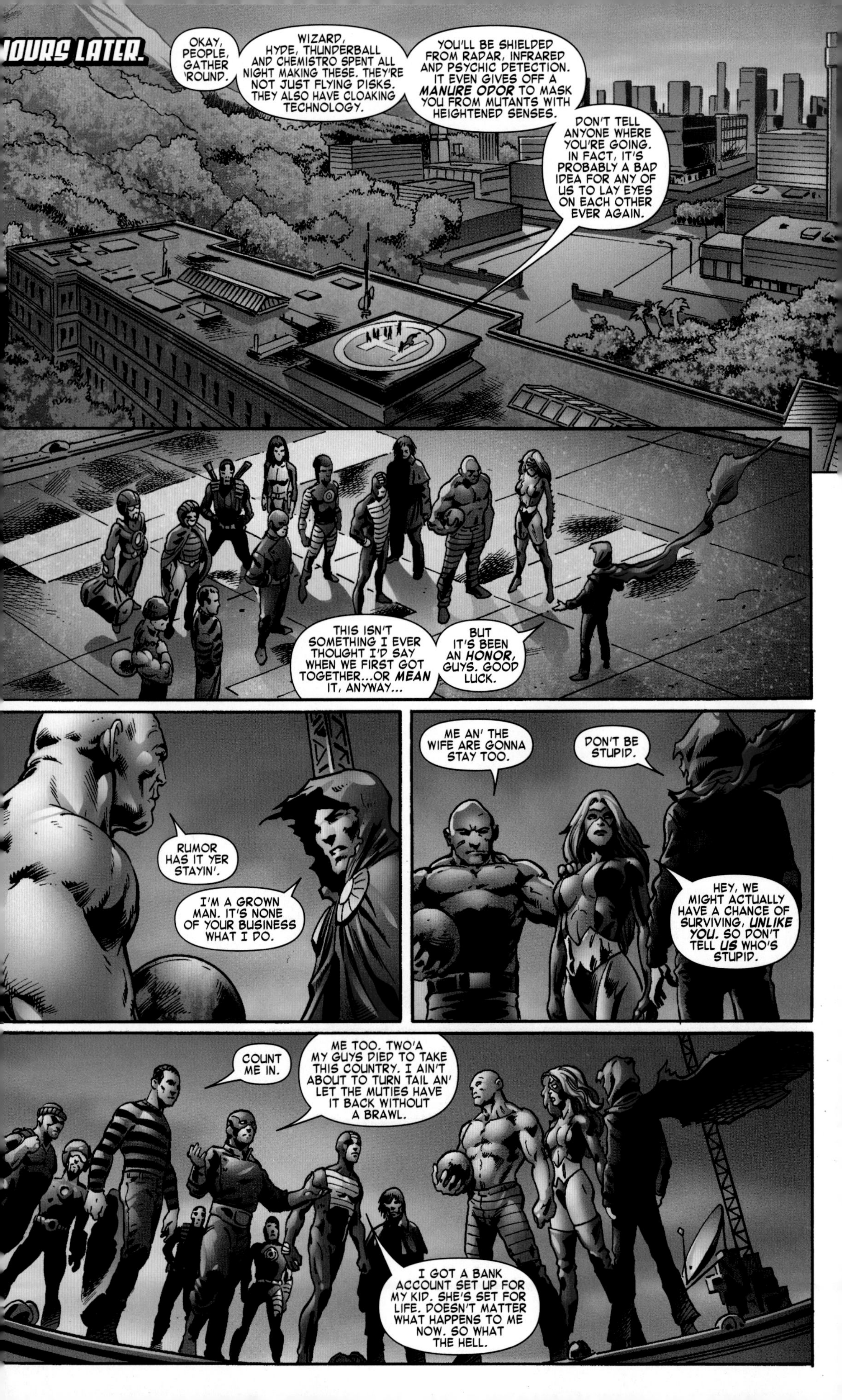

OURS LATER.
OKAY, PEOPLE, GATHER 'ROUND.
WIZARD, HYDE, THUNDERBALL AND CHEMISTRO SPENT ALL NIGHT MAKING THESE. THEY'RE NOT JUST FLYING DISKS. THEY ALSO HAVE CLOAKING TECHNOLOGY.
YOU'LL BE SHIELDED FROM RADAR, INFRARED AND PSYCHIC DETECTION. IT EVEN GIVES OFF A **MANURE ODOR** TO MASK YOU FROM MUTANTS WITH HEIGHTENED SENSES.
DON'T TELL ANYONE WHERE YOU'RE GOING. IN FACT, IT'S PROBABLY A BAD IDEA FOR ANY OF US TO LAY EYES ON EACH OTHER EVER AGAIN.
THIS ISN'T SOMETHING I EVER THOUGHT I'D SAY WHEN WE FIRST GOT TOGETHER...OR **MEAN** IT, ANYWAY...
BUT IT'S BEEN AN **HONOR**, GUYS. GOOD LUCK.
RUMOR HAS IT YER STAYIN'.
I'M A GROWN MAN. IT'S NONE OF YOUR BUSINESS WHAT I DO.
ME AN' THE WIFE ARE GONNA STAY TOO.
DON'T BE STUPID.
HEY, WE MIGHT ACTUALLY HAVE A CHANCE OF SURVIVING, **UNLIKE YOU.** SO DON'T TELL **US** WHO'S STUPID.
COUNT ME IN.
ME TOO. TWO'A MY GUYS DIED TO TAKE THIS COUNTRY. I AIN'T ABOUT TO TURN TAIL AN' LET THE MUTIES HAVE IT BACK WITHOUT A BRAWL.
I GOT A BANK ACCOUNT SET UP FOR MY KID. SHE'S SET FOR LIFE. DOESN'T MATTER WHAT HAPPENS TO ME NOW. SO WHAT THE HELL.

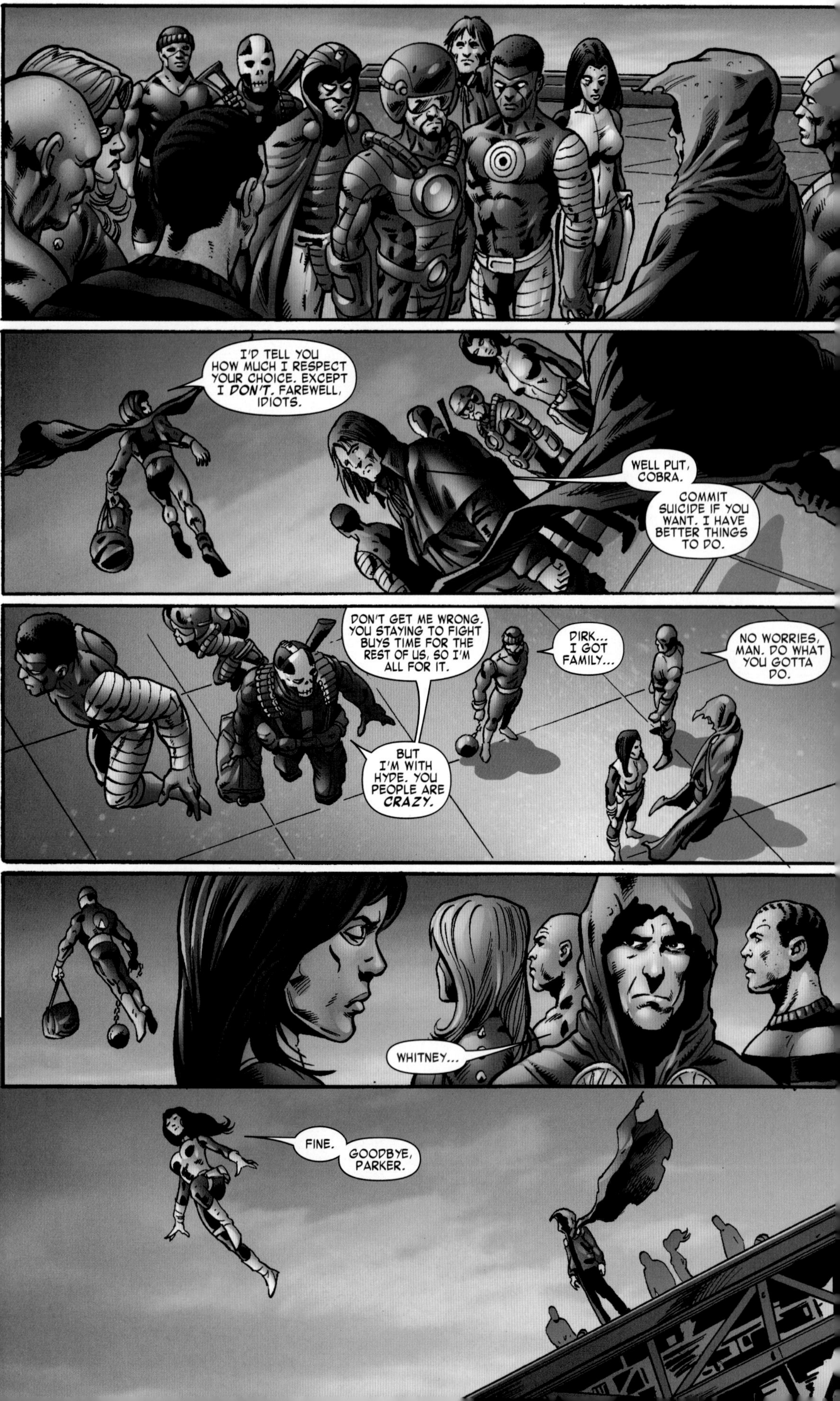
I'D TELL YOU HOW MUCH I RESPECT YOUR CHOICE. EXCEPT I *DON'T*. FAREWELL, IDIOTS.
WELL PUT, COBRA.
COMMIT SUICIDE IF YOU WANT. I HAVE BETTER THINGS TO DO.
DON'T GET ME WRONG. YOU STAYING TO FIGHT BUYS TIME FOR THE REST OF US, SO I'M ALL FOR IT.
BUT I'M WITH HYDE. YOU PEOPLE ARE *CRAZY*.
DIRK... I GOT FAMILY...
NO WORRIES, MAN. DO WHAT YOU GOTTA DO.
WHITNEY...
FINE.
GOODBYE, PARKER.

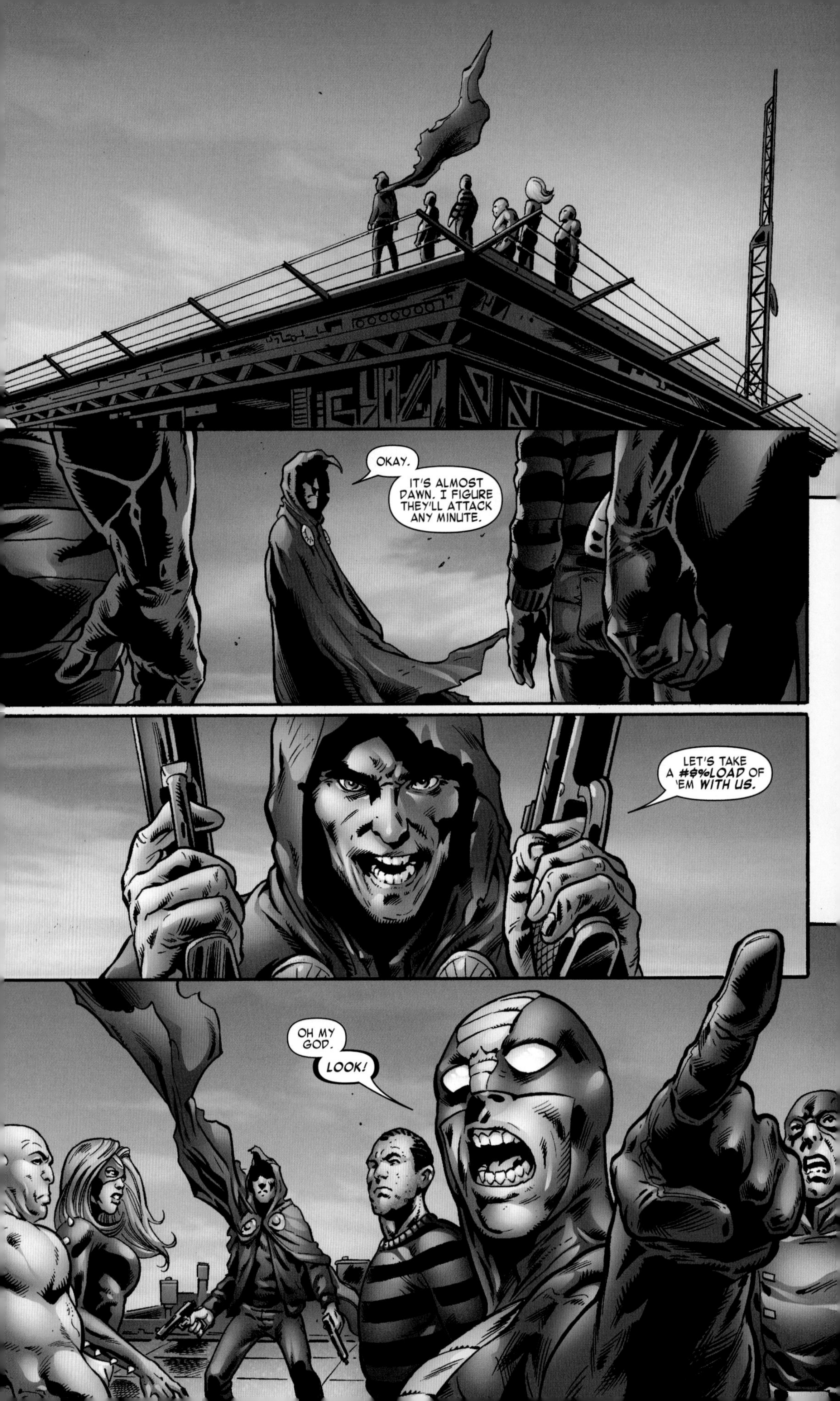
OKAY.
IT'S ALMOST DAWN. I FIGURE THEY'LL ATTACK ANY MINUTE.
LET'S TAKE A #$%LOAD OF 'EM WITH US.
OH MY GOD.
LOOK!

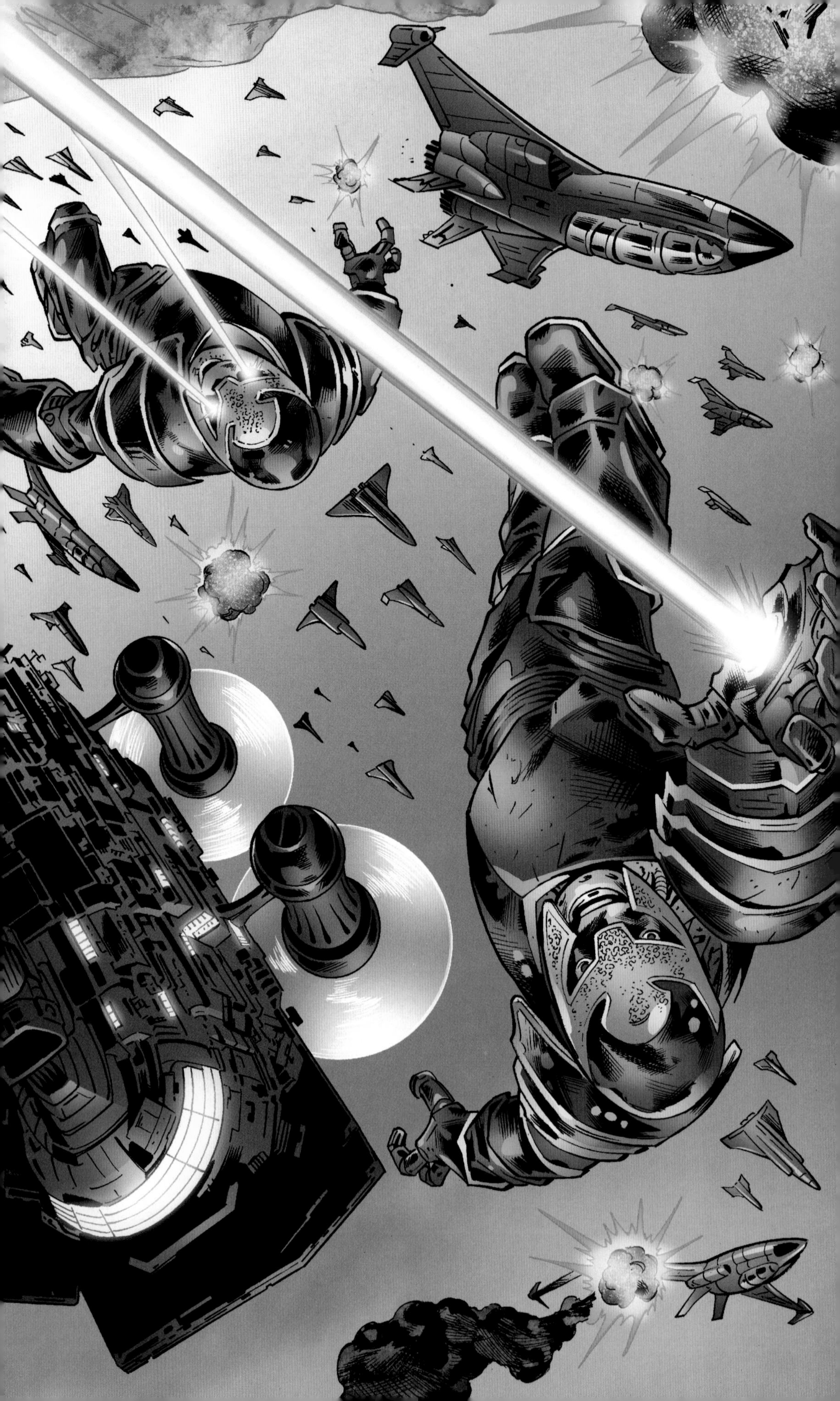

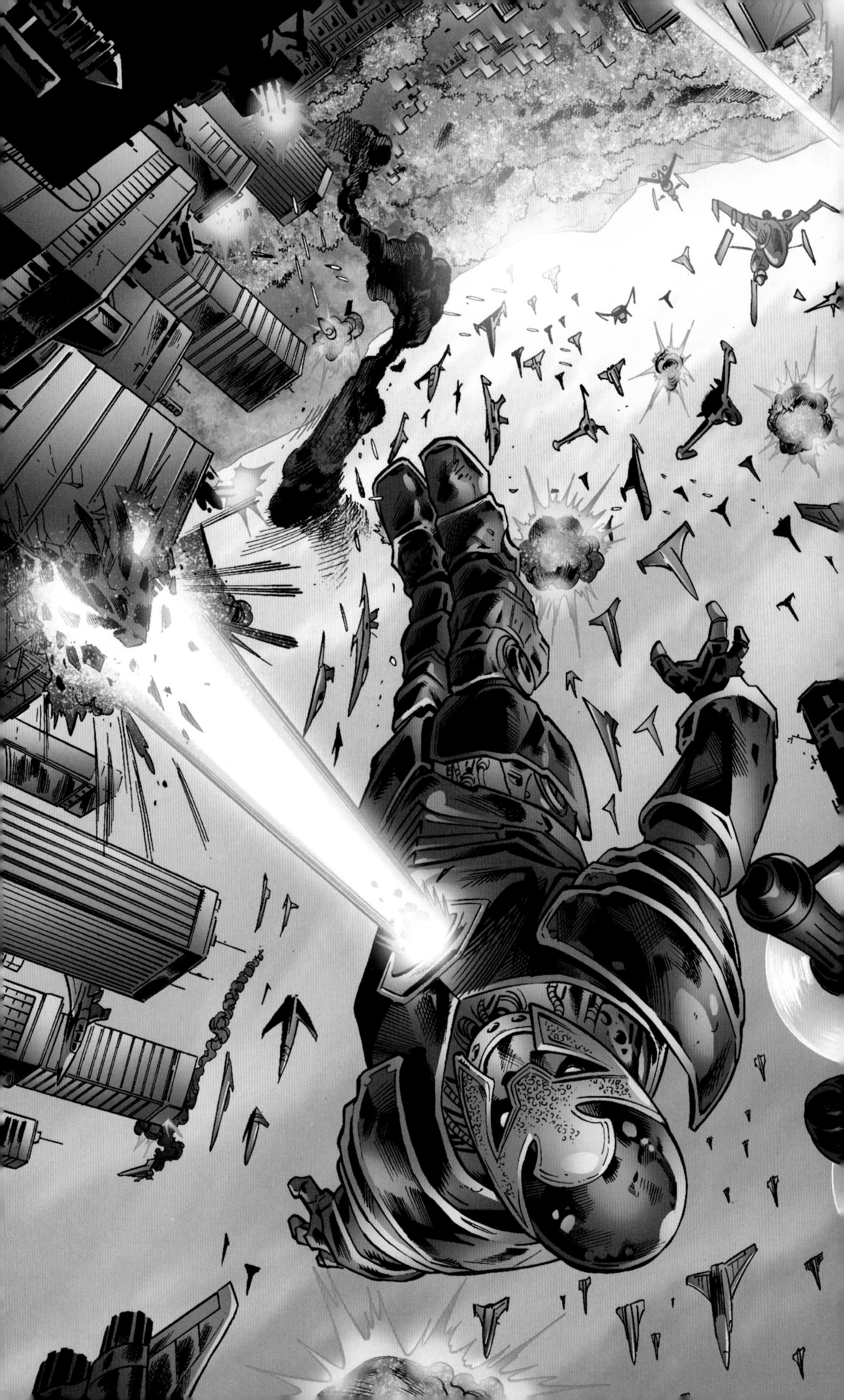

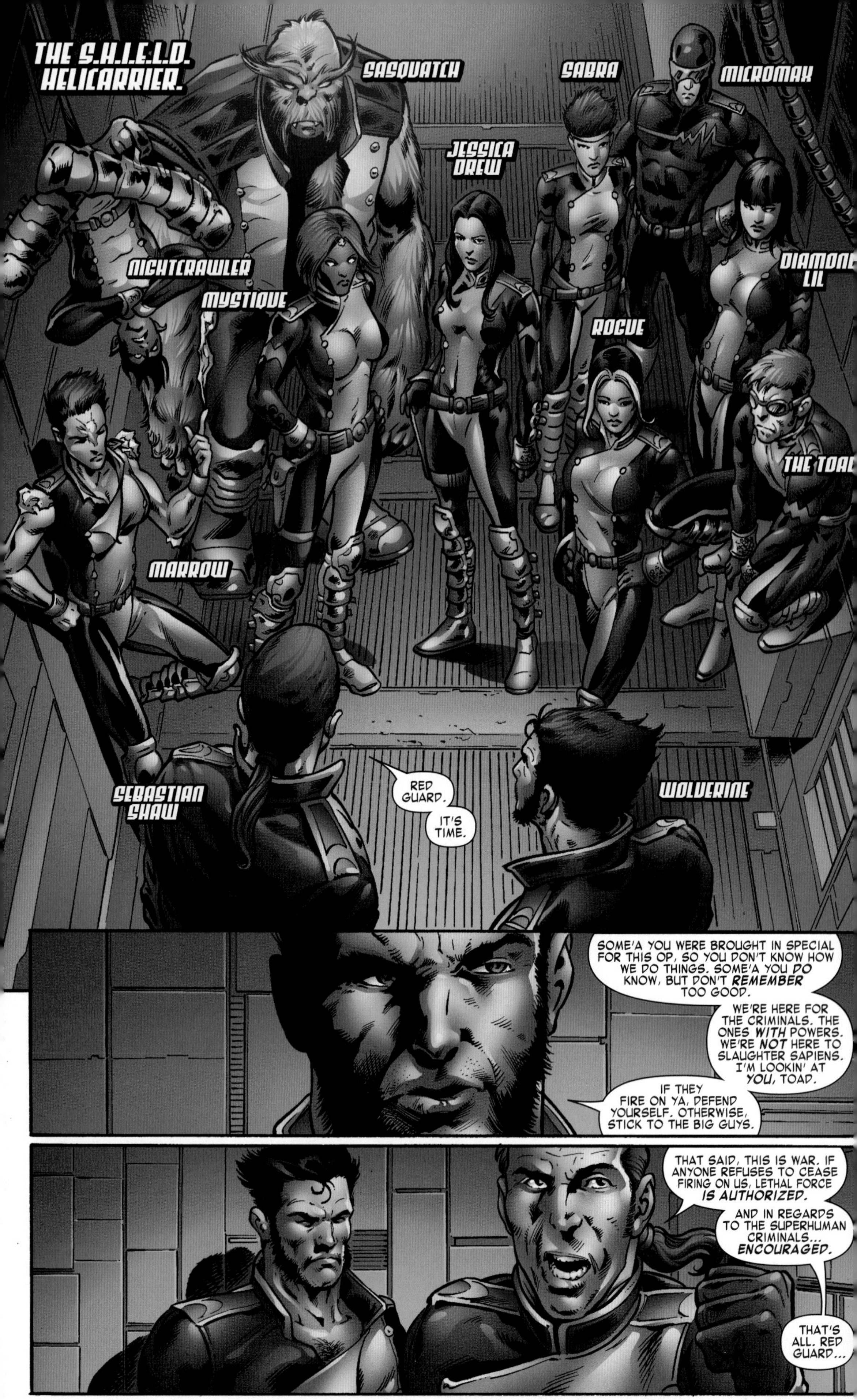
THE S.H.I.E.L.D. HELICARRIER.
SASQUATCH
SABRA
MICROMAX
JESSICA DREW
NIGHTCRAWLER
MYSTIQUE
DIAMONE LIL
ROGUE
THE TOAI
MARROW
SEBASTIAN SHAW
RED GUARD.
IT'S TIME.
WOLVERINE
SOME'A YOU WERE BROUGHT IN SPECIAL FOR THIS OP, SO YOU DON'T KNOW HOW WE DO THINGS. SOME'A YOU DO KNOW, BUT DON'T REMEMBER TOO GOOD.
WE'RE HERE FOR THE CRIMINALS. THE ONES WITH POWERS. WE'RE NOT HERE TO SLAUGHTER SAPIENS. I'M LOOKIN' AT YOU, TOAD.
IF THEY FIRE ON YA, DEFEND YOURSELF. OTHERWISE, STICK TO THE BIG GUYS.
THAT SAID, THIS IS WAR. IF ANYONE REFUSES TO CEASE FIRING ON US, LETHAL FORCE IS AUTHORIZED.
AND IN REGARDS TO THE SUPERHUMAN CRIMINALS... ENCOURAGED.
THAT'S ALL. RED GUARD...

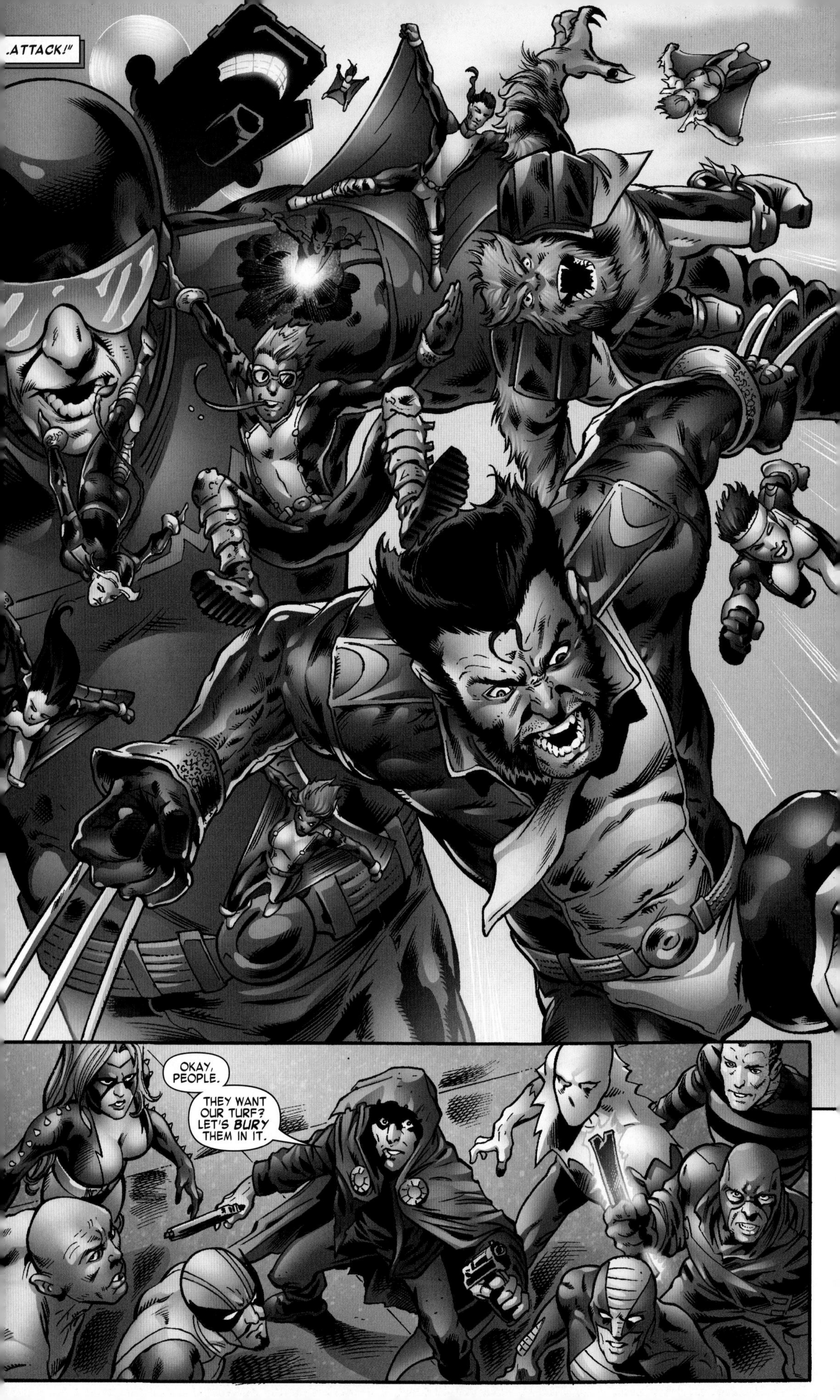
...ATTACK!"
OKAY, PEOPLE.
THEY WANT OUR TURF? LET'S BURY THEM IN IT.

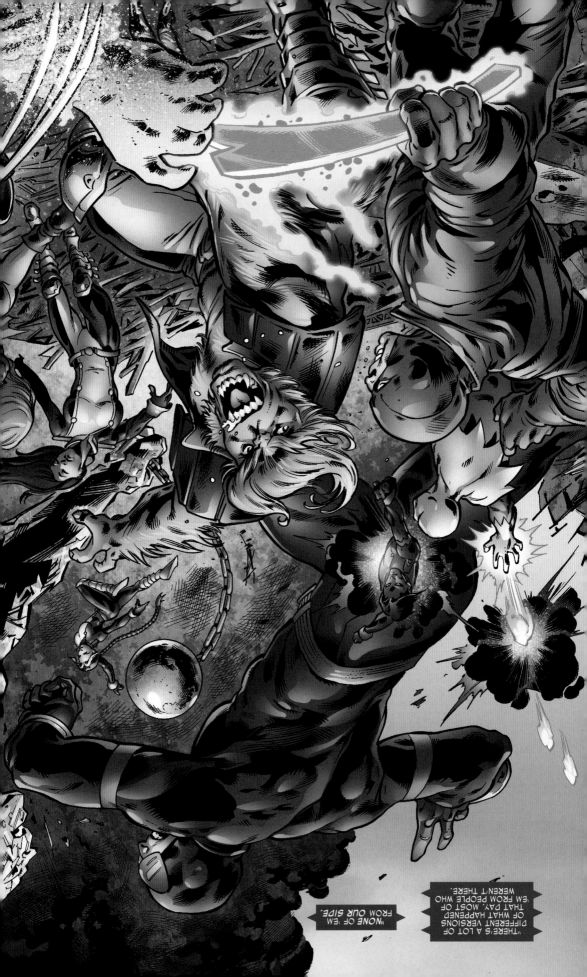

"THERE'S A LOT OF DIFFERENT VERSIONS OF WHAT HAPPENED THAT DAY. MOST OF 'EM FROM PEOPLE WHO WEREN'T THERE.

"NONE OF 'EM FROM OUR SIDE.

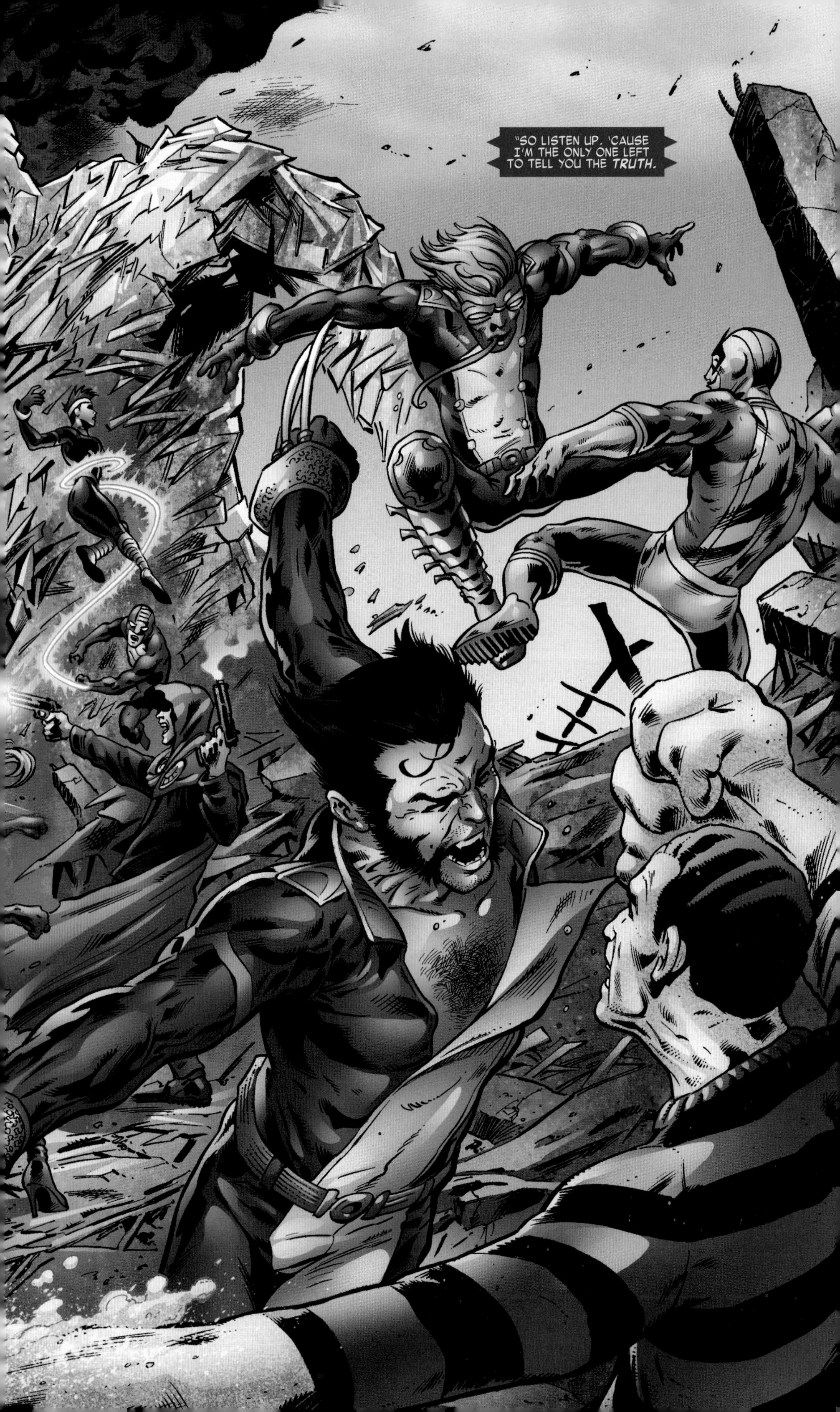
"SO LISTEN UP. 'CAUSE I'M THE ONLY ONE LEFT TO TELL YOU THE *TRUTH*.

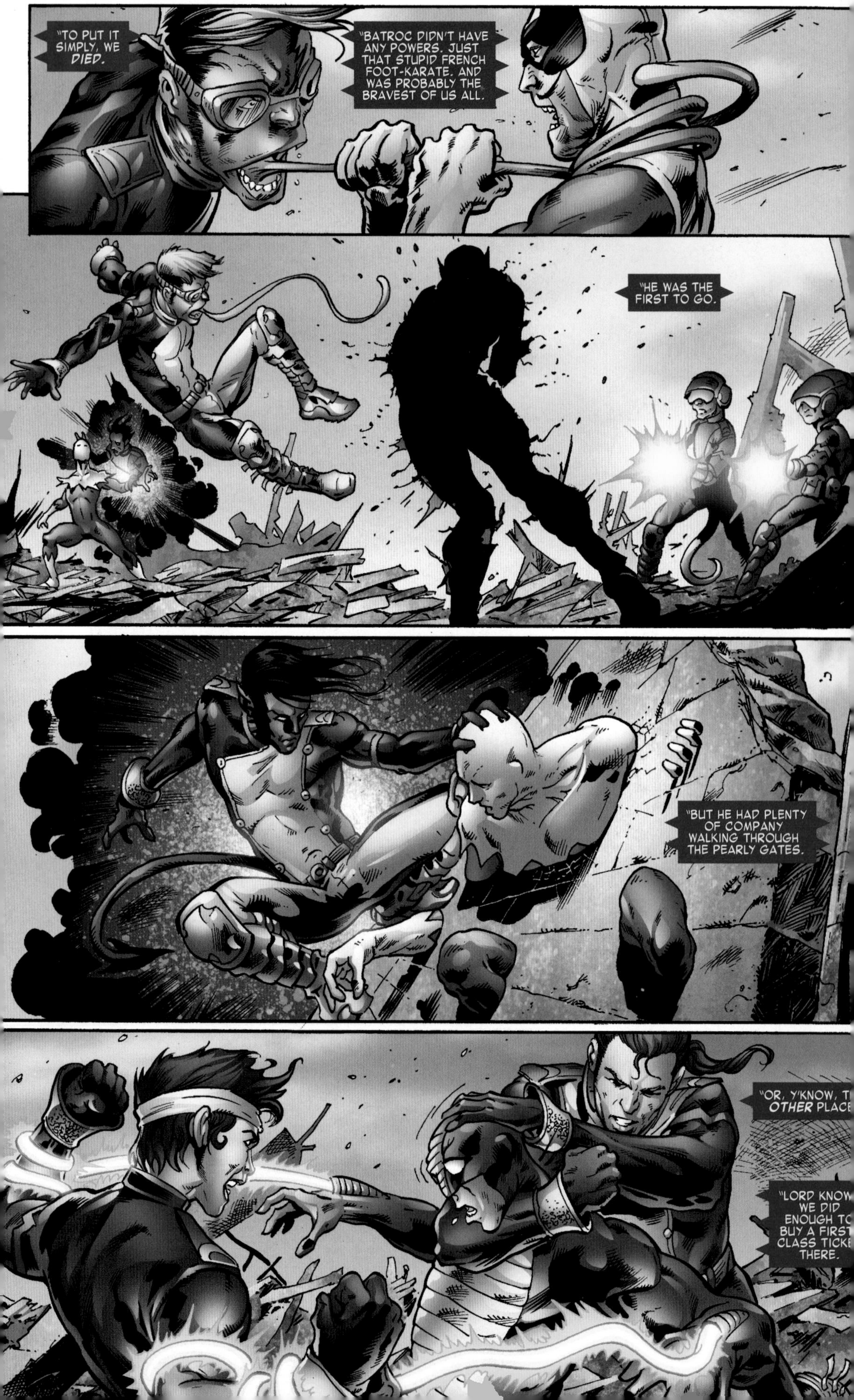
"TO PUT IT SIMPLY, WE *DIED*.
"BATROC DIDN'T HAVE ANY POWERS. JUST THAT STUPID FRENCH FOOT-KARATE. AND WAS PROBABLY THE BRAVEST OF US ALL.
"HE WAS THE FIRST TO GO.
"BUT HE HAD PLENTY OF COMPANY WALKING THROUGH THE PEARLY GATES.
"OR, Y'KNOW, T *OTHER* PLACE
"LORD KNOW WE DID ENOUGH TO BUY A FIRST CLASS TICKE THERE.

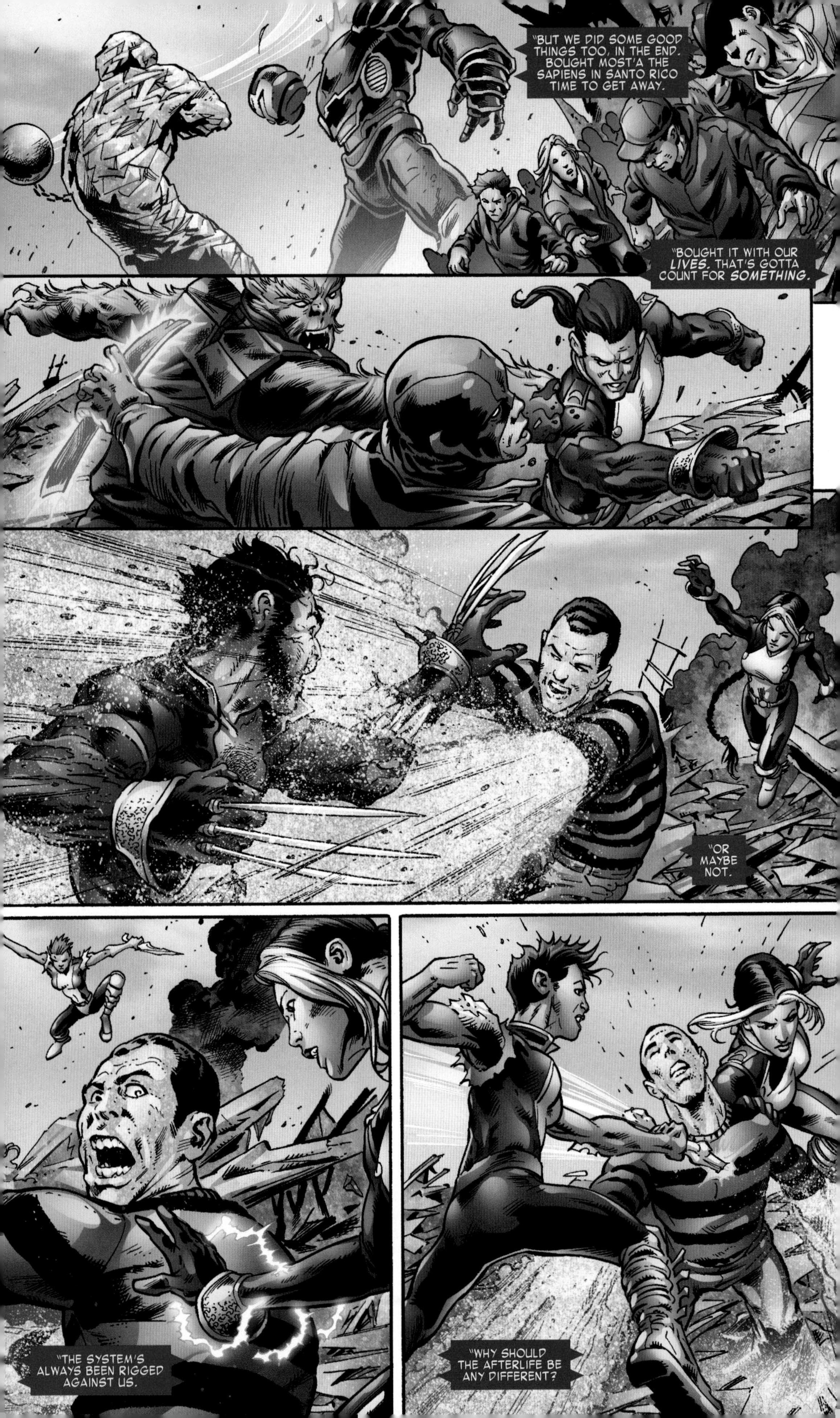
"BUT WE DID SOME GOOD THINGS TOO, IN THE END. BOUGHT MOST'A THE SAPIENS IN SANTO RICO TIME TO GET AWAY.
"BOUGHT IT WITH OUR *LIVES.* THAT'S GOTTA COUNT FOR *SOMETHING.*
"OR MAYBE NOT.
"THE SYSTEM'S ALWAYS BEEN RIGGED AGAINST US.
"WHY SHOULD THE AFTERLIFE BE ANY DIFFERENT?

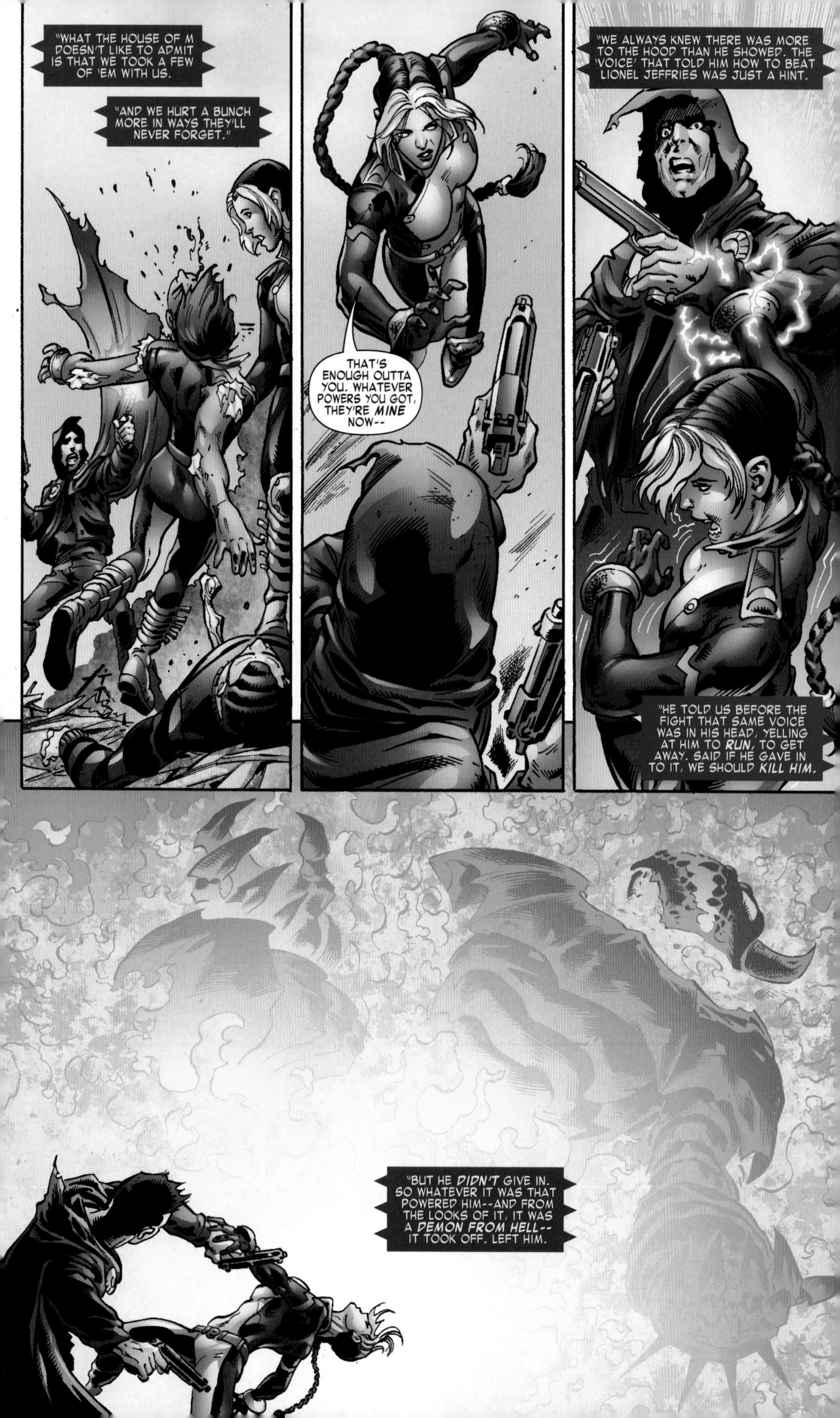
"WHAT THE HOUSE OF M DOESN'T LIKE TO ADMIT IS THAT WE TOOK A FEW OF 'EM WITH US.
"AND WE HURT A BUNCH MORE IN WAYS THEY'LL NEVER FORGET."
THAT'S ENOUGH OUTTA YOU. WHATEVER POWERS YOU GOT, THEY'RE *MINE* NOW--
"WE ALWAYS KNEW THERE WAS MORE TO THE HOOD THAN HE SHOWED. THE 'VOICE' THAT TOLD HIM HOW TO BEAT LIONEL JEFFRIES WAS JUST A HINT.
"HE TOLD US BEFORE THE FIGHT THAT SAME VOICE WAS IN HIS HEAD, YELLING AT HIM TO *RUN*, TO GET AWAY. SAID IF HE GAVE IN TO IT, WE SHOULD *KILL HIM*.
"BUT HE *DIDN'T* GIVE IN. SO WHATEVER IT WAS THAT POWERED HIM--AND FROM THE LOOKS OF IT, IT WAS A *DEMON FROM HELL*--IT TOOK OFF. LEFT HIM.

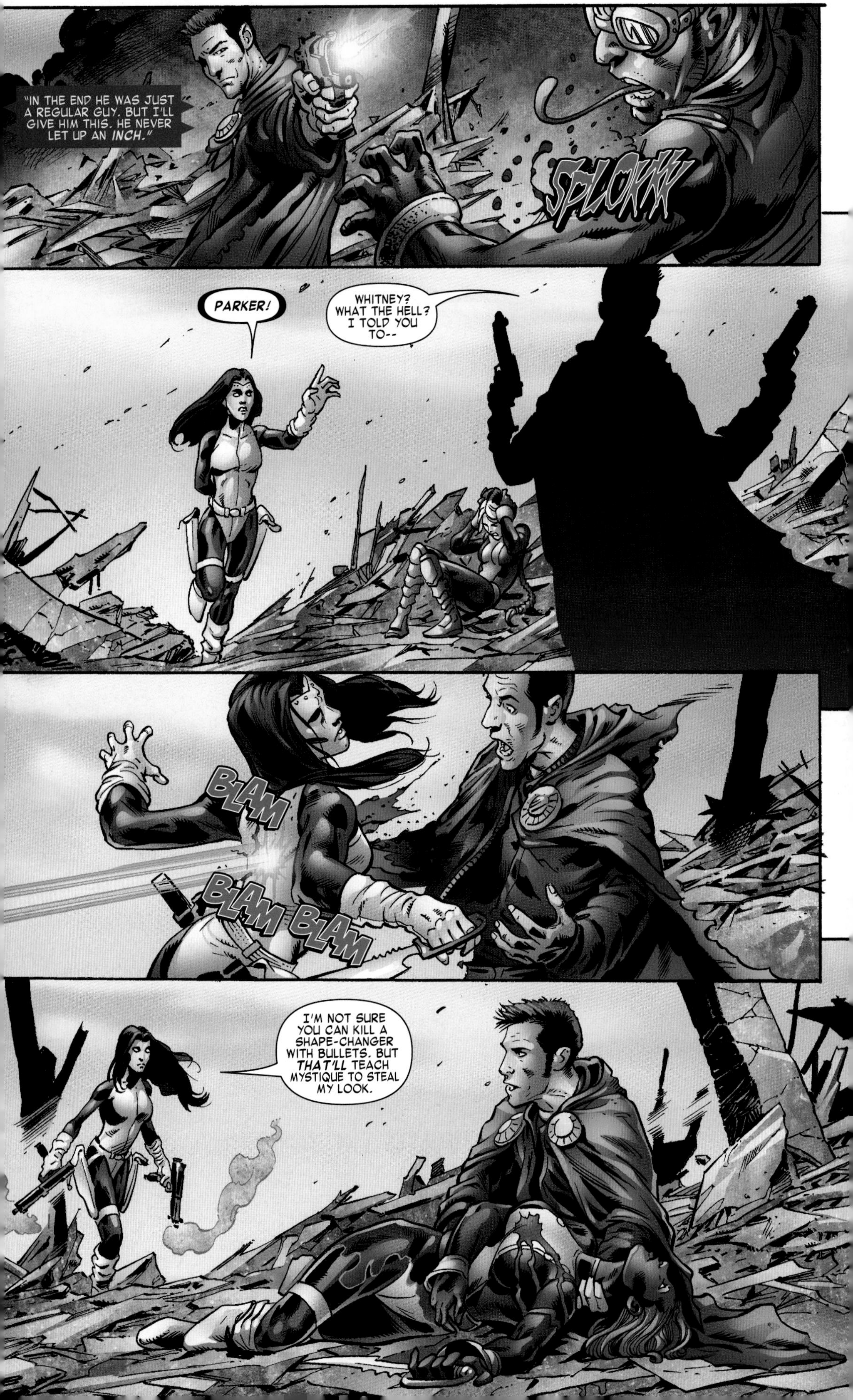
"IN THE END HE WAS JUST A REGULAR GUY. BUT I'LL GIVE HIM THIS. HE NEVER LET UP AN *INCH*."
SPLOKK
PARKER!
WHITNEY? WHAT THE HELL? I TOLD YOU TO--
BLAM
BLAM BLAM
I'M NOT SURE YOU CAN KILL A SHAPE-CHANGER WITH BULLETS. BUT *THAT'LL* TEACH MYSTIQUE TO STEAL MY LOOK.

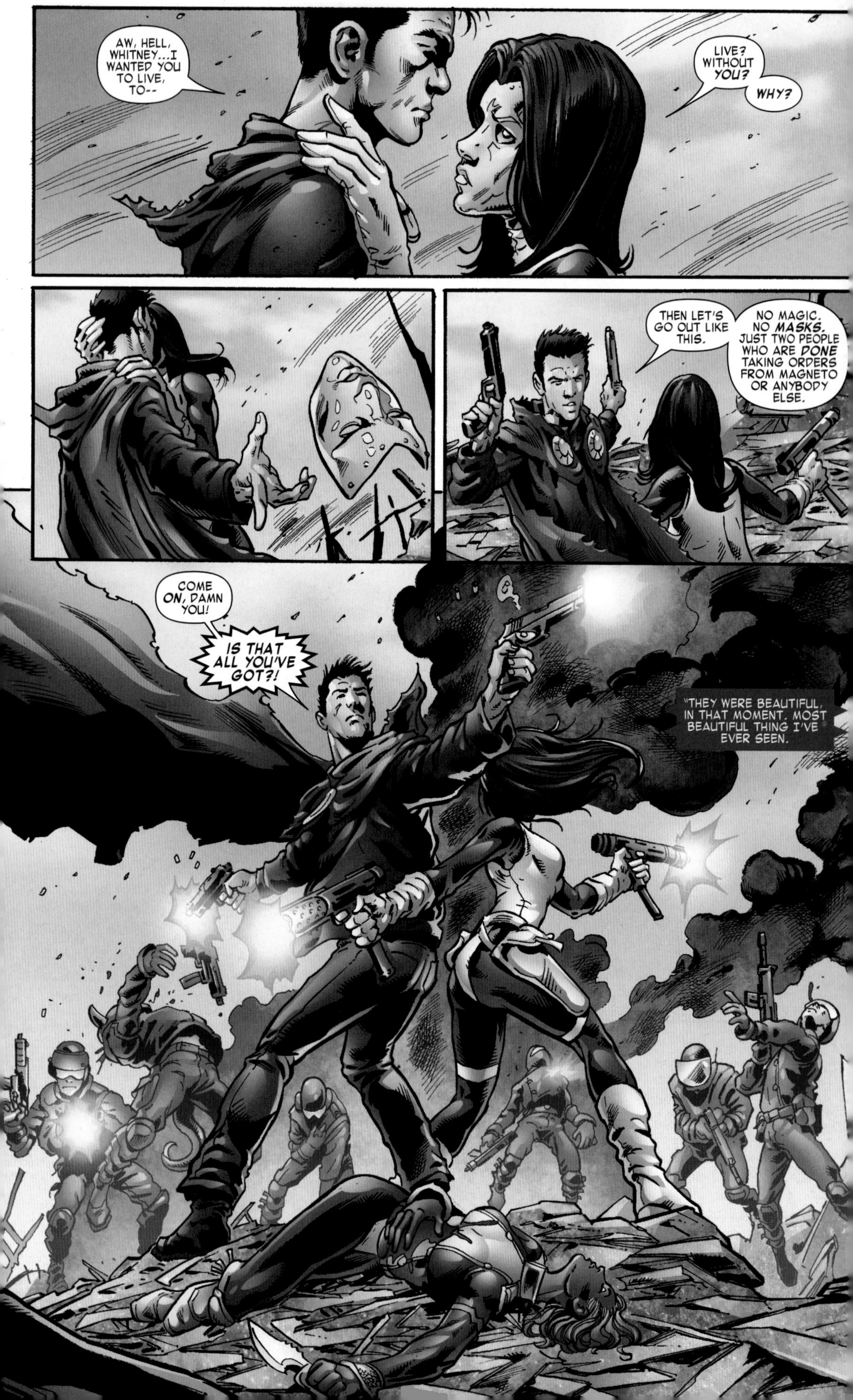
AW, HELL, WHITNEY...I WANTED YOU TO LIVE, TO--
LIVE? WITHOUT *YOU?*
WHY?
THEN LET'S GO OUT LIKE THIS.
NO MAGIC. NO *MASKS.* JUST TWO PEOPLE WHO ARE *DONE* TAKING ORDERS FROM MAGNETO OR ANYBODY ELSE.
COME *ON,* DAMN YOU!
IS THAT ALL YOU'VE GOT?!
"THEY WERE BEAUTIFUL, IN THAT MOMENT. MOST BEAUTIFUL THING I'VE EVER SEEN.

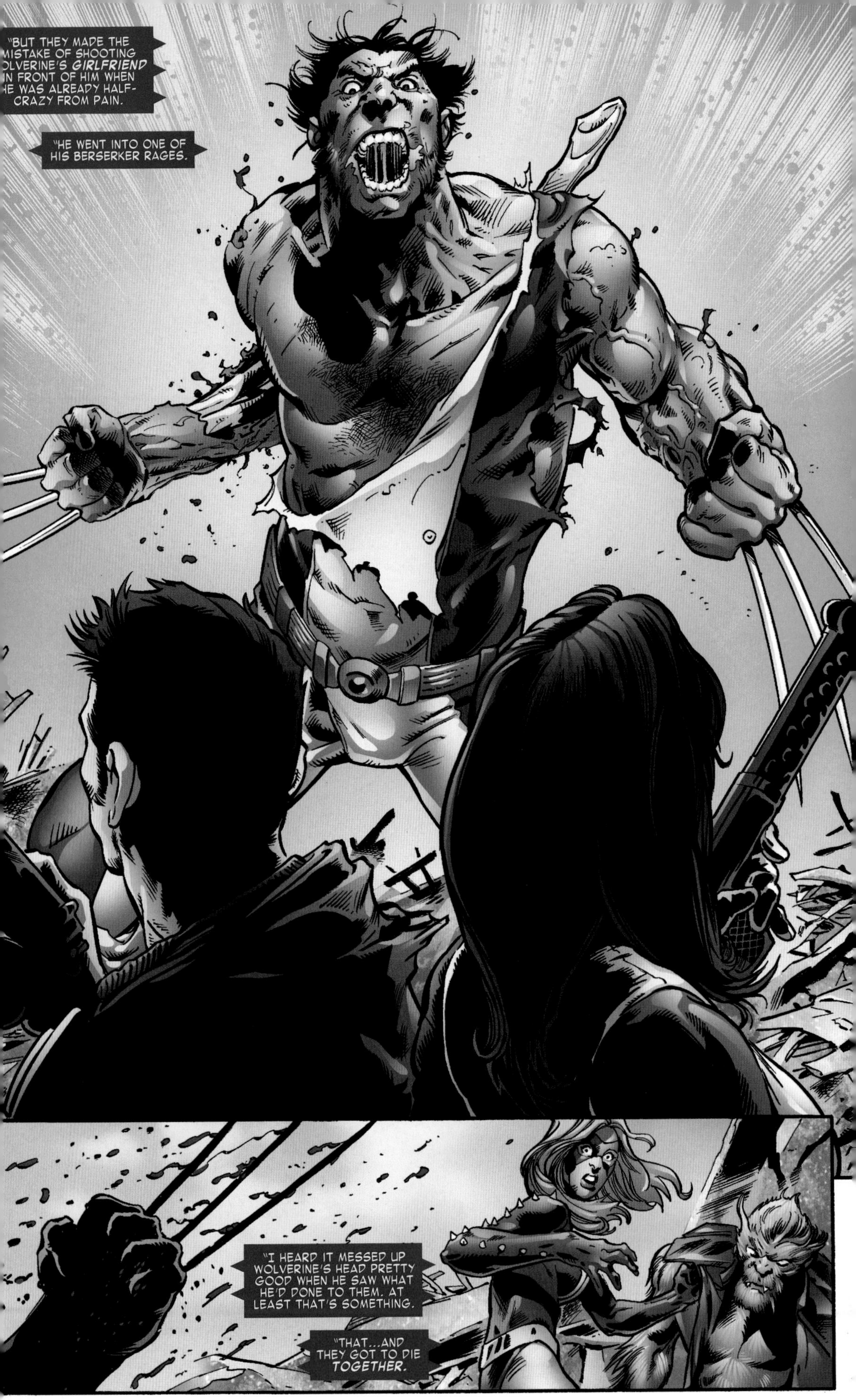
"BUT THEY MADE THE MISTAKE OF SHOOTING OLVERINE'S *GIRLFRIEND* N FRONT OF HIM WHEN E WAS ALREADY HALF-CRAZY FROM PAIN.
"HE WENT INTO ONE OF HIS BERSERKER RAGES.
"I HEARD IT MESSED UP WOLVERINE'S HEAD PRETTY GOOD WHEN HE SAW WHAT HE'D DONE TO THEM. AT LEAST THAT'S SOMETHING.
"THAT...AND THEY GOT TO DIE *TOGETHER*.

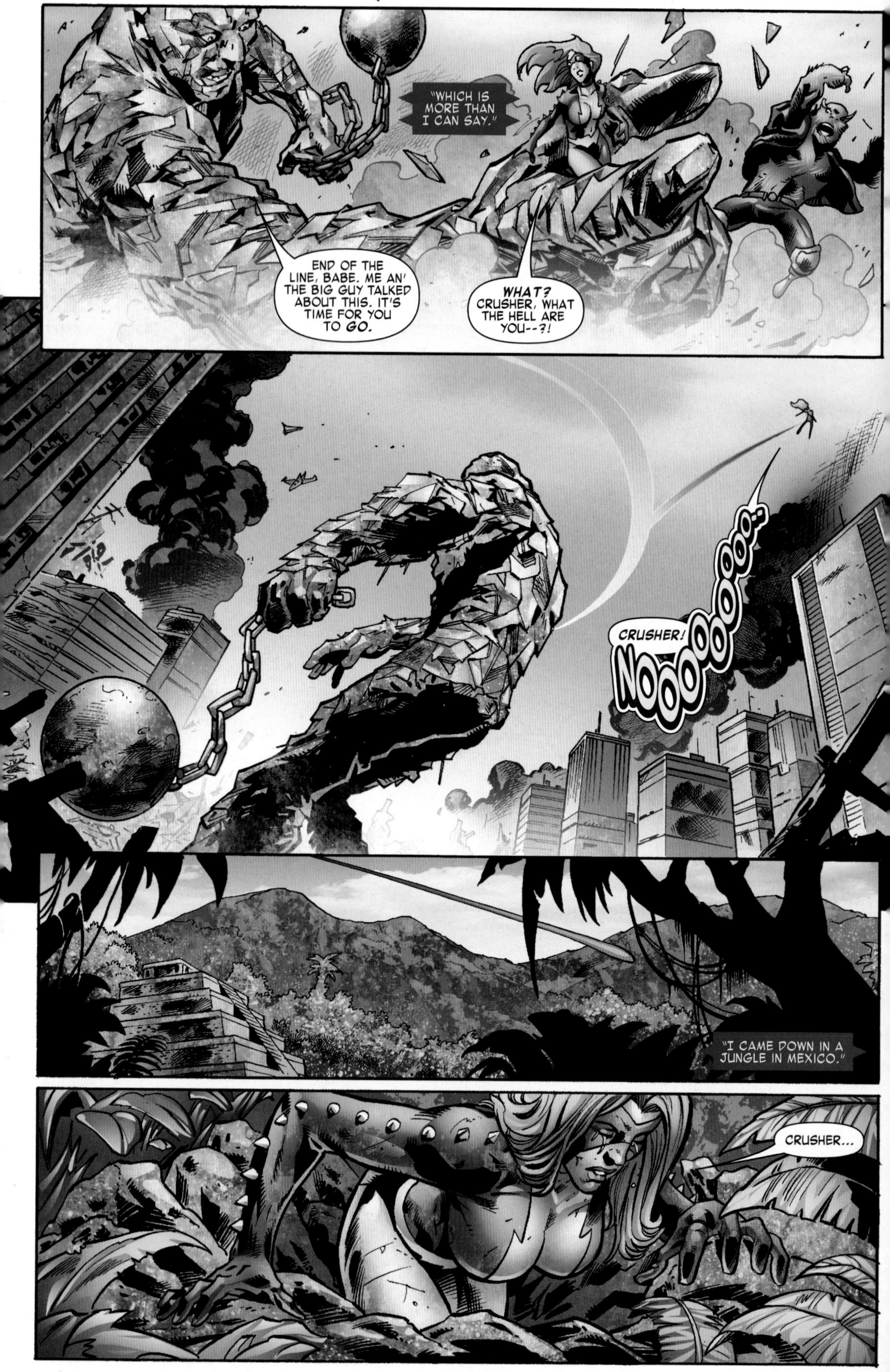
"WHICH IS MORE THAN I CAN SAY."
END OF THE LINE, BABE. ME AN' THE BIG GUY TALKED ABOUT THIS. IT'S TIME FOR YOU TO GO.
WHAT? CRUSHER, WHAT THE HELL ARE YOU--?!
CRUSHER!
NOOOOOOOOO-
"I CAME DOWN IN A JUNGLE IN MEXICO."
CRUSHER...

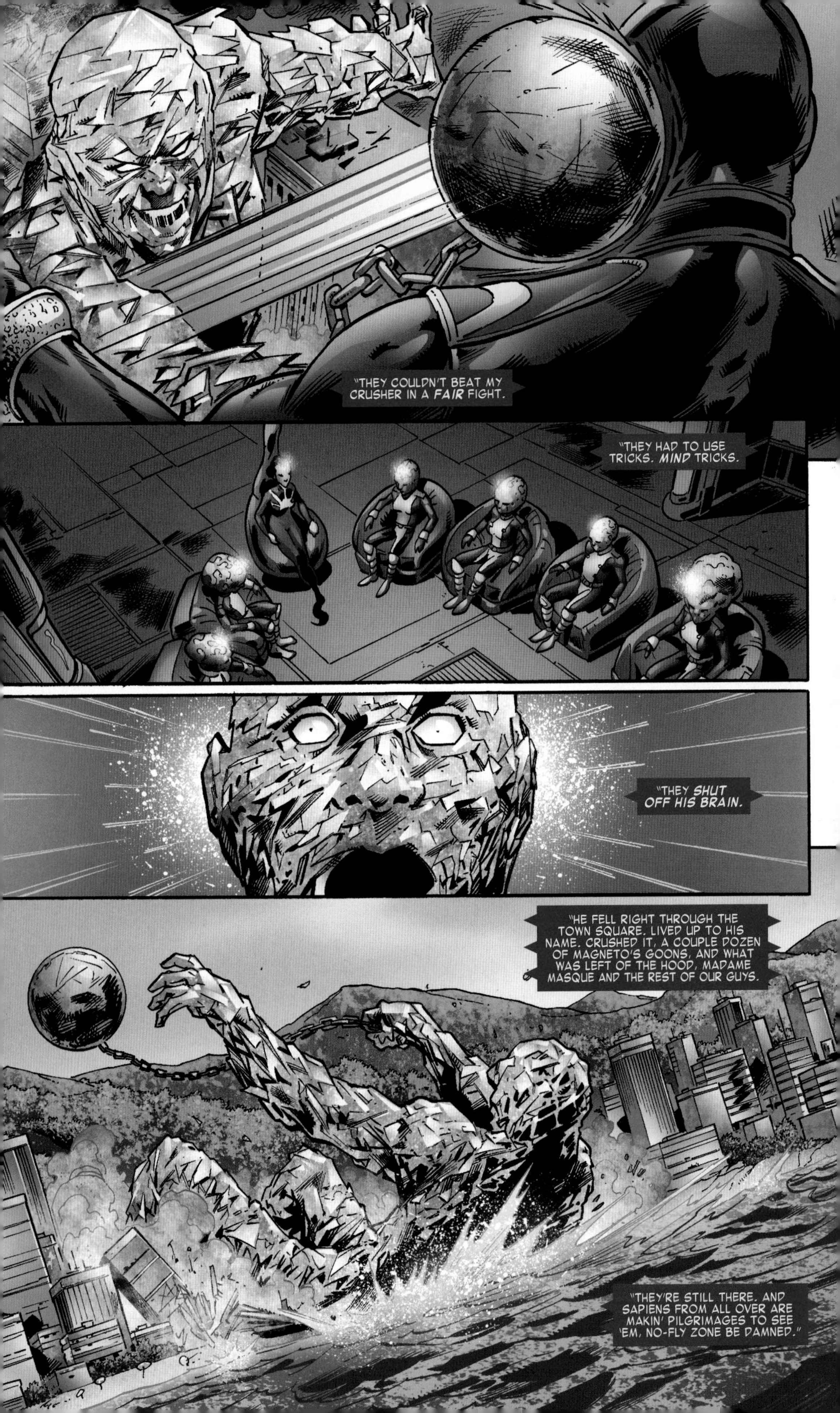
"THEY COULDN'T BEAT MY CRUSHER IN A FAIR FIGHT.
"THEY HAD TO USE TRICKS. MIND TRICKS.
"THEY SHUT OFF HIS BRAIN.
"HE FELL RIGHT THROUGH THE TOWN SQUARE. LIVED UP TO HIS NAME. CRUSHED IT, A COUPLE DOZEN OF MAGNETO'S GOONS, AND WHAT WAS LEFT OF THE HOOD, MADAME MASQUE AND THE REST OF OUR GUYS.
"THEY'RE STILL THERE. AND SAPIENS FROM ALL OVER ARE MAKIN' PILGRIMAGES TO SEE 'EM, NO-FLY ZONE BE DAMNED."

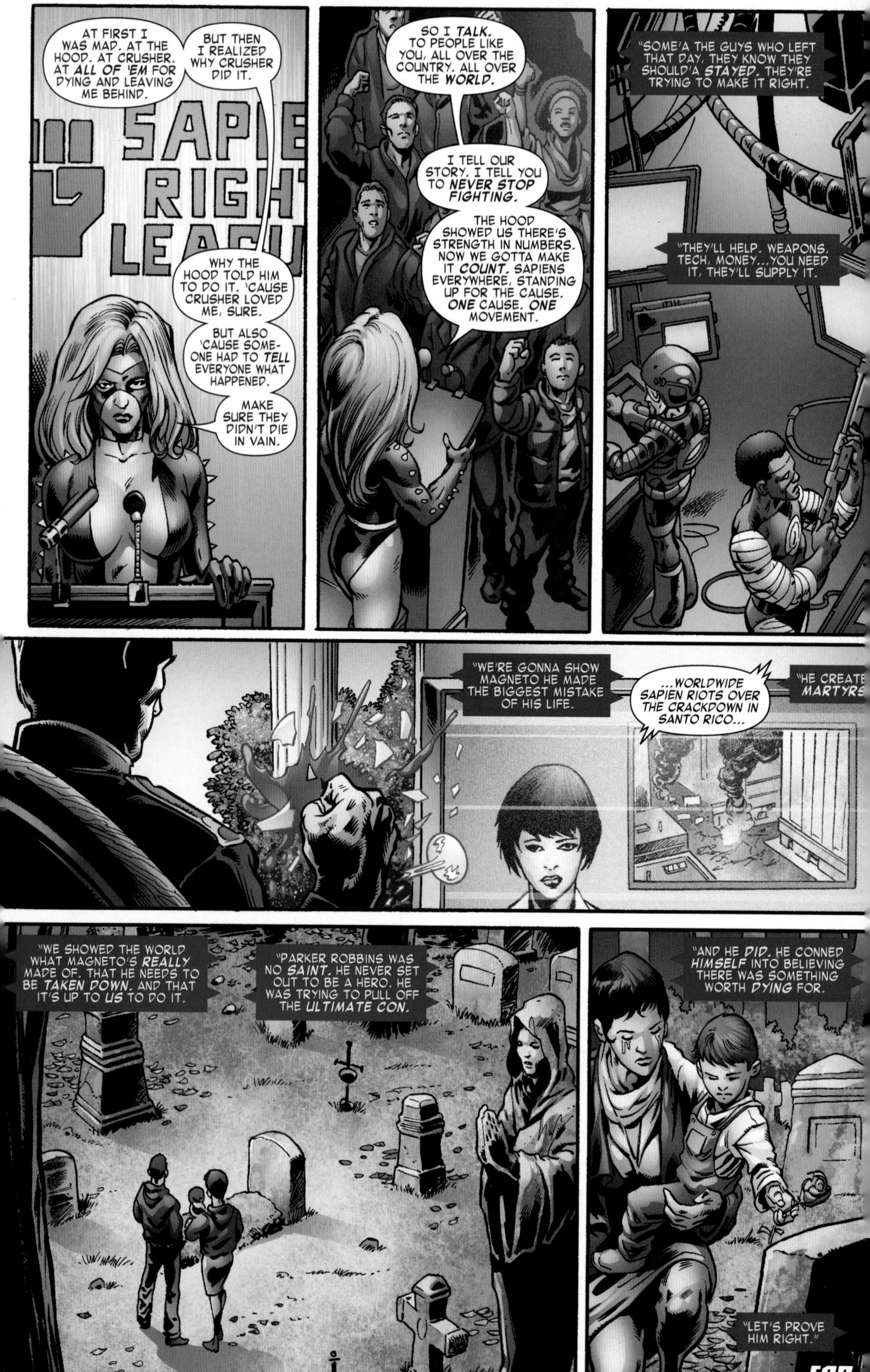
AT FIRST I WAS MAD. AT THE HOOD. AT CRUSHER. AT ALL OF 'EM FOR DYING AND LEAVING ME BEHIND.
BUT THEN I REALIZED WHY CRUSHER DID IT.
WHY THE HOOD TOLD HIM TO DO IT. 'CAUSE CRUSHER LOVED ME, SURE.
BUT ALSO 'CAUSE SOMEONE HAD TO TELL EVERYONE WHAT HAPPENED.
MAKE SURE THEY DIDN'T DIE IN VAIN.
SO I TALK. TO PEOPLE LIKE YOU, ALL OVER THE COUNTRY. ALL OVER THE WORLD.
I TELL OUR STORY. I TELL YOU TO NEVER STOP FIGHTING.
THE HOOD SHOWED US THERE'S STRENGTH IN NUMBERS. NOW WE GOTTA MAKE IT COUNT. SAPIENS EVERYWHERE, STANDING UP FOR THE CAUSE. ONE CAUSE. ONE MOVEMENT.
"SOME'A THE GUYS WHO LEFT THAT DAY, THEY KNOW THEY SHOULD'A STAYED. THEY'RE TRYING TO MAKE IT RIGHT.
"THEY'LL HELP. WEAPONS, TECH, MONEY... YOU NEED IT, THEY'LL SUPPLY IT.
"WE'RE GONNA SHOW MAGNETO HE MADE THE BIGGEST MISTAKE OF HIS LIFE.
...WORLDWIDE SAPIEN RIOTS OVER THE CRACKDOWN IN SANTO RICO...
"HE CREATE MARTYRS
"WE SHOWED THE WORLD WHAT MAGNETO'S REALLY MADE OF. THAT HE NEEDS TO BE TAKEN DOWN. AND THAT IT'S UP TO US TO DO IT.
"PARKER ROBBINS WAS NO SAINT. HE NEVER SET OUT TO BE A HERO. HE WAS TRYING TO PULL OFF THE ULTIMATE CON.
"AND HE DID. HE CONNED HIMSELF INTO BELIEVING THERE WAS SOMETHING WORTH DYING FOR.
"LET'S PROVE HIM RIGHT."
END.

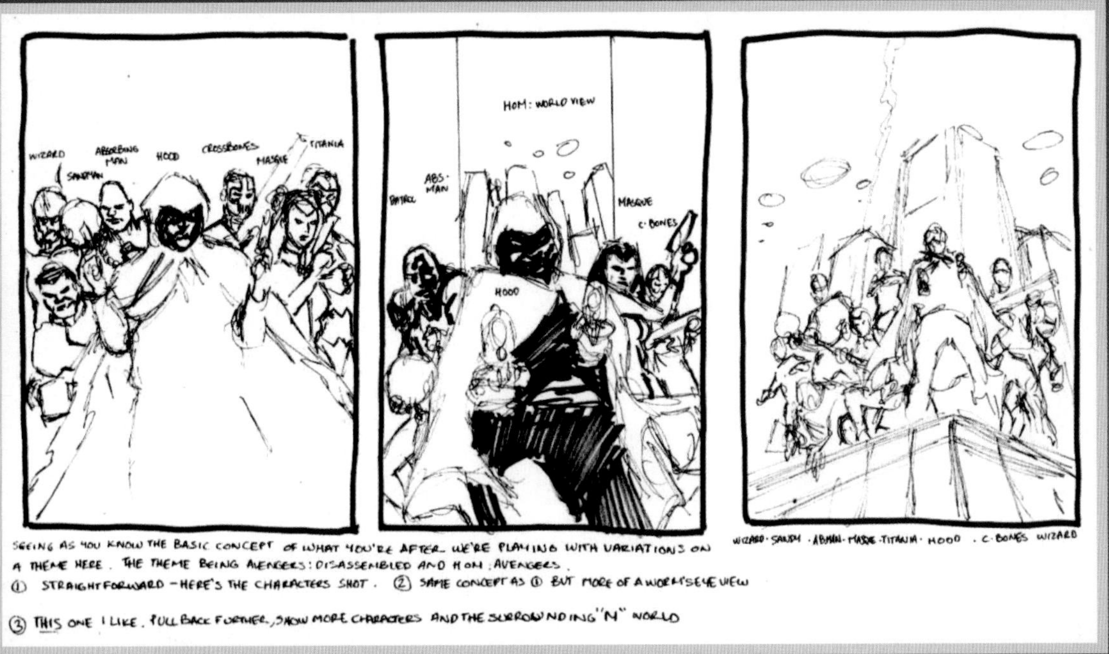
WIZARD
SANDMAN
ABSORBING MAN
HOOD
CROSSBONES
MASQUE
TITANIA
HOM: WORLD VIEW
PATROL
ABS-MAN
HOOD
MASQUE
C. BONES
WIZARD · SANDY · ABMAN · MASQUE · TITANIA · HOOD · C. BONES WIZARD
SEEING AS YOU KNOW THE BASIC CONCEPT OF WHAT YOU'RE AFTER. WE'RE PLAYING WITH VARIATIONS ON A THEME HERE. THE THEME BEING AVENGERS: DISASSEMBLED AND HOM: AVENGERS.
① STRAIGHTFORWARD – HERE'S THE CHARACTERS SHOT. ② SAME CONCEPT AS ① BUT MORE OF A WORM'S-EYE VIEW
③ THIS ONE I LIKE. PULL BACK FURTHER, SHOW MORE CHARACTERS AND THE SURROUNDING "M" WORLD

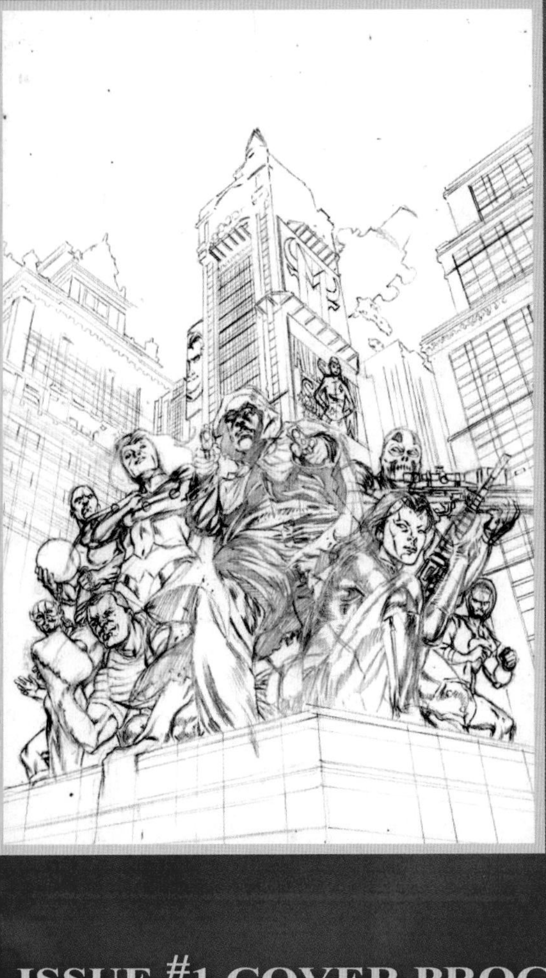

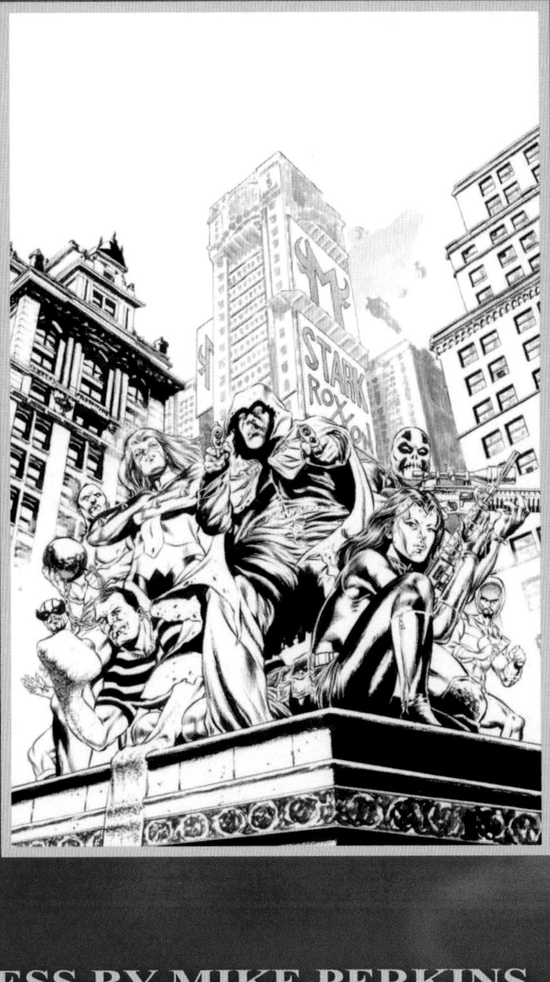
STARK
ROXXON

ISSUE #1 COVER PROCESS BY MIKE PERKINS

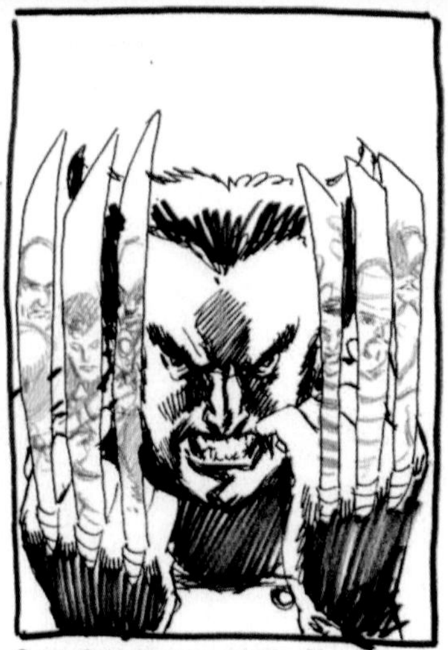

① WOLVERINE WITH CLAWS RAISED - REFLECTED IN THEM - THE MASTERS OF EVIL

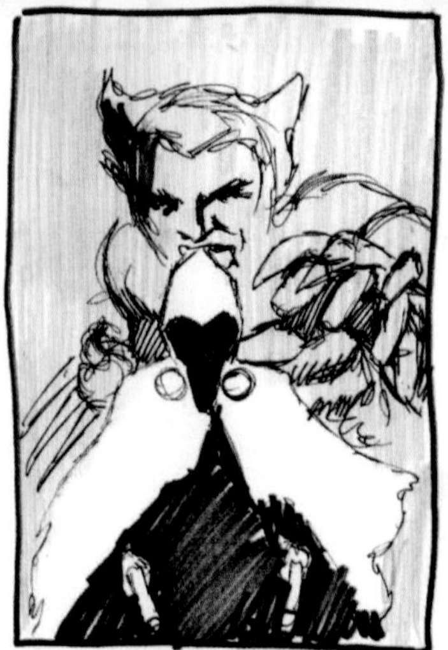

② A STARK RED AND BLACK IMAGE OF THE HOOD WITH GUNS AND WOLVERINE - HIGHLY DETAILED IN GREYTONES - BEHIND HIM. MORE OF A MONTAGE COVER.

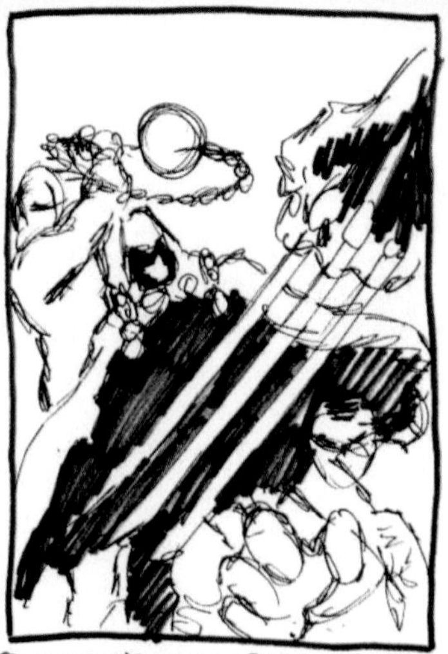

③ WOLVERINE'S CLAWS IN FOREGROUND WITH MASTERS OF EVIL ATTACKING.

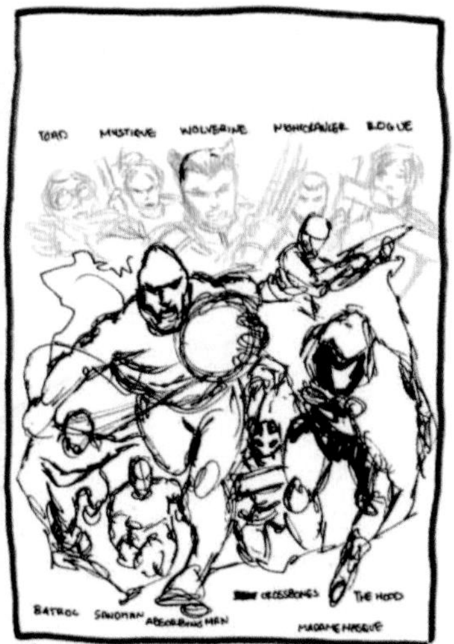
TOAD
MYSTIQUE
WOLVERINE
NIGHTCRAWLER
ROGUE
BATROC
SANDMAN
ABSORBING MAN
CROSSBONES
THE HOOD
MADAME MASQUE

④ A FUN COVER. X-MEN GIANT SIZE #1 RIP-OFF (A-HEM... I MEAN, HOMAGE) WITH MASTER OF EVIL BREAKING THROUGH AND WOLVERINES "M" SQUAD ABOVE.

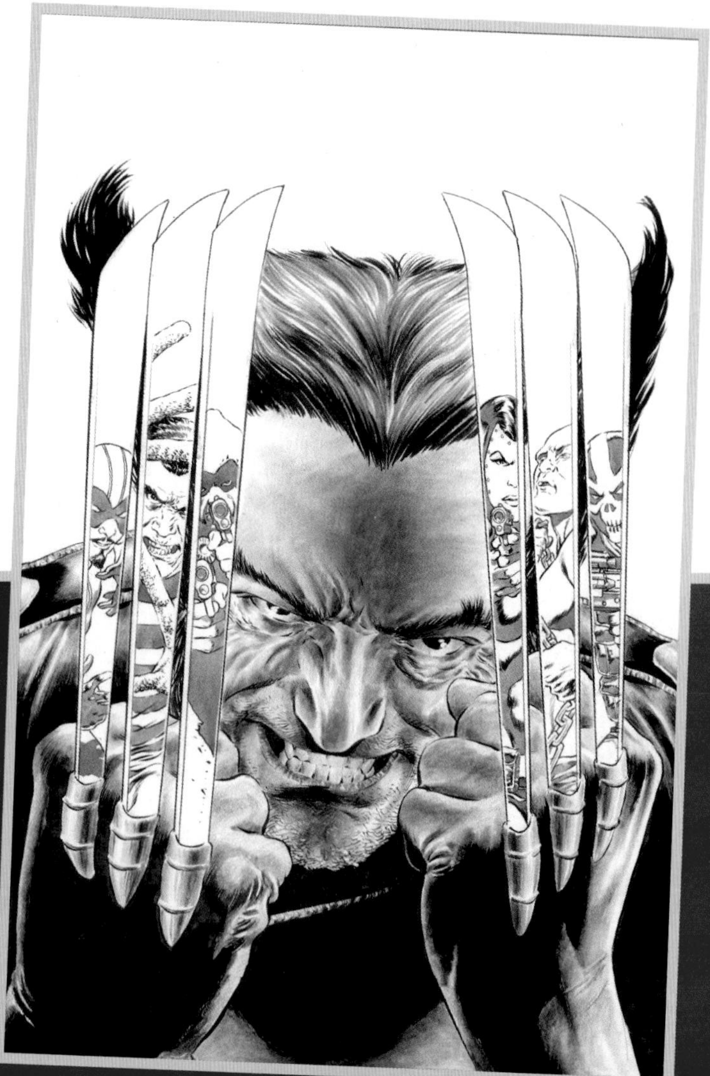

ISSUE #2 COVER PROCESS BY MIKE PERKINS

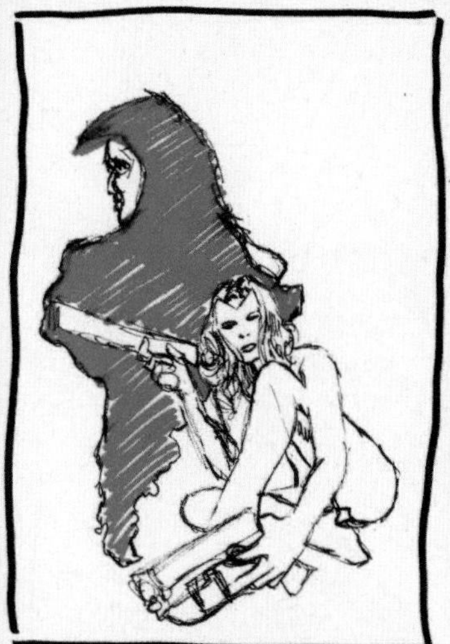

①. POSED SHOT WITH HOOD'S CAPE IN THE SHAPE OF SOUTH AMERICA.

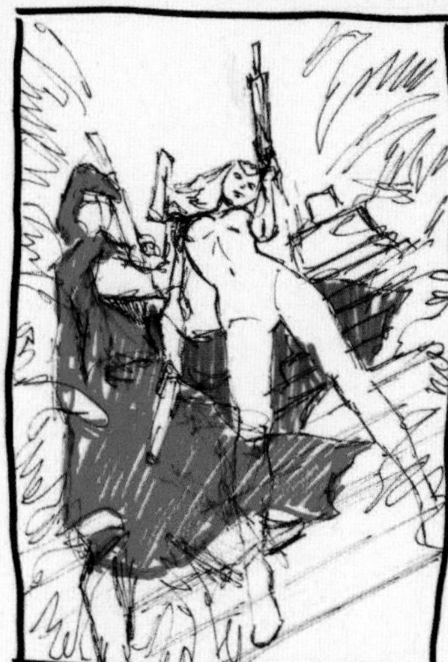

② IN THE JUNGLE ON THE STEPS OF AN AZTEC TEMPLE.

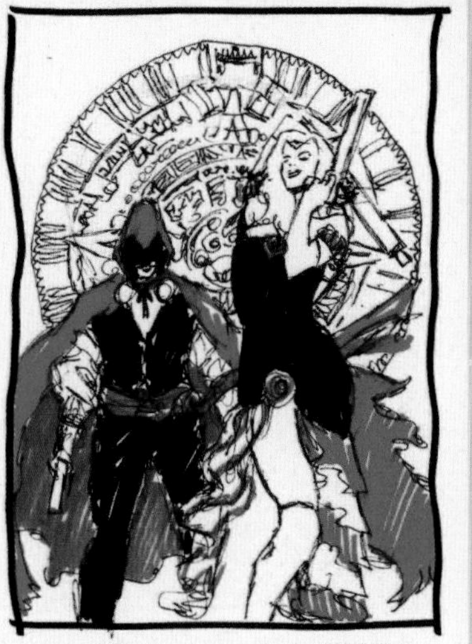

③ IN LATIN AMERICAN OUTFITS WITH AN AZTEC CALENDER BEHIND THEM.

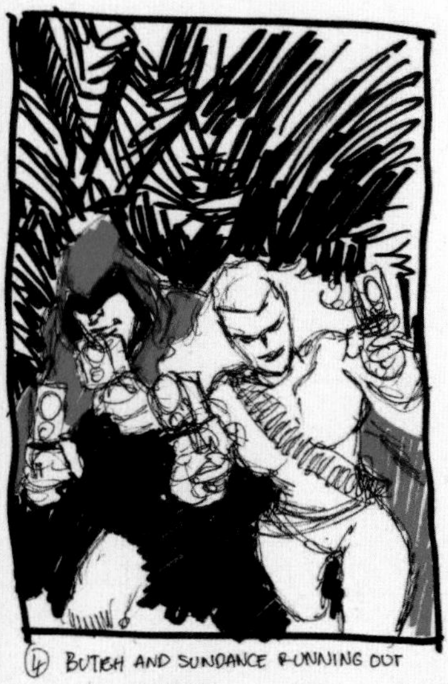

④ BUTCH AND SUNDANCE RUNNING OUT OF JUNGLE

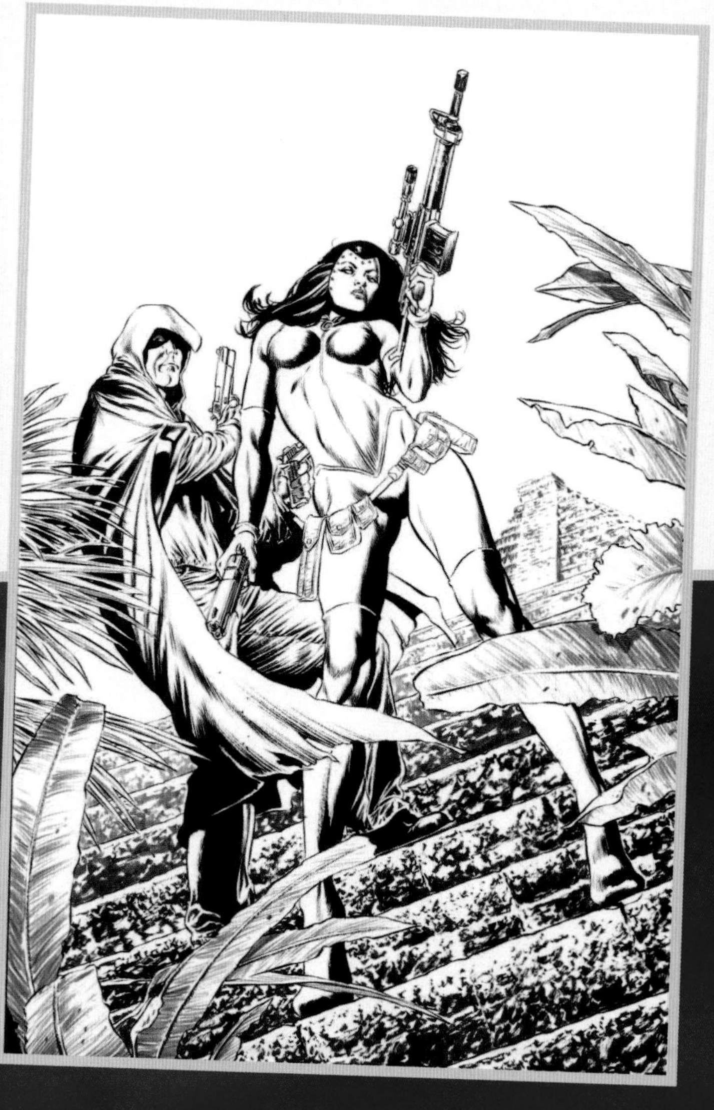

ISSUE #3 COVER PROCESS BY MIKE PERKINS

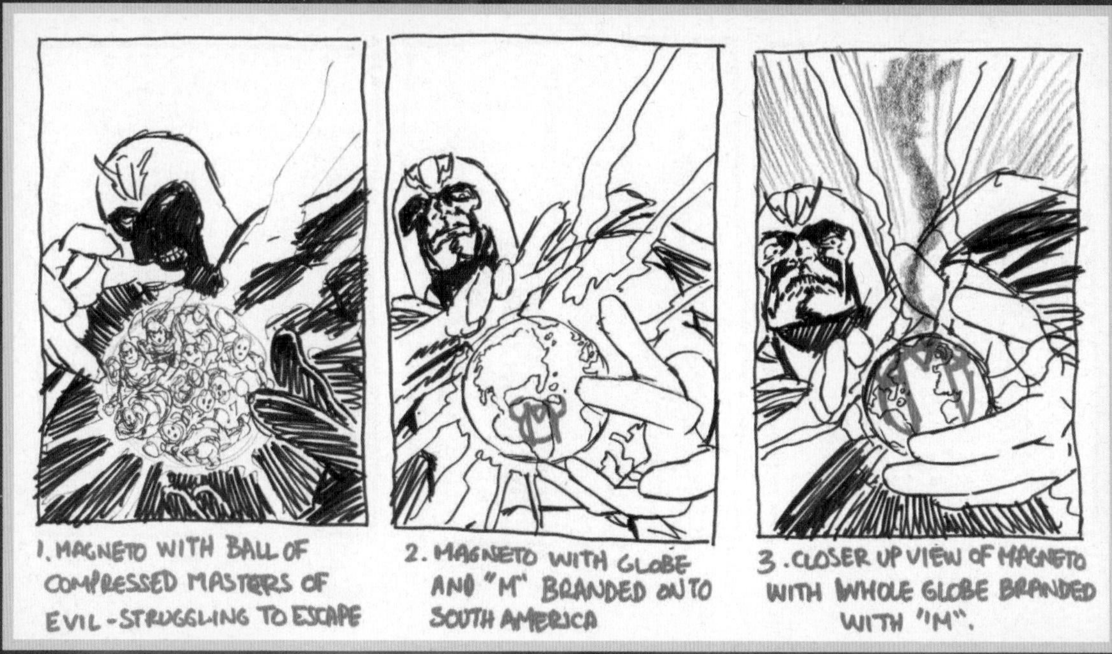
1. MAGNETO WITH BALL OF COMPRESSED MASTERS OF EVIL - STRUGGLING TO ESCAPE
2. MAGNETO WITH GLOBE AND "M" BRANDED ONTO SOUTH AMERICA
3. CLOSER UP VIEW OF MAGNETO WITH WHOLE GLOBE BRANDED WITH "M".

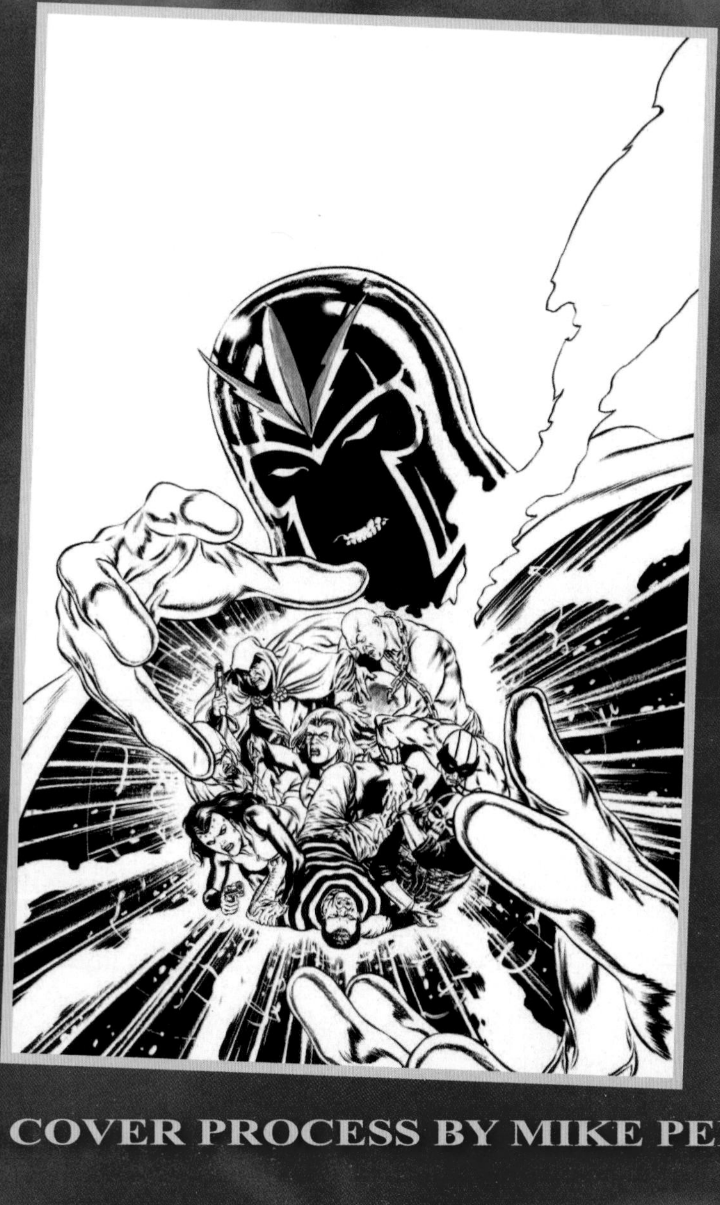

ISSUE #4 COVER PROCESS BY MIKE PERKINS